Journey to the Orient

Gérard de Nerval

Journey to the Orient

Selected, translated from the French
and with an Introduction by
Norman Glass

New York University Press
New York 1972

I feel the need to liken myself unto the entire universe of nature . . . foreign women. . . . Memories of having lived there.

To pursue the same characteristics in different kinds of women.

The double : child of heaven, child of hell.

The hero : son of Cain.

From Nerval's travel notebook

Contents

The Background   11
Introduction : Voyage Within a Voyage   15

PART ONE : ZETNAYBIA

1   Sunrise   23
2   The Khowals   25
3   The Dervishes   28
4   A Decision   31
5   The Slave-Merchants   33
6   The Barber's Shop   36
7   The Caravan from Mecca   38
8   Abd-el-Kerim   43
9   Zetnaybia   48
10   My First Arabic Lesson   51
11   A Domestic Revolution   53
12   Zetnaybia's French Lesson   57
13   The Afrites   60
14   Departure   63
15   Mutiny   65
16   Farewell   73

PART TWO : THE TALE OF THE CALIPH HAKIM

Introduction   83
1   Hashish   85
2   Famine   92
3   The Lady of the Kingdom   95
4   The Moristan   100
5   The Fire of Cairo   105
6   The Two Caliphs   111
Conclusion   118

PART THREE : THE TALE OF THE QUEEN OF THE MORNING
AND SOLIMAN THE PRINCE OF THE GENII

Introduction   123
1   Adoniram   124
2   Balkis   129
3   The Temple   139
4   Millo   150
5   The Sea of Bronze   157
6   The Apparition   164
7   The Subterranean Kingdom   168
8   The Pool of Siloam   176
9   Phanor, Amrou and Methuselah   186
10 Soliman and Adoniram   192
11 Soliman and Balkis   196
12 Makbenash   204
Conclusion   212

Glossary   215

Illustrations

FACING PAGE 92

Coffee Shop
Lithograph by Louis Haghe

FACING PAGE 93

Slave Market
Lithograph by Louis Haghe

FACING PAGE 124

Mosque of Sultan Hassan
Lithograph by Louis Haghe

FACING PAGE 125

Hacine
Drawing by Gérard de Nerval

The lithographs by Louis Haghe are from drawings by
David Roberts, R.A. They appear in *Egypt and Nubia*,
published 1849, and are reproduced by courtesy of the Victoria
and Albert Museum, London.

The Background

1807　Étienne Labrunie marries Marie-Antoinette-Marguerite Laurent; her family are from the Valois.

1808　Birth of Gérard Labrunie, on 22 May, at 96, rue Saint-Martin, Paris.

1809　A military doctor in the Rhine Army, Étienne Labrunie is sent to Poland and Austria. His wife accompanies him. Gérard is nursed at Loisy, near Mortefontaine, in the Valois '*où pendant plus de mille ans a battu le coeur de France*'.

1810　Dr Labrunie is superintendent of the Hanover hospital, then of the Glogau hospital. Marie-Antoinette Labrunie dies at the age of twenty-five from a fever which she caught '*en traversant un pont chargé de cadavres*', according to Gérard. She is buried in the Catholic cemetery of Gross-Glogau, in Silesia. '*Je n'ai jamais vu ma mère,*' Nerval would write, '*ses portraits ont été perdus ou volés; je sais seulement qu'elle ressemblait à une gravure du temps, d'après Prud'hon ou Fragonard, qu'on appelait* La Modestie.'
Gérard grows up at Mortefontaine, at the home of his maternal uncle, Antoine Boucher, who has a large library which includes many esoteric works. He will return to visit him during his holidays and it is here, at Mortefontaine, that Gérard meets Sophie Dawes, baronne Adrien de Feuchères, daughter of a fisherman from the Isle of Wight.

1812　THE RUSSIAN CAMPAIGN.

1814　Dr Labrunie returns to France.

1815　SECOND ABDICATION OF NAPOLEON. THE RESTORATION OF THE BOURBONS.

1820　Gérard lives with his father in Paris, on rue Saint-Martin. He studies Classics at the Lycée Charlemagne and becomes friendly with a fellow-pupil, Théophile Gautier. Death of Antoine Boucher.

1826　Publication of Nerval's *Élégies Nationales* and *L'Académie ou les Membres Introuvables*.

1828　At the age of twenty, Nerval publishes his first important work, a translation of Goethe's *Faust*, which is highly praised by the author himself. Death of his maternal grandmother.

1830　Gérard attends the première of Hugo's *Hernani*. Publishes his

Choix des Poésies de Ronsard and a translation, *Poésies allemandes.*

THE JULY REVOLUTION. THE JULY MONARCHY.

1832   Gérard is a member of the Petit Cénacle around Jehan Duseigneur; it includes Petrus Borel, Victor Hugo, Charles Nodier, Célestin Nanteuil, etc. A medical student (under his father's influence), he looks after victims of the April cholera epidemic.

1833   The year when Gérard probably sees Jenny Colon for the first time. She sings at the Variétés. They are both twenty-five years old. Gautier describes Jenny as '*forte et grasse . . . à l'embonpoint potelé et soutenu . . . aux cheveux rutilants et flaves*'.

1834   On the death of his maternal grandfather, Gérard inherits 30,000 francs and travels to the south of France and Italy — Florence, Rome, Naples.

1835   At the impasse du Doyenné, with Esquiros, Gautier, Arséne Houssaye, Camille Rogier, etc., Gérard founds *Le Monde Dramatique* to glorify Jenny Colon. Sale of Antoine Boucher's house, at Mortefontaine, to Sophie Dawes.

1836   Failure and bankruptcy of *Le Monde Dramatique*. From now on Gérard will have financial difficulties. A journalist, through necessity, he writes for *Le Figaro* and *La Charte de 1830*. Travels to Belgium with Gautier.

1837   Gérard writes for the drama column of *La Presse*. Jenny Colon plays Sylvia in the première of *Piquillo* by Nerval and Dumas.

1838   On 11 April, Jenny Colon marries Louis-Gabriel Leplus, a flutist, and ends her relationship with Gérard. He travels to Germany — Baden, Strasbourg, Karlsruhe, Mannheim, Frankfurt — and works on his play *Léo Burckart*.

1839   Première of *l'Alchimiste* by Nerval and Dumas. *Léo Burckart* is performed at the Porte Saint-Martin. Gérard is sent on diplomatic business to Austria — Lyon, Geneva, Berne, Zurich, Constance, Lindau, Munich, Salzburg, Linz, Vienna. Here, in Vienna, he meets the pianist Marie Pleyel whose features were like '*le pâle reflet de la lune*'. Everyone who knew Gérard would have endorsed the terms in which she referred to him in a letter to Jules Janin : '*Que fait ce bon petit Gérard? . . . J'ai beaucoup d'amitié pour ce doux poète. . . . Quand j'étais triste de ne pas recevoir de vos nouvelles, il me consolait avec une parfaite bonté.*'

1840   Gérard returns to Paris and works on his translation of the *Second Faust*. He travels to Belgium. *Piquillo* is performed in

Brussels where Marie Pleyel arranges for Gérard and Jenny to meet again and be reconciled. Death of Sophie Dawes.

1841 Gérard's first psychic crisis (21 February?). He is taken to Madame Saint-Marcel, rue de Picpus, then, following a relapse, to Dr Esprit Blanche's clinic at Montmartre where he stays until the end of November. The periods of psychic disorder, which Gérard will suffer intermittently until his death, are excruciatingly painful and culminate in that '*épanchement du songe dans la vie réelle*', recorded in the pages of *Aurélia*.

1842 On 5 June, Jenny Colon dies. Gérard wanders around Paris, living, perhaps, on rue de Douai. He leaves for the East in December.

1843 The Voyage to the East — Marseille, Malta, the Archipelago — puts into port at Syros in the Cyclades; Egypt — Cairo, Alexandria; Lebanon — Acre, Beirut; Syria; Cyprus, Rhodes, Smyrna, Constantinople, Malta. Stays in Naples at the end of November and returns to Marseille on 5 December.

1844 Works on *Voyage en Orient*. Travels to Belgium and Holland with Arsène Houssaye.

1845 August, a week in London.

1846 Gérard visits the Valois, works on *Angélique, Sylvie*, and *Promenades et Souvenirs*.

1848 He becomes friendly with Heine, in Paris, and translates some of his poems; they are published in the *Revue des Deux Mondes*.
LOUIS-PHILIPPE ABDICATES. 1848 REVOLUTION.

1849 April, Gérard suffers another crisis and is looked after by Dr Aussandon. He goes to London in June.

1850 Gérard is looked after once again by Dr Aussandon. He travels to Germany — Leipzig; Belgium — Brussels.

1851 The definitive edition of *Voyage en Orient* is published by Charpentier. Another crisis, in September, takes Gérard to a clinic in Passy belonging to Dr Émile Blanche, son of Dr Esprit Blanche. Highly amiable and enlightened, Dr Émile Blanche will look after Gérard during the following years and encourage him to write as a means of therapy.
Première of *L'Imagier de Harlem* at the Porte Saint-Martin.
THE DECEMBER COUP D'ÉTAT.

1852 THE SECOND EMPIRE.
Ill, Gérard is hospitalized at the maison Dubois, a municipal mental home. He travels to Holland in May and visits the Valois again in August. *Les Illuminés* is published in November. Gérard is under severe mental and financial stress.

1853   He works on *Sylvie*. Suffering from 'fever', he stays at the
maison Dubois. He visits the Valois for the last time. On
15 August, *Sylvie* is published in the *Revue des Deux Mondes*.
Following a further crisis, on 25 August, Gérard is taken to
the Hôpital de la Charité, then to Dr Blanche's clinic. He
leaves prematurely, suffers a relapse and returns. *El Desdi-
chado* is published in *Le Mousequetaire*. Publication of *Petits
Chateaux de Bohême* and *Contes et Facéties*. December,
Gérard finishes *Les Filles du Feu* and *Les Chimères*; they are
published the following year.

1854   He plans to travel East again. In May he departs for Germany
where he probably makes a pilgrimage to his mother's tomb in
Gross-Glogau. From Strasbourg he goes to Baden, Karlsruhe,
Stuttgart, Munich, Augsburg, Nuremberg, Neuenmarkt,
Leipzig, Weimar, Gotha, Frankfurt, returning to Paris, however, late July. August, Gérard stays at Dr Blanche's clinic
again and works on *Aurélia*. He leaves on 19 October and
wanders through the streets of Paris, cold, lonely, hungry,
and without any fixed abode.

1855   The streets of Paris are covered with snow, the temperature is
down to −18°. On 26 January, Gérard is found hanging from
the railings of the dingy rue de la Vieille-Lanterne.
'The Saviour himself says : He that is near me is near the fire.
He that is far from me is far from the kingdom.' Origen,
Agrapha

Voyage Within a Voyage

Le soir, lorsque l'heure fatale semblait
s'approcher, je dissertais avec deux amis,
à la table d'un cercle, sur la peinture et
sur la musique, définissant à mon point de
vue la génération des couleurs et le sens
des nombres. L'un d'eux, nommé Paul,
voulut me reconduire chez moi, mais je
lui dis que je ne rentrais pas.
'Où vas-tu?' me dit-il. 'Vers l'Orient!'

Gérard de Nerval, *Aurélia*

On 1 January, 1843, when Gérard, leaving for the East, boarded the
Mentor at Marseille, the literary and artistic atmosphere of Paris was
impregnated by Orientalism. This was the epoch of Chateaubriand's
Itinéraire, Lamartine's *Voyage en Orient*, Hugo's *Les Orientales*.
Gautier had dedicated *La Péri* to his friend Gérard; he later published
Le Club des Hachischim in *La Presse*. And in 1781 the Englishman,
William Beckford, had written in French that sombre masterpiece of
Orientalism, *Vathek*. On the surface, then, Gérard was giving in to
the mode; he disclosed his underlying motives, however, in his corres-
pondence, especially in two letters to his father. Writing to him from
Lyons, on Christmas Day, 1842, Gérard confessed that he had spent
a deplorable summer. Dissatisfied with the little work that he was
doing, he feared that he could inspire nothing but commiseration
because of his *'terrible maladie'*. The voyage would efface all past
suffering from his memory, he trusted, and help him prepare a
'physionomie nouvelle' for the eyes of his friends. *'Sois donc un peu
content,'* he wrote later from Marseille, *'de me voir tiré de ma
végétation de Paris pours des travaux utiles et instructifs.'*
    We can picture him sitting on deck, absorbed in an Arabic Gram-
mar. He is of less than medium height and rather stout; his hair is
thin, but he sports a rich auburn beard à la Van Dyck. *'Il conservait
l'allure jeune et les manières chevalresques'* of the 1830s generation.
He looks up from his book, and we are struck by his expression; it is
sweet, humble, and mischievous. There is about his features a firm-
ness, however, which indicates a purposeful will, while the high arch
of his forehead testifies to his metaphysical ruminations and the
nobility of his character. His eyes are deeply set, his gaze is keen; he

15

looks out at the world around him with steady knowledge of the world within. Suddenly he sighs and bends his head.

Two of Gérard's friends have died, Sophie Dawes and, more recently, Jenny Colon. Whatever her character (she is reputed to have murdered her lover), baronne Adrien de Feuchères,* by her mysterious and beautiful presence, exerted a subtle influence over the young Gérard during those early years in his beloved Valois; he will recall her when he creates Adrienne in *Sylvie*. Whether or not Jenny Colon was his mistress is debatable, but she had certainly enraptured him; her sudden death, some fifteen months after his first mental crisis, wounded Gérard deeply. Sophie Dawes, Jenny Colon, Marie Pleyel, all played fundamental roles in Gérard's life : his imagination was kindled no less than his affections were stirred. He glimpsed in each of them an aspect, a quality of the Eternal Female who is at once Mother, Sister, and Bride, the one who redeems the hero and is at the same time directly or indirectly responsible for his death. Robert Graves has called her the White Goddess. And in Balkis, Queen of the Morning, she comes close to incarnation. Balkis is more than a legendary figure, however, she is, like Zetnaybia, a flesh and blood creation. If the women he knew contributed to the lifelike characteristics of Nerval's heroines, the tragic, early death of his mother influenced the pattern of his relationships and intensified his emotional needs. His search was always more than a literary one, for he was guided by an acute, personal sorrow. Throughout his life he was haunted by an absence.

Gérard puts aside his Arabic Grammar and asks his travelling companion, Fonfrède, who, incidentally, is never mentioned in the *Voyage*, how much longer they have to wait; but Fronfrède doesn't know, doesn't care, either, for his attention is fixed on a vivacious looking girl who has just stepped aboard. Does she resemble the Javanese slave, Zetnaybia, whom he, in fact, not Gérard, will purchase soon in Cairo? . . . Gérard smiles and turns to his notes.

A period of intensive reading preceded Nerval's departure for the East and he continued his researches during the voyage and afterwards. Considering his interests and learnings, his fiery enthusiasm and spiritual aspiration, it was inevitable that he would set off, one day, for '*la terre des coexistences religieuses . . . la patrie des convergences sacrées*'. In the Orient, moreover, originated much that enchanted and inspired him in the works of Apuleius (whose *Golden Ass* was one of Nerval's favourite books), Picus de Mirandula, Silvestre de Sacy, Emanuel Swedenborg, and the eighteenth century Illuminés to whom he would devote an important work in 1852. Gérard was eager to reach the source. He already planned to write

* Sophie Dawes.

a book based upon his voyage, and well might he have had an intuition that it would be his first major work : the time was ripe. In *Voyage en Orient* Nerval affirms his own particular genre, one which is at once a novel yet a tale, an autobiography yet a poem. . . . But the boat is moving, the coast of France recedes. Now begins the enterprise of great pith and moment.

Turning to the entry for 1843 on the background chart, the reader will note the actual route which Gérard took on his travels to the East; it is not the one taken in the original *Voyage*, which opens with a long *Introduction* describing a journey from Geneva to Constance, Munich, and Vienna, then down the Adriatic from Trieste to Cythera. The first part was based on Gérard's 1839 visit to Austria where he had met Marie Pleyel in Vienna. Strict chronology and factual reality were set aside for the sake of symbolic substructure and imaginative reality. '*Quoi qu'il en soit,*' Nerval would write in *Aurélia,* '*je crois que l'imagination humaine n'a rien inventé qui ne soit vrai, dans ce monde ou dans les autres.*' The visit to Cythera aptly enabled Gérard to retell the story of Francesco Colonna's 'neoplatonic love' for Lucrezia Polia, in homage, perhaps, to Marie Pleyel. At all events, this was the first of the '*ponctuations poétiques*' in the *Voyage,* another being an excursion to the pyramids; they prepared the way for, and anticipated the tone of, the two major Tales which are included in the present volume. The main part of the original *Voyage* follows Gérard's real itinerary; the first Tale is inserted before his departure for Beirut, the second concludes the book.

Ostensibly, the narrator in our 'Zetnaybia' is Gérard; in reality, he is the author's invention, a dramatization of Gérard : without his mirrors Nerval would be blind. When Fonfrède bought the girl, whom he kept for about a week, Gérard at once appreciated her potential as copy; he developed her as a character who would offset the heroines of the Tales. Although the *Voyage* owes much of its realistic humour and spice to Zetnaybia, she is, paradoxically, scarcely less fictitious than Setalmulc and Balkis. After the hasty conclusion of the narrator's adventures with Zetnaybia it was Nervalian logic that Gérard should turn to legendary women for fulfilment. A work of careful juxtapositions, *Voyage en Orient* may be read as Nerval's discovery of himself as a poet : ultimately, reality proves a sham; salvation abides in myth.

Few readers today would have patience enough to wade through the whole of the *Voyage,* which consists of some 680 pages in the Classiques Garnier edition. Many of the descriptions of Lebanon and Syria are familiar to us through cinema, television, and standard travel books; they no longer hold the novel and exotic appeal that they did for Nerval's contemporaries. Moreover, for Nerval himself

the two Tales formed the real marrow of the *Voyage* and they
remain, in fact, its most significant landmark. 'The Queen of the
Morning' had already been in embryo form for nearly twenty years:
in 1835 Nerval had written a rough draft for an opera in which Jenny
Colon would star as Balkis. (An early version of *Hakim* appeared in
the *Revue des Deux Mondes*, in 1847, and of *Balkis et Salomon* in
Le National, in 1850.) In making a selection, then, I have respected
the design of the original, in spirit if not by the letter. I must acknowledge two particular instances of editor's licence which I trust the
reader will excuse for the sake of perspective and construction. I have
curtailed to a hint the narrator's short but dramatic declaration of
his feelings for the daughter of the Druze sheikh and left Zetnaybia
at Madame Carlès' rather than reintroduce her later in the book as
Salèma's servant. 'Zetnaybia' contains the best reporting in, and the
most animated scenes of, *Voyage en Orient*; it bubbles with sensuous
appreciation of the palpable world. Impressionistic and lively, immediate and nervous, the style is well tuned for modern ears. With
his wild fluctuations of mood, the swashbuckling narrator reminded
me, at times, of Henry Miller. The Tales are translated in their
entirety. Charged with occult preoccupations, tender with mystic
undertones, and revealing, at the same time, especially in 'Caliph
Hakim', a keen sense of social reality and a concern for justice, they
form two of the brightest and most valuable links on a chain which
includes the translation of *Faust*, the plays *Léo Burckart* and
L'Alchimiste, *Les Illuminés*, the marvellous sonnets *Les Chimères*,
and the confessional *Aurélia*. The second Tale represents the synthe-
sis of Nerval's esoteric thought, but I do not wish to spoil the reader's
enjoyment by any attempt at exegesis. Suffice to say that it 'places'
the author somewhere between William Blake and Helena Blavatsky.

Both Tales reflect not only Gérard's quest for the Eternal Female,
but also the painful search for his own identity : '. . . *la même quête
de soi, et cette quête, il faut l'écrire pour exister*'. Where Gérard's
identity is at stake a principle issue is, on one level — Am I a son of
Lucifer or of Jehovah? on another — Do I commit the sacrifice or
am I the victim? A Freudian viewpoint — identity shattered in childhood, a mother fixation, sado-masochistic ambivalence, sexual impotence, homosexual inclinations — may well increase contemporary
understanding of Nerval, but in no way can it diminish or appease
the drama that he lived, transmuted, and gave exceptional utterance
to. '*Sous la paleur d'Abel, hélas! ensanglantée, / J'ai parfois de Caïn
l'implacable rougeur!*' (*Antéros*) And in his suicide, too, did he not
confirm that he was both. Gérard, then, is Hakim in the first Tale
(where the Moristan scenes are based on his own experiences) and
Adoniram in the second. This personal motivation behind the Tales

makes them ring with a particularly authentic note and renders the heroes highly sympathetic. The best of Nerval's writing is inspired by dire necessity.

To estimate Nerval's importance in the history of literature is beyond the scope of the present Introduction. May I simply remind the reader, in passing, that Proust was strongly influenced by the evocation of past time in *Sylvie*, while the Symbolists and the Surrealists were equally indebted to Nerval, for the form and content of their work. And I close with tributes from Baudelaire, André Breton, and Apollinaire. '. . . *l'intelligence brilliante, active, lumineuse de Gérard de Nerval*'. '*Il semble en effet que Nerval posséda à merveille l'esprit dont nous nous réclamons.*' '*Esprit charmant! Je l'eusse aimé comme un frère!*'

rue Casimir Delavigne, Paris   Norman Glass
1972

Part One *Zetnaybia*

1 Sunrise

Life is strange indeed and wonderful! Every morning, during those uncertain moments when reason gradually triumphs over the frenzy of the dream world, I expect nothing more natural, nothing more logical and in keeping with my Parisian background, than waking up to the feeble light of a grey and cheerless sky. My ears listen for the noise of wheels pounding the road, while my eyes prepare to focus on the dismal view of a hotel room, crammed with such knobby furniture that my imagination, like an imprisoned fly, will collide against one window after the other. Consider, then, for an instant, my increasing delight and astonishment as I discover myself a thousand leagues away from my homeland and let my senses slowly absorb the confused impressions of a world which is the perfect antithesis of ours. The chanting of the Turk at the nearby minaret, the small bell and the heavy trot of a passing camel, which utters, now and then, an uncanny howl, the rustling and the barely audible hissing that animate air, woodwork and high walls, the precocious dawn projecting the innumerable indentations of the windows across the ceiling, the morning breeze, which, laden with a smack of perfume, lifts up the door-curtain to display the swaying crests of palm-trees above the courtyard walls . . . imagine, then, my amazement and my rapture! But occasionally I'm saddened, it depends upon the day; I don't wish to assert that an eternal summer implies a life that is never anything but joy. The black sun of melancholy, which sheds its gloomy rays over the countenance of Albert Durer's pensive angel, rises too, at times, over the luminous plains of the Nile, as it does over the banks of the Rhine and the chilly countryside of Germany. Although there is no mist and fog, the dust can settle, I'm bound to confess, like a mournful veil, over the brightness of a day in the Orient.

Sometimes I climb up on to the terrace of my house, in the Coptic district of Cairo, so that I can watch the sun's early beams kindle the distant plain of Heliopolis and the slopes of mount Mokatem, where the City of the Dead stretches out between Cairo and Mataray. Generally this is a magnificent sight, above all when the dawn starts

23

tinting the cupolas and slender arches of the tombs consecrated to the three dynasties of caliphs, soudans and sultans who have governed Egypt since A.D. 1000. One of the obelisks from the ancient temple of the sun has remained in this plain, standing upright like a neglected sentinel; erect in the midst of a tufted clump of palm-trees and sycamores, it still welcomes the first rays of the god who was worshipped long ago at its foot.

In Egypt daybreak lacks those lovely vermilion hues that embellish the Cyclades or the coasts of Candia; without any warning, except a faint glimmer of white, the sun suddenly splits the horizon. Often it seems to struggle, though, as it hoists up the long folds of a slate-coloured shroud; it appears pale to us, at such times, and robbed of its rays, like the subterranean Osiris; its faded imprint augments the sadness of the arid sky, which is then the very image of an overcast sky in Europe, but instead of bringing down rain, this sky will absorb every drop of humidity. The turbid dust that clogs the horizon never breaks up into fresh clouds, as our European mists do; even at zenith the sun only just manages to pierce a course through the cinereous atmosphere in the form of a fiery red disk that might well have emerged from the Libyan forges of the god Phta. At this prospect you understand the melancholia of ancient Egypt, preoccupied, as it so often was, by sorrow and tombs, that profound melancholia which is also transmitted to us through the extant monuments. Now Typhon triumphs for awhile over the benevolent divinities; he irritates your eyes, parches your throat, and hurls a swarm of insects over the fields and orchards.

I saw them, in fact, this morning, descending like messengers of death and famine; they congested the air. Looking up, and never having seen anything comparable, I took them at first for a flock of birds. Abdullah, my dragoman, joined me on the terrace; he made a circle in the air with the long stem of his chibouk and knocked down two or three of them. He shook his head as he looked at these enormous, red and green cicadas.

'Have you ever eaten any?' he asked me.

I could not resist a grimace of disgust at the mere thought of such a meal; nevertheless, if you remove their wings and legs, they must look almost exactly like shrimps.

'They're very handy in the desert,' Abdullah informed me. 'Smoke them, salt them, and they taste very much like red herrings. Add a little *dourah* paste and they make a delicious dish.'

'Talking about food, wouldn't it be possible to do a little Egyptian cooking for me here?' I asked him. 'It's too much trouble having to go twice a day to eat at the hotel.'

'You're quite right,' Abdullah replied, 'you should hire a cook.'

'But what about Ibrahim, surely he can do something?'

'No,' Abdullah said, 'I told you when you employed him that he's just a barbarin (ordinary domestic). His job is to open the door and keep the house clean, he isn't qualified for anything else.'

'And what about you,' I suggested, 'wouldn't you be able to put a piece of meat on the fire and cook up something?'

'You are speaking to me!' Abdullah exclaimed, as though my words had mortally wounded him. 'I fear you're forgetting my rank, sir.'

'That's a pity,' I replied, as though I had only been joking, 'otherwise we could have had a breakfast of cicadas this morning. Seriously, though, I would prefer to take my meals here. After all, there are butchers in the city, fishmongers, fruiterers . . . it's not as though I'm asking for the impossible.'

'It can all be arranged quite simply,' Abdullah assured me, 'hire a cook. But a European cook will cost you one talari (five francs) a day. Even the beys, the pashas, and the hotel-keepers themselves have difficulty in getting hold of one.'

'I want a local cook, one who'll prepare me the kind of dishes he'd eat himself.'

'All right,' said Abdullah, 'I can find one for you at Monsieur Jean's. He's one of your compatriots and he runs a tavern not far from here. There are lots of people there waiting for a job.'

2 The Khowals

I lunched that day, however, as usual, at the hotel, and then I went to rest for awhile at the luxurious Mousky café, where, for the first time, I saw almas dancing in public.

I would like to project the footlights, so to speak, on this café, but in fact it is adorned neither with trefoils, columns, porcelain lining, nor with ostrich eggs dangling from the ceiling. Only in Paris do you find such Oriental cafés! Imagine, instead, a plain, modest, white-washed shop, where the only arabesque is a picture, reproduced several times, of a pendulum hanging between two cypress-trees in a meadow. The rest of the decoration consists of mirrors, which are also painted; they serve to reflect a small palm-tree planted in a pot and surrounded by dishes of oil full of floating night-lights. The overall effect is delightful in the evening.

Hard, wooden divans are arranged around the room and close to them are cages of palm-tree wood, which serve the customers as foot-stools while they enjoy their fines-janes (elegant cups) of coffee. Here, the fellahs in their blue overalls, the Copts in their black turbans, or the Bedouins in their striped cloaks, take a seat along the wall and look without any surprise or suspicion at the Frank sitting among them, but they all smile at the bizarre preparation which the kahwadji (proprietor) knows he must add to the foreigner's coffee . . . sugar! The cooking-range takes up one of the shop corners and it is generally the most precious ornament in the place. There is a cupboard above it fixed to the wall and stocked with painted crockery; embellished by festoons and rock-work, it looks something like a German stove. The cooking-range is always crammed with innumerable, small copper coffee-pots, since a whole coffee-pot has to be heated to boiling point for each one of those fines-janes which is as big as an egg-cup. . . . But here come the khowals (almas) in a cloud of dust and tobacco smoke!

First of all I was struck by the brilliant colours of the skull-caps which topped their glossy tresses. Small bells rang and rings jangled as their heels beat the floor, while their raised arms whirled in time with the boisterous rhythm and their hips quivered voluptuously. Under the transparent muslin their waists were naked between their short blouses and their ornate, low hanging girdles, but so rapidly did they turn and spin that I could scarcely make out the features of these seductive dancers. Two of them, however, were intoxicating beauties . . . that much I could perceive; quickly inflamed by them, I was already planning to pay them homage by fastening a handful of ghazis (small gold coins worth up to five francs) on to their fore-heads, following the true traditions of the Levant. Their expression was proud, their Arabic eyes glittered with kohl, their plump but delicate cheeks were lightly painted; but the third one, I have to admit, evidently belonged to the less tender sex . . . he had a week's growth of beard! When the dance was over I was at last able to examine the features of the two girls more attentively, as though I were Paris about to offer the apple, and then, despite my initial incredulity, I was obliged to recognize that, like their partner, these two potential Venuses were . . . males!

On my return home Abdullah greeted me in such a state of excite-ment that I was unable to understand him. Exasperated by my feeble powers of comprehension, he began again, in Arabic this time, with-out permitting me to interrupt him for a single moment, and when he finished, I hinted that his French was not exactly free of faults.

He was, of course, outraged at this suggestion, but I was able to calm him and even make him laugh by telling him how I had been taken in by the khowals. He finally explained to me in an intelligible manner what had occurred during my absence.

My neighbour, a khanoun (mistress of the house) and a sixty-year-old widow at that, had summoned the sheikh to inform him that she could no longer tolerate the risk of living next to a French bachelor, and she reminded him that I was breaking Muslim rules of etiquette by refusing to live with a woman. The sheikh agreed and assured her that he had warned me about my situation when he had allowed me to rent the house; he added that he would have me evicted unless I took a wife or a slave-girl into my household within a few days.

'You should convert to Mohammedanism and get married,' Abdullah advised me, 'otherwise you'll be obliged to live in a noisy okel.* You've already said that you can't afford the prices at the French hotel.'

'Not only can't I afford the prices, but as I've already told you, I don't intend to cut myself off from everyday life in such a fashion.'

'The solution is simple, then,' Abdullah assured me, 'convert to Mohammedanism.'

I replied that I would reach a decision in a day or two.

If I converted to Mohammedanism, I reasoned, I would thereby lose my nationality and become a Turkish subject in every respect. Among us Europeans, religion is completely separated, for better or for worse, from the civil law, but the two principles merge into one among the Mohammedans; I would therefore fall out of French jurisdiction and, so to speak, fall under the baton and the sabre. Moreover, according to Turkish law, I would be condemned to death if I reverted to Christianity. When you become a Mohammedan you lose not only your former faith, but also your name, your family and your country; you are no longer the same man, you are now a Turk.

I had already lived long enough in the Orient to realize that slavery is basically nothing more than a kind of adoption. The condition of a slave is certainly better than that of a free fellah or a rayah (non-Muslim subject of the Ottoman Empire). Indeed, as far as I could see, there was little difference between an Egyptian girl, who was sold by her parents to a husband whom they chose for her, and an Abyssinian girl on display at the slave bazaar. Furthermore, a European who takes a slave-girl thereby earns the legal right to practise almost any of the regular professions, though in such an instance he must first ask the slave if she consents, for she has the right, if she is unsatisfied with her master for one reason or another,

* Native inn or caravanserai. — N.G.

to order him to resell her at the bazaar. This particular detail indicates better than any other the mildness of slavery in the Orient. . . . But none of these general reflections helped me to reach a decision about my own situation !

3 The Dervishes

Late that evening I went out alone for a walk, but soon I wished that I had asked the erudite and enlightened Abdullah to accompany me, for Abdullah, like most dragomen, considers himself quite a scholar and he believes that in revealing his knowledge he is conferring great honours upon me . . . and for only twenty piastres a day ! On this particular occasion he would certainly have been able to explain why there was such a jostling crowd in the streets, an exceptional phenomenon at this hour of night. The cafés were open and packed ; the mosques were illuminated, and a solemn chant resounded from them, while their slender minarets were ringed by light ; tents were pitched on Esbekieh Square, and the sound of drums and reed flutes reverberated in every corner. Leaving the Square, I elbowed my way with some difficulty through the crowds and joined the people hurrying down the main street ; the shops were open, as though it were daytime, and each one was lit up by hundreds of candles and decked with garlands of flowers made of gold or coloured paper. In front of a small mosque in the middle of the street, there was an immense candelabrum with innumerable, pyramid-shaped, little glass lamps upon it, and intermingled among them were bunches of grapes hanging from lanterns. About thirty singers were seated in an oval below and around the candelabrum ; they formed the chorus to four other singers who were standing up in the midst of them, and one pellucid voice after another pealed forth the strophes of a song. A sweet and even amorous note marked this nocturnal hymn as it rose up to the sky with that undertone of melancholy with which the Orientals sanctify joy as well as sorrow. I noticed that the majority of the audience were Copts (they could be identified by their black turbans) ; it was clear, then, that the Turks willingly permitted Christians to attend this ceremony.

I was suddenly disturbed from my reverie by a familiar slap on the back, and turning round I found myself confronting a pair of bleary but amiable eyes, which doubtless belonged to one of my compatriots.

'You must be the gentleman who was looking for a cook,' he said to me in fluent French.

'I am,' I replied, 'but how do you know about that?'

'Didn't your dragoman tell you?' he asked in surprise.

Then I realized that this must be Monsieur Jean, the tavern proprietor whom Abdullah had told me he would consult. I explained that my dragoman, preoccupied by other urgent matters, had forgotten to tell me the result of his visit. Fortunately, Monsieur Jean was in a festive mood, and he wasn't at all offended by this oversight.

'Well,' he declared, 'you have a cook, his name is Mustapha and he'll report for duty early tomorrow morning.'

I thanked him, but as I was much more interested at present in the sight before us than in my household problems, I asked Monsieur Jean if he could explain the reasons for this unexpected festival.

He told me that we were assisting at a ceremony in honour of a Dervish saint who was buried in the nearby mosque. As this mosque was situated in the Coptic district the wealthier members of the sect were responsible every year for the expenses of the ceremony.

That explained the mingling of black turbans with those of other colours.

He informed me, furthermore, that the more vulgar class of Christians were only too ready to enjoy a celebration for certain religious Dervishes and Santons whose strange rules and conduct often form no part of any particular cult, but date back, perhaps, to the superstitions of antiquity.

The ceremony, in fact, had now grown even more extraordinary. The thirty Dervishes were holding hands and bobbing up and down like boats, while the zikkers (chorus leaders) gradually worked themselves up into a poetic frenzy which was as tender as it was savage; their long curled hair, which they preserved, contrary to the Arabic custom, flowed in all directions as they swung their heads to and fro; they wore, instead of tarbooshes, caps of an antique shape which resembled the Roman petasus; soon, their humming psalmody was regularly punctuated by highly dramatic notes and it adopted the form of a dialogue in verse, while the performance itself was addressed with gentleness and lamentation to some unknown being or object worthy of veneration and love. Perhaps this was how the priests of ancient Egypt celebrated the mysteries of the lost or recovered Osiris; the incantations of the Corybants were no doubt similar to these sounds of lamentation, while this weird chorus of howling Dervishes rhythmically pounding the ground were still obeying, perhaps, that age-old tradition of ecstasy and rapture which resounded long ago across the entire eastern shore, from the oasis of Ammon to cold Samothrace. Just listening to them, I felt my eyes brim with tears, while in their turn, all the bystanders were gradually overwhelmed by an enthusiasm bordering on abandon.

Monsieur Jean, however, an old sceptic of the republican army, did not participate in the general excitement; he found the performance quite ridiculous and assured me that the Mohammedans themselves took pity on the Dervishes.

'It's the common people who encourage them,' he said. 'Nothing could be less in keeping with true Mohammedanism, and as for their songs, they don't mean anything at all.'

'All the same,' I suggested, 'could you translate one of them for me?'

'It's all nonsense,' he replied, 'a lot of gushy love songs with no purpose behind them. I know quite a few of them, here's one which they were singing : "My heart is harrowed by love, and my eyelids refuse to close. Shall I never again behold my beloved?

"Sorrow consumes me at night, for absence is the grave of hope. I am weighed down by a necklace of tears, and my heart scorches my blood.

"Tell me, O dove, why do you lament in this fashion? Is absence the fount of your grief, too, or do your wings bewail the lack of space?

"Yes, she replies, our sorrows are alike; I, too, am consumed by love, O alas! we share the same affliction, for the absence of my beloved is the source of my lamentation!"

'And the thirty Dervishes always accompany these couplets with the same refrain : "There is no God but Allah!"' '

'It seems to me,' I said, 'that this song may well be addressed to the Divinity, in fact. There's no doubt that the subject is divine love.'

'Oh! not at all,' Monsieur Jean replied, 'for you hear the same refrain pop up with other couplets when they compare their beloved to the gazelle of the Yemen . . . she has blooming skin, she has spent most of her time drinking milk and whatnot. . . . They're no better than our Music-hall songs,' he concluded.

I was not convinced, and when he quoted other songs, I more than once recalled the Song of Songs.

'Anyhow,' Monsieur Jean said, 'you'll see them again, the day after tomorrow, giving way to all kinds of lunacy during the festival of Mohammed. Though if I were you I'd put on Arabic costume, for this year the festival falls on the same day as the pilgrims' return from Mecca. There'll be lots of Maghrebians (Muslims from the west) among them who won't appreciate the sight of French clothes, especially,' he chuckled, 'since the conquest of Algiers,' and he returned to his tavern for further stimulus.

I decided to follow his advice. I watched for awhile longer, then started making my own way home. The ceremony continued until dawn.

4 A Decision

Early the following morning, I told Abdullah to order the cook to make my breakfast, but Mustapha replied that he couldn't prepare anything until the necessary kitchen utensils were purchased. That was true enough, and I must admit that the set of things which I went out to buy, under my dragoman's guidance, was neither superfluous nor expensive. As for provisions, the female fellahs are lined up all along the streets with cages full of chickens, pigeons, and ducks; they even sell by the bushel chickens that have been hatched in those famous egg ovens of Egypt; in the morning, Bedouins bring heathcocks and quail into the city, holding the feet between their fingers and thereby forming a wreath around their hands. All of which, not to mention fish from the Nile, the vegetables and the enormous fruits from this ancient earth, is sold at prodigiously cheap prices. Since a chicken cost only twenty centimes and a pigeon ten, I calculated that I would certainly be able to avoid hotel meals for a long time to come.

Unfortunately it was impossible to find any plump poultry; there was nothing on sale except little feathered skeletons. The fellahs find it more profitable to sell them in this condition instead of filling them up beforehand with lots of maize. Abdullah advised me to buy quite a number of cages; we would then have the opportunity to fatten up all the birds ourselves. On our return home we set the chickens free in the courtyard and the pigeons in a room; Mustapha noticed a small cock that was less bony than the others, and, on my request, he got ready to prepare a couscous.

I shall never forget the sight of this Arab ferociously whipping out his yataghan from under his belt in order to slaughter a miserable cock. The poor bird was skinnier than it looked, and beneath its plumage, which was as brilliant as a golden pheasant's, there was precious little meat. At the stab of Mustapha's knife, it shrieked itself hoarse until my soul shuddered. Mustapha cleanly cut off its head, then let the cock drag itself along for awhile with an occasional helpless flutter; it reached a corner, stopped, stiffened its legs and fell down. This gory performance robbed me of my appetite; I appreciate a good dish as long as I don't see how it's prepared, and I considered myself infinitely more guilt laden for the death of the little cock than I would have if it had perished in the hands of a hotel-keeper. A coward's reasoning? . . . I couldn't free myself from recollections of ancient Egypt, and I must confess that for a day or two after this incident I thought twice before thrusting my table-knife into a vegetable, for fear of offending some god of long ago.

I didn't intend, however, to let myself be overcome by pity for the death of a skinny cock to the extent of overlooking man's legitimate need to nourish himself. There are many other provisions in the centre of Cairo; fresh dates and bananas would always suffice for an agreeable breakfast or even for lunch. The butchers, however, sell nothing but mutton, while those in the suburbs add, for the sake of variety, camel meat, and you can see huge slabs of it hanging from the ceiling at the back of the shop. There is no mistaking camel meat, but Abdullah claimed that the mutton was often dog meat . . . and that was his mildest joke about it! Frankly, I am sure that I would have recognized the difference. What I could never understand, though, was the weighing operation and the preparations; all I learned was that every dish cost me about ten piastres, but this did include the requisite condiments and dressing : *meloukia* or *bamie*, savoury vegetables indeed; the first resembles spinach, as for the other, there is nothing like it in Europe.

In short, I soon reached the conclusion that in the Orient the hotel-keepers, the shop-keepers, the dragomen, the servants and the cooks were all faithfully united against the traveller. Without a great deal of determination and even imagination, you require a colossal fortune in order to afford a lengthy sojourn. M. de Chateaubriand admits that he was ruined in the Orient; M. de Lamartine spent a quite extravagant amount of money here; as for other travellers, most of them didn't even risk leaving the port, while those who did crossed through the country as quickly as possible. As for me I'm going to undertake what I consider a much better project : I shall buy a slave-girl, who will soon be able to replace Abdullah and Ibrahim (besides, it was my dragoman who insisted that I had to employ the latter); I shall then be able to settle accounts squarely with Mustapha, and, in all, decrease my daily expenses. Moreover, I shall have a woman in the house, at last, and the sheikh will bother me no longer. With a slave-girl rather than a wife, I shall remain independent and at the same time be able to maintain a better economic situation. Once I had made this decision I told Abdullah to lead me to the slave-bazaar.

5 The Slave-Merchants

We had to cross the whole of Cairo to reach the district of the main bazaars; when we arrived, we followed a small, dark, winding street off the corner of the principal one, and we soon emerged into an irregularly shaped courtyard, without being obliged to dismount from our donkeys. In the middle of the courtyard was a well, shaded by a sycamore. To the right, standing up and lined against the wall, were a dozen Negroes who looked restless rather than sad; they wore the blue, sleeveless tunic of the common people, and, most striking of all, each one of them revealed a physique distinct from the others and boasted his own particular hue of black. We turned to the left where there was a long row of little rooms on each side of an inlaid floor which reached right into the courtyard, forming a stage, about two feet above ground level. Here we dismounted and tied our donkeys to a nearby post. We were already surrounded by swarthy merchants.

'Essouad? Abesch? (Negresses? Abyssinians?),' they exclaimed. And we made our way to the first room.

We were greeted by storms of laughter from six or seven Negresses, who were squatting on mats in a circle and smoking. They were dressed in scant, blue rags, and you could hardly accuse the dealers of glamorizing their merchandise. Their hair, which was divided up into hundreds of tight little tresses, was kept together by a red ribbon which separated it into two voluminous tufts, while the parting was tinted with cinnabar; they wore pewter bracelets around their arms and legs, and necklaces of glass beads; some of them had large copper rings dangling from the fleshy tip of their nose or ear-lobe : this gave them a barbaric appearance, which was emphasized by differently coloured tattoos all over their faces. They were Negresses from Sennaar, and indeed no species could be so far removed from our standard conceptions of beauty. The prominence of their jaws, their flattened foreheads, and their thick lips are characteristics which class these poor creatures in an almost bestial category; nevertheless, apart from this strange physiognomy which nature had endowed them with, their bodies were of a rare and exceptional beauty; pure and virginal forms were clearly visible under their tunics; their voices

33

were sweet and vibrant like the shrill but subdued sounds of fresh mountain springs. All the same, I was hardly inflamed by these lovely monsters, and I asked to see other women with a more open facial angle and a less pronounced shade of black.

'That depends on how much money you're prepared to spend,' Abdullah said. 'Those you're looking at cost only two hundred and fifty centimes. They're guaranteed for eight days and you have the right to resell them during that period if you find they have any defects or infirmities.'

'But I don't have to be so stingy,' I assured Abdullah. 'After all, it won't cost me any more to feed a really pretty girl than it will to feed one of these.'

Abdullah said nothing, but his silence indicated that he didn't share my opinion on that particular subject.

In the other rooms we visited all the girls were still from Sennaar; there were some younger ones, it's true, and quite a few beauties, but the same physiognomy prevailed with depressing uniformity.

The merchants were ready to have them strip; they poked open their mouths so that I could examine their teeth; they made them walk up and down and pointed out, above all, the elasticity of their breasts. These poor girls responded in the most carefree manner, and the scene was hardly a painful one, for most of them burst into uncontrollable laughter. I realized, moreover, that they would prefer any circumstances to a long sojourn in the bazaar and, perhaps, to the existence which they had previously led in their own country.

Seeing only pure Negresses around me, however, I asked Abdullah if there were no Abyssinian girls on display.

'They're not on public display,' he informed me. 'You have to go into the merchant's house and convince him that you haven't come here out of mere curiosity, the way most travellers do. Besides, they're much more expensive, and perhaps you'll be able to find a woman who suits you among the slaves from Dangola. We've still got the smaller bazaars to visit.'

One of the merchants approached us and told me that some Ethiopians had just arrived. They had been installed outside the city, in order to avoid paying the entrance duty, in the countryside beyond the gate of Bab-el-Madbah. I told him that I wanted to go and see them before I made a decision, and Abdullah untied our donkeys.

We trotted through a deserted district, and, after making our way up and down many narrow, winding streets, we found ourselves in the plain, that is to say, amidst the tombs, for they happened to surround this side of the city. To our left were the monuments of the caliphs. We passed between hills of drifting dust which were full of potholes and formed by the remains of ancient edifices. We halted

our donkeys at the gate of a small circumference of walls which were
probably the ruins of a mosque. Three or four Arabs, dressed in costumes which I had not seen in Cairo, told us to come inside, and I
found myself in the midst of a sort of tribe whose tents were pitched
in this enclosure, which was sealed off on every side. I was greeted,
as I had been at the main bazaar, by a storm of laughter from a
number of Negresses; these naïve natures never hesitate to reveal all
their impressions, but I don't know why they should find European
clothes so ridiculous. All of them were busy at various household
chores, and in their midst was a very tall and extremely beautiful girl;
she was carefully stirring the contents of a huge cauldron which was
placed upon the fire. As nothing could divert her, I had some of the
other girls displayed; they quickly abandoned their jobs and didn't
hesitate to draw my attention to their most alluring features. Not the
least of their attractions was their hair; arranged in enormous plaits,
it was also entirely saturated in butter which streamed down on to
their shoulders and breasts. To protect their heads from the sun, I
thought, but my dragoman informed me that it was a question of
fashion; their hair was glossier, this way, and their faces more
dazzling.

'But,' he said, 'as soon as you've bought them, you send them to the
hammam with orders to disentangle all those tresses, for such a hair-
style is only in fashion around the Mountains of the Moon.'

It didn't take me long to inspect them, for though their savage
appearance was interesting it hardly encouraged cohabitation. Most
of them were disfigured by a mass of tattoos, grotesque incisions, blue
stars and suns cut into the greyish black of their skin. Moreover, I
noticed that their gestures, their attitudes, and their feet, which were
elongated and expanded, probably from their practice at climbing
trees, made them bear a close resemblance to the monkey, that disowned relative whom we insist on spurning through our racial pride.

'Bakchis! Bakchis! (a tip!),' they all cried, and I hesitantly took
some piastres from my pocket, suspecting that their masters would be
the only ones to profit from them. But in order to reassure me, the
men now distributed dates, water-melons, tobacco, and even brandy:
the girls were immediately overcome by joy, and several of them
started dancing to the melancholy sounds of the tarabouk and zom-
marah, the drum and the fife of the African tribes.

The tall, beautiful girl in charge of the cooking merely glanced
round, however, while she continued stirring a thick pap of *dourah*
in the copper cauldron. I drew nearer to her; she looked at me disdainfully, but her attention was suddenly aroused when she caught
sight of my black gloves. Then she crossed her arms and uttered cries
of admiration. She failed to understand how I could have a white

face and black hands! And her astonishment reached a peak when I suddenly took off one of my gloves.

'Bismallah!' she exclaimed. 'Enti effrit? Enti Sheytan?' (Save me, Allah! Are you an afrite? Are you Satan?)

The other girls were equally amazed, and you can imagine how these ingenuous souls were struck by all the details of my European attire. Evidently I could have earned a fortune in their country by simply putting myself on display. The chief beauty, however, quickly returned her attention to the cauldron, like a fickle monkey which is distracted by everything but quite unable to concentrate on any particular subject for more than a second.

I thought of asking how much she would cost, but I was persuaded otherwise by my dragoman who informed me that she was the merchant's favourite; he did not wish to sell her, for he hoped to have a child by her. If he did agree to sell her, the price would be exorbitant.

'Anyhow,' I said to Abdullah, 'I find their colour too dark, let's look at some lighter tints. Are Abyssinians so rare on the market?'

'There aren't very many at present,' he replied, 'but look! the big caravan from Mecca is arriving. It has halted at Birket-el-Hadji, it will enter Cairo tomorrow at daybreak. We'll have a fine selection to choose from then, for many of the pilgrims will be short of money to complete their journey, so they'll sell some of their women, and there'll be slave-merchants, too, that's for sure, coming home from Hedjaz.'

We left the enclosure without anyone being at all offended or surprised at my not having purchased a slave.

6 The Barber's Shop

Early the following morning, I decided to prepare myself for the coming festivities which would welcome the pilgrims and honour the prophet Mohammed. I already possessed the essential article of Arabic dress, the machla, a patriarchial cloak, which can either be worn over the shoulders, or draped over the head, while it still envelops the whole body; but in this case your legs are uncovered, and, thanks to the hood, you look like a dignified sphinx. My first intention, however, was to reach the Frankish district where, Abdullah told me, I would find a barber to attend to my total transformation.

The barber's shop was a marvel of ornamentation, one of the last monuments of the ancient Arabic style, which is being usurped everywhere, in decoration and in architecture, by the Turkish style of Constantinople, which is a cold, dreary jumble, partly Tartar, partly European. The windows of this delightful shop were gracefully denticulated and they overlooked the Calish or canal of Cairo.

Here it was that I lost my European hair-style. The barber applied his razor most skilfully, and, following my instructions, he left me a single tuft on the top of my head, like the one worn by the Chinese and the Muslims. People have different opinions as to the origins of this custom; some claim that it enables the Angel of Death to take a firm grip, while others have a more practical explanation : the Turk always foresees an instance when he could have his head cut off, and, since it would then be exhibited to the people, he doesn't want it to be lifted up by the nose, the beard, or the mouth; the very thought of such ignominious treatment upsets him. The Turkish barbers are malicious enough to razor a Christian's head quite bare. As for me, my scepticism is so solid that I don't feel obliged to rebuff any superstition.

When the job was done, the barber had me hold a pewter basin under my chin, and then I felt a jet of cold water streaming over my neck and ears. Standing on a bench, the barber poured out the whole contents of a huge kettle hanging from the ceiling just above my head. No sooner had I recovered from the shock than I had to submit to a thorough wash in soapy water, then my beard was cut and trimmed in the latest Constantinople fashion.

Next I had to be hatted; this presented no problem, for the street was full of tarboosh dealers and female fellahs making small white caps; these takias, as they are called, are placed directly upon the skin; some of them are very delicately quilted with yarn or silk, while others even have a lace border which hangs down from under the edge of the red cap. The latter are generally of French manufacture, and, if I'm not mistaken, our city of Tours has the privilege of hatting the entire Orient.

With the two caps superposed, my neck uncovered and my beard trimmed, I hardly recognized myself in the exquisite shell-encrusted mirror which the barber held up in front of me. He was only too glad to accompany me as I left the shop to complete my transformation; I purchased from the old clothes dealers a very spacious pair of blue cotton breeches and a red waistcoat embellished by quite clean silver embroidery. The barber told me that I could now pass for a Syrian highlander from Saide or Taraboulous. The bystanders hailed me as *tchelby*, which is the title they bestow upon the dandies of the country. Totally transfigured, I joyfully went my way, proud that I was no longer defiling this beautiful city with my sack of an overcoat and my chimney-pot of a hat!

7 The Caravan from Mecca

As many as thirty thousand people were about to swell the population of Cairo. The streets of the Muslim district were already thronged with crowds, but I managed to make my way to Bab-el-Fotouh, the Gate of Victory; the whole of the main street which leads there was crammed with bystanders who were kept in orderly lines by government troops. The sound of trumpets, cymbals and drums directed the advancing procession; the various nations and sects were distinguished by their trophies and flags. The long files of harnessed dromedaries, which were mounted by Bedouins armed with long rifles, followed one another, however, at a fairly monotonous pace, and it was only when I reached the countryside that I was able to appreciate the full impact of a spectacle which is unique in the whole world.

A whole nation on the march was merging into the huge population which adorned the knolls of mount Mokatam on the right, and, on the left, the thousands of usually deserted edifices of the City of the Dead; streaked with red and yellow bands, the turreted copings of the walls and towers of Saladin were also swarming with onlookers. I had the impression that I was present at a scene during the crusades, and this illusion of living in another age was perfected by the sight of the flashing breastplates and knightly helmets worn by the viceroy's guards, interspersed in groups among the crowd. Farther ahead, in the plain where the Calish meanders, stood thousands of chequered tents where the pilgrims halted to refresh themselves; there was no lack of dancers and singers; all the musicians of Cairo, in fact, competed with the horn-blowers and kettledrummers of the procession, an enormous orchestra whose members were perched on top of camels.

Most awesome of all was the vast multitude of Maghrebians which consisted of people from Tunis, Tripoli, Morocco, and also of our 'compatriots' from Algiers; I was sure that I would never again have the opportunity to admire such a bearded, shaggy and ferocious assortment. The majority of the Santon and Dervish brotherhoods were among them, too, ecstatically howling their canticles of love which were punctuated by the name of Allah. Flags of a thousand different colours, hampers overloaded with personal property and weapons, and, here and there, in their magnificent apparel, the emirs and sheikhs mounted upon caparisoned horses streaming with gold and precious stones . . . all enhanced the overwhelming splendour of this somewhat disorderly advance. The numerous palanquins for the women were also a picturesque sight, to say the least; this singular apparatus, consisting of a bed surmounted by a tent, was fixed across the back of a camel. Entire families, with lots of children and furniture, appeared to be comfortably settled within these pavilions which, for the most part, were embellished by gorgeous tapestries.

Late in the afternoon, the booming of the citadel cannons and a sudden blast of trumpets proclaimed that the Mahmil, a holy ark which contains Mohammed's robe of golden cloth, had arrived within sight of the city. The most imposing members of the caravan, the most magnificent horsemen, the most inspired Santons, and the aristocracy of turbans, which was indicated by the colour green, surrounded this palladium of Islam. Seven or eight dromedaries approached, one after the other; their heads were so richly adorned with plumes, and they were covered by such brilliant trappings and rugs, that beneath all this attire, which disguised their shape, they resembled the salamanders or dragons which carry elves and pixies. The first ones bore young kettledrummers whose arms were bare up to their shoulders; in the midst of a bundle of flowing flags, which were arranged around the saddles, they lifted high their golden rods and brought them down with a flourish. Next came an old man with a long white beard; he was symbolically crowned with foliage and seated in a kind of chariot, which was likewise fixed on to the back of a camel. And then came the Mahmil; it consisted of an opulent pavilion, in the form of a square tent, which was embroidered all over with inscriptions and surmounted not only on the top but also at the four corners by enormous bells of silver.

From time to time the Mahmil came to a halt, and the entire population prostrated themselves in the dust, cupping their heads in their hands. An escort of guards struggled to drive back the Negroes who were more fanatical than the other Muslims; they aspired, in fact, to the honour of being trampled to death beneath the camels, but the only share of martyrdom bestowed upon them was a volley of baton blows. As for the Santons, who are an even more ecstatic species of saints than the Dervishes and whose orthodoxy is more questionable, several of them pierced their cheeks with long, pointed nails and walked on, showered in blood; others devoured live serpents, while a third group stuffed their mouths with burning coals. Hardly any of the women participated in these exercises, but among the crowd of pilgrims were troupes of almas who formed part of the caravan; they sang their unending, guttural lamentations, and did not hesitate to lower their veils and expose their faces, which were tattooed red and blue, while their noses were pierced by heavy rings.

I joined the motley host which followed the Mahmil, crying Allah! like the crowds at the various stations of the sacred camels, which swung their embellished heads majestically up and down and thereby appeared to bless the people with their long, curved necks and their strange whinnying. As we entered the city the cannons boomed forth their salute again, and we jostled through the streets on our way to the citadel, while the caravan continued filling up Cairo with its thirty thousand believers who, from now on, had a right to the title of *hadjis*.

It did not take long to reach the main bazaars and the immense Salahel road, where the mosques of El-Hazar, El-Moyed, and the Moristan display their architectural marvels and cast up to the sky their sheaves of minarets interspersed with cupolas. At each mosque that we came to a large number of the pilgrims withdrew from the procession; mountains of babouches piled up in front of the doors, for nobody was admitted unless his feet were bare. The Mahmil, however, didn't come to a halt; taking to the narrow streets which lead up to the citadel, it entered by the north gate, acclaimed by the people gathered together in Roumelieh Square as it passed through the assembled lines of troops. Unable to approach the precincts of Mehemt-Ali's palace, a recent edifice, incidentally, built in the mediocre Turkish style, I climbed up on to the terrace which towers over the whole of Cairo. The view from here dumbfounds you; it is one of the most stunningly beautiful in the entire world. Your eyes are first struck by the huge expanse of the Sultan Hassan mosque, in the foreground, which is streaked and striped with red; it still preserves traces of the French grape-shot, dating from the famous Cairo uprising of 1798. The city takes up the whole horizon in front of you and terminates in the green shade of Choubrah; to the west you see the straggling city of Muslim tombs, the countryside of Heliopolis, and the vast, spacious tract of the Arabian desert, interrupted by the Mokatam range; to the east wind the reddish waters of the Nile with its meagre border of date-trees and sycamores. Boulac stands on the bank, serving, half a league away from the city, as Cairo's port; you

can also make out the green and blossoming island of Rodda, a cultivated landscape garden at the edge of which is the Nilometer structure, opposite the cheerful houses of the Giza countryside; and at last
you see the pyramids in the distance, set on the ultimate slopes of the
Libyan range. Farther south, at Saqqarah, other pyramids, intermingled with hypogea, are visible, and beyond them is the forest of
palm-trees which covers the ruins of Memphis. As your eyes return
towards the city you see, on the opposite bank of the Nile, the old
Cairo built by Amrou to replace the ancient Babylon of Egypt; it is
half hidden by the arches of a gigantic aqueduct, at the foot of which
the Calish opens, skirting the plain of the tombs of Khafre.

The exuberance of the people rallied in the Square and swarming
over the neighbouring countryside animated this vast panorama. But
night was drawing near, the sun had already buried its countenance
in the sands of the lengthy ravine of the desert of Ammon, which the
Arabs name Sea Without Water. I could no longer see anything in
the distance except the course of the Nile, where thousands of cangias
traced silvery networks as they had long ago during the celebrations
of the Ptolemies. It was time for me to climb down from the terrace
and turn my eyes away from that mute antiquity whose eternal
secrets are guarded by a sphinx which has almost vanished into the
sand. We shall see whether the pomp and faith of Islam will repeople
that double solitude of desert and tombs, or whether we shall be
obliged to weep one again over the poetry of an epoch under eclipse.
Ancient Greece disintegrated. Three centuries in arrears, will this
Arabian Middle Ages soon collapse in its turn at the heedless foot of
Pharaoh's monuments?

We shall see . . . and indeed I saw ! for turning round I spied above
my head the last red columns of Saladin's old palace. A rigidly square
construction in marble and alabaster, lacking even a hint of elegance
or character, has recently been built upon the remains of that amaz-
ingly bold and graceful architecture, which is, however, like the
works of the genii, both fragile and transient. Looking like a grain
market, it claims to be a mosque; it is, in fact, as much a mosque as
the Madelaine is a church : modern architects always take the precaution of raising up to God edifices which can serve another purpose
when nobody believes in Him any longer.

Nevertheless the government appeared to have celebrated the
arrival of the Mahmil to everybody's satisfaction; reverently, the
pasha and his family had welcomed the Prophet's robe, which had
been brought back from Mecca, the holy water from the well of
Zemzem, and other treasures of the pilgrimage; the robe had been
displayed to the people at the door of a small mosque behind the
palace. Illuminated now, the city was a magnificent sight; revived

by light, the architectural details of the huge edifices emerged from the shadows; beaming chaplets wreathed the domes of the mosque, while the minarets were again adorned by those dazzling necklaces which had struck me once before; traced in coloured glass, verses from the Koran shone all over the main façade of the mosques. With a last look at these wonders I hurried to Esbekieh Square, which had now become the centre of the festivities.

The nearby districts were lit up by the glare from the shops; specialists in fried dishes, pastry cooks and fruit dealers had invaded all the ground floors; the confectioners exposed sugary marvels in the form of edifices, animals, and other more imaginative inventions. The pyramids and girandoles of light illuminated everything; it might have been the middle of the brightest day. Small, brilliant vessels hung from taut cords stretched across the street, a custom whose origins went back, perhaps, to the festivals of Isis and was still treasured, like so many others, by the good Egyptian people. The south side of the Square, which adjoins the Frankish district, was the heart of the rejoicings. Tents were pitched all around, not only for the cafés but also for the zikkers. Arranged four in a row, firmly fixed into the ground and topped by chandeliers, large flagstaffs (sarys) aided the whirling Dervishes in their exercises; they are distinct from the howlers, for each group has its own manner of attaining that state of enthusiasm which provokes ecstatic visions. Round these poles, then, the Dervishes gyrated, without linking hands to form a dancing circle. Allah zeht! (By the living Allah!) was their only muffled cry. Elsewhere the crowd pushed forward to see the jugglers and rope-dancers, or listen to the rhapsodists who recited selections from the epic novel *Abou-Zeyd*. Swings and see-saws, games of skill and all kinds of caragheuz (puppet-shows and shadow-theatres) formed the final lively attractions of this turbulent fun fair, which would last for another two days, during the celebrations for the anniversary of Mohammed's birth, El-Mouled-en-neby.

I was more than willing to remain there until dawn, but it was already close to the hour when I would have to solve my domestic problem, so, like a child who is obliged to withdraw in the middle of a party, I started walking regretfully home.

8 Abd-el-Kerim

Early the following morning I set off with Abdullah to the slave bazaar at Souk-el-Ezzi. I had chosen a very handsome donkey, streaked like a zebra, for this occasion, and arranged my new costume with a measure of affectation. Buying women is no reason for frightening them, as I had learnt from the scornful laughter of the Negresses.

We arrived at a quite splendid house that must have once belonged to a kachef (bey's deputy) or a mameluke bey; the hall extended into a colonnaded gallery along one side of the courtyard, at the end of which was a wooden divan adorned with cushions. Here a good-looking, elegantly dressed Muslim was holding court; nonchalantly he fingered his rosary of aloes, while a Negro boy rekindled his narghile for him; a Coptic scribe, seated at his feet, probably served him as a secretary.

'This,' Abdullah announced, 'is his honour Abd-el-Kerim, the most illustrious of slave-merchants. He can procure you the loveliest women, if he wants to . . . he's wealthy and he often keeps them for himself.'

'*Saba-el-kher,*' Abd-el-Kerim greeted me, graciously nodding his head and touching his chest with his hand.

I replied with a similar Arabic formula, but my accent revealed my origins; nevertheless, he invited me to take a seat beside him and told the Negro boy to bring me a narghile and a cup of coffee.

'It's because he sees you in my company,' Abdullah didn't hesitate to assure me, 'that he already has a good opinion of you. I'll tell him you've come to settle in the country and want to arrange your household in a lordly style.'

My dragoman's words did, in fact, appear to make a favourable impression on Abd-el-Kerim, who addressed me politely in bad Italian.

His features were refined and distinguished, his eyes penetrating, and his manners courteous; it was only natural that he should conduct me through his palace where he devoted himself, however, to a very dismal trade. He was an affable prince and at the same time a pitiless, resolute freebooter : a strange and fascinating mixture, indeed. He had to dominate the slaves with a fierce glance from his melancholy eyes, even make them suffer, and finally have them leave him full of regrets that he was no longer their master. Clearly enough, any woman sold to me by Abd-el-Kerim would leave him like a mistress forced to leave her lover, but this prospect didn't deter me, for I was already so struck myself by his character and expression that I was almost sure I would settle my business with him and no other.

The square courtyard, where a large number of Nubian and Abyssinian males were wandering around, was full of porticoes and upper galleries whose architecture was highly impressive; huge moucharabies in carved woodwork overhung a staircase hall, decorated by Moresque arcades, which led to the suite occupied by Abd-el-Kerim's most beautiful women.

Many buyers had already entered the courtyard to examine the deep black Negroes; the latter were told to walk up and down, their backs and chests were tested by light smacks, and their tongues, in particular, were closely examined. Dressed in a yellow and blue striped machla, one of these youngsters, whose hair was flat and plaited in the style of the Middle Ages, wore a heavy chain upon his arm, and loudly it clanked as he proudly walked from one end of the courtyard to the other. An Abyssinian from the nation of Gallas, he had no doubt been captured in the war.

There were several low rooms around the courtyard full of carefree Negresses who laughed crazily at the slightest provocation, just like those whom I had seen in the other bazaars. But I saw another woman, draped in a yellow cloak, weeping and hiding her face against a column in the hall, while the mournful serenity of the sky and the glittering embroidery, woven by the rays of the sun in the corners of the courtyard, protested in vain against her eloquent despair.

Passing behind the column I noticed, although her face was covered, that her skin was almost white; moreover, her arms tightly held a baby who was half hidden within her cloak. Sick at heart I was ready to buy her and restore her at once to liberty.

'Don't bother about her,' Abdullah said. 'This woman is the favourite slave of an effendi. She did something wrong, so he sent her here as a punishment, pretending he was going to have her sold along with the child. He'll arrive in a few hours, probably, to take her home and pardon her.'

So the one really miserable slave was crying in the belief that she had lost her master, while the others appeared troubled only by the fear that they would stay here too long without finding one. Here indeed is something which speaks well in favour of the Muslims, especially when you compare such a situation to the fate of slaves in America.

Abd-el-Kerim had left us for a moment to discuss business with one of the Turkish buyers. The Abyssinian women were being dressed, he told me when he returned, and he wanted to show them to me.

'They're in my harem,' he said, 'they're treated just like the members of my family, taking their meals in company with my wives. While we're waiting for them I can show you some very young girls who you may find quite appealing.'

He opened a door and a dozen copper-coloured mites rushed into the courtyard like school children ready for playtime. They were encouraged to have fun with the ducks and guinea-fowl splashing around in the basin of a sculptured fountain under the stairway casing.

I looked at these poor girls . . . how large and dark their eyes were! They were dressed up like young sultanas and had doubtless been torn away from their mother's arms to gratify the lusts of the wealthy inhabitants of Cairo. But Abdullah told me that several of them didn't belong to the merchant; they had been put up for sale by their parents, who had a statement drawn up with Abd-el-Kerim to that effect; they had actually made a special journey to Cairo with the intention of preparing the happiest situation possible for their children.

'You should also know,' Abdullah said, 'that they cost much more than the nubile women.'

'*Queste fanciulle sono cucite!*' Abd-el-Kerim exclaimed in his odd Italian.

What he meant, I supposed, was that these were first-class little girls, but even if I had been a philologist I wouldn't have been able to decipher the phrase with any certainty.

'Oh, you don't have to worry at all,' Abdullah said in the tone of a connoisseur, 'you can buy them with absolute confidence. Their parents carefully checked everything before bringing them here.'

Well, I told myself, I'll leave these children to other hands. The Muslim, who lives according to his laws, can answer to God with a quiet conscience for the fate of these poor young souls, but as for me, if I buy a slave I plan to allow her freedom, even to leave me if she wants.

Abd-el-Kerim now invited me to enter the private section of his house, and Abdullah was discreet enough to remain behind at the foot of the staircase.

In a spacious room with a carved ceiling, which enriched a number of painted and gold arabesques, I saw lined up against the wall five quite beautiful women whose tints recalled the glowing bronze of

Florence; their features were symmetrical, their noses straight, their mouths small; the perfect oval of their heads, the graceful lines of their necks and the serenity of their expression made them resemble those Italian paintings of the Madonna which time has faintly tarnished. They were Catholic Abyssinians, descendants, perhaps, of Father John or Queen Candicia.

To make a particular choice was by no means an easy matter, for they all looked alike, which is what generally occurs among these primitive races. Seeing me hesitate, Abd-el-Kerim thought they didn't attract me, so he had another one brought in; indolently, she walked towards the wall and then turned round to face us.

I was unable to suppress a cry of enthusiasm as I immediately recognized the almond-shaped eyes and the slanting eyelids of a Javanese, while her complexion confirmed that she belonged to the yellow race. Nor can I explain my sudden, overwhelming inclination for the strange and unexpected which quickly led me to decide in her favour. Moreover, she was extremely beautiful, and I didn't hesitate to admire her firm but supple body; the metallic glint of her eyes, the whiteness of her teeth, the elegance of her hands, and her dark mahogany-coloured hair, which she revealed when, obeying the merchant's orders, she insolently took off her tarboosh, far from offered me any cause to object to Abd-el-Kerim's eulogies :

'*Bono! Bono!*' he exclaimed.

We descended the staircase and discussed business, with Abdullah acting as interpreter. This woman had arrived the day before along with the caravan's retinue.

'But,' I said to Abdullah, 'if Abd-el-Kerim put her among his wives yesterday. . . .'

'But what? . . .' my dragoman insisted, looking at me with surprise.

I had evidently made a banal remark.

'Do you mean to say,' Abdullah exclaimed, finally understanding my line of thought, 'that his legitimate wives would allow him to flirt with another woman? . . . And then he's a merchant, just think for a moment! Why, if anything like that ever got known he'd lose all his clientele !'

That made sense enough, and Abdullah swore, moreover, that Abd-el-Kerim, as a good Muslim, must have spent the whole of the previous night praying at the mosque, to be ready for the solemn celebrations in honour of Mohammed.

One question remained, then : the price. Abd-el-Kerim asked for 625 francs; at first, I thought of offering only five hundred, but bargaining for a woman struck me as a rather squalid affair. And anyhow, Abdullah informed me, a Turkish merchant never has two prices.

I asked what her name was, for the price of her name would naturally be included in the net sum.

'Z't'n'b,' Abd-el-Kerim said.

'Z't'n'b,' Abdullah repeated with a tremendous nasal contraction.

I was unable to understand how the sneezing of four consonants represented a name; it took me some time to figure out that Z't'n'b could more reasonably be pronounced Zetnaybia.

I gave Abd-el-Kerim a deposit and said that I would return as soon as I had drawn the balance from my bank in the Frankish district. I even left my handsome donkey there as a further guarantee, but my dragoman untied his and went his separate way.

As I crossed Esbekieh Square I witnessed an extraordinary spectacle. A large crowd had gathered together to watch the *Dohza* ceremony. The sheikh of the caravan was about to ride over the bodies of the Dervishes, both the dancers and the howlers, who had been performing around the poles and close to the tents since the previous evening. These poor wretches were now stretched out flat on their stomachs all along the way which led to the extreme south of the Square, ending at the house of the sheikh El-Bekry, the chief of all the Dervishes; they formed a human highway of over sixty bodies.

This ceremony is considered a miracle which should convince the infidels; the Franks are therefore willingly permitted to occupy the front row of spectators. A public miracle has become a rarity ever since man ventured to look, as Heine says, into the sleeves of the good Lord's mantle, but this, if it is a miracle, is incontestably one. With my own eyes I saw the old sheikh of the Dervishes, wrapped in a white *benich* and wearing a yellow turban, ride his horse over the backs of these sixty or so believers who, with their arms crossed over their heads, were squeezed together without the slightest space between them. The hooves of the horse were shod with iron. Then, simultaneously, they all stood up again in a straight line and cried out, Allah!

According to erudite inhabitants of the Frankish district, this phenomenon is similar to the one which formerly enabled convulsionists to endure the blows of iron fire-dogs right in the belly. The state of exaltation which these people reach acts upon their nervous system and renders them insensible to pain; it reinforces all their organs, which thus develop exceptional powers of resistance.

The Muslims don't accept this explanation; they claim that the sheikh has also ridden his horse over glass bottles and that it wasn't able to break any of them . . . something I would certainly have liked to see, but despite this spectacle, I had not forgotten my acquisition.

Early in the afternoon, then, I triumphantly took the veiled Zetnaybia to my house in the Coptic district. And just in time, for it was the last day of grace which the district sheikh was prepared to allow me. One of Abd-el-Kerim's servants followed the slave, leading a donkey which carried a green trunk on its back.

'It belongs to her,' Abd-el-Kerim had managed to explain to me, 'there are two quite perfect costumes inside. The trunk was given to her by a Mecca sheikh to whom she previously belonged, and now she belongs to you.'

In all, Abd-el-Kerim had behaved with the utmost delicacy.

9 Zetnaybia

There is something extremely captivating and irresistible in a woman from a faraway country; her costumes and habits are already singular enough to strike you, she speaks an unknown language and has, in short, none of those vulgar shortcomings to which we have become only too accustomed among the women of our own country. I gave way, then, for some hours to my fascination for local colour; I listened to Zetnaybia's chatter, I watched her display the motley of her clothes; I had the impression — but would it last for long? I asked myself — that I owned a magnificent bird in a cage.

If the merchant had deluded me about the slave's merits, if she revealed any kind of physical defect, I had eight days, I had been told, in which to annul the agreement. I hardly thought that any European would wish to profit from this infamous clause even if he had been deceived. But I was grieved to see that under her red headband, from where her hair began, the poor girl had on her forehead a burn mark, much bigger than the usual size of a French crown. There was another burn of the same size between her breasts, it reached almost up to her neck, and both marks were tattooed by a design in the shape of a sun. There was also a lance-head tattoo on her chin, while her left nostril was pierced, ready to be fitted with a ring. As for her hair, starting at her temples it was trimmed in front and around her forehead, so that it fell to her eyebrows in a straight line which was interrupted only by the burn, while her eyebrows themselves were prolonged and joined together in the centre according to custom. As for her arms and feet, they were tinted orange, but this, I knew, was the effect of a henna preparation which would disappear within a few days, leaving no traces behind.

What should I do now? To dress a yellow woman in European clothes would be the most ridiculous thing in the world; for the moment, then, I did no more than indicate to her that she should let her hair grow again in the middle of her forehead. She looked at me in astonishment but raised no objections. The part of the burn which would still remain visible on her forehead and the burn between her breasts could be concealed by a jewel or any kind of ornament. These two burns probably originated in one of her native customs, for nothing similar was to be seen in Egypt. When I had completed my inspection I was glad to acknowledge that I had no particular cause for complaints.

Zetnaybia had fallen asleep while I was still examining her hair like a zealous proprietor who's upset by the chips and dents he discovers in his newly acquired merchandise.

Abdullah's sudden arrival ended my solicitude, however, and made me think of more practical matters. Whenever I had no need of his services he offered them to English tourists in one hotel or another. I now went to tell him that I wished to employ him only on certain days, for I would quickly learn to communicate with my slave. My dragoman, who believed to the contrary that he would now prove more indispensable than ever, was quite amazed by my decision, but he took things in his stride and informed me that I would be able to find him at the Hotel Waghorne on the occasions when I needed him. He was no doubt hoping to make at least the acquaintance of the slave by serving us as interpreter, but jealousy is only too well appreciated in the Orient, and reserve, even caution, is so natural and habitual in all matters where women are concerned, that Abdullah, without making any reference to the subject, quietly left the house.

I returned to the room where I had left Zetnaybia sleeping. She had woken up and was now sitting on the window-sill, turning her head from right to left, as she looked at the street through the latticework of the moucharaby. Two houses away several young men were leaning against a gate and nonchalantly smoking; they wore the Turkish uniform of the Reform and were probably the officers of an important personage. There appeared to be a certain danger on that side of the street. I wracked my brains to try and find a word which would make the slave understand that it was incorrect to look at soldiers in the street, but the only one I hit upon was the universal Tayeb (very good, very well, et cetera), an optimistic interjection which perfectly characterizes the mentality of the most affable people on the earth; you only have to say Tayeb and the whole of Egypt smiles at you, but it was evidently not the appropriate word in the present circumstances. Now, on the rare occasions when an Egyptian is displeased by something, he says Lah! and placidly lifts his hand to his forehead. But how could I say Lah! in a firm enough tone and at the same time accompany this order by a languid gesture of my hand? There was no alternative, however, and once I had addressed the slave in this manner, I led her back to the divan and indicated that it was more suitable for her to remain there rather than at the window, and I quickly added, by means of appropriate gestures, that we were about to have an early supper, for I didn't know when she had eaten last.

The next question was to decide whether I should let her remain unveiled in the presence of the cook, Mustapha. This seemed contrary to custom, and I remembered that the dragoman himself had not accompanied me when Abd-el-Kerim had invited me into his home to see the Abyssinian women; it was clear, then, that I would run the risk of being unrespected if my own household behaviour differed from what was standard in the country.

When supper was ready, Mustapha cried Sidi! from the other side of the door. I went out and he showed me the contents of an earthenware saucepan : a carved chicken garnished with rice.

'Tayeb!' I said to him, then I returned to the room and signalled to the slave to adjust her veil, which she did immediately.

Mustapha entered and set the table, spreading a green cloth over it, then, having arranged his pilaff pyramid on a dish, he brought us a variety of vegetables on little plates, lots of koulkas (a kind of arum with edible roots), chopped up and served in vinegar, and thick slices of onion floating in a mustard sauce. This somewhat unusual mixture looked very tasty indeed. After a final glance at his handiwork, in which he managed to encompass the slave, Mustapha discreetly withdrew.

10 My First Arabic Lesson

As I had been rash enough to buy a number of chairs I now made a sign to the slave to draw one of them near. She shook her head; my idea was ridiculous, I realized, considering how low the table was. Putting some cushions on the floor, I sat down and invited her to take a place opposite me, but nothing could persuade her to do so; she turned her head aside and covered her mouth with her hand.

'My child,' said I, 'surely you don't want to die of hunger.'

Convinced that she wouldn't understand anything, I still thought it better to speak, rather than perform an absurd dumb-show. She replied with a few words which no doubt signified exactly that : she didn't understand a word. And I replied in turn with the famous Tayeb . . . a perfect opening for a dialogue !

According to Lord Byron's experience the best way to learn a language is to live alone for some time with a woman. I would add to this excellent advice that you should use some elementary books as well, otherwise you will learn only nouns, no verbs at all; moreover, it is very difficult to remember words without writing them down, and Arabic isn't written with our alphabet; if you do employ the latter you will gain a far from perfect idea of the pronunciation. As for learning how to write in Arabic, it is such a complicated business because of the elisions,* that the scholar Volney found it simpler and more practical to invent a mixed alphabet, but other scholars unfortunately discouraged its use. The erudite love to retain and foster difficulties; they are quite hostile to what they consider the over-popularization of learning. After all, if you taught yourself, what would happen to all the professors?

But what about this girl ! Born in Java, perhaps she follows the Hindu religion and will smile only at the sight of fruits and herbs. So, making a sign of reverence, I uttered interrogatively the name of Brahma, but still she didn't appear to understand. My pronunciation was no doubt faulty. Carefully I now recited all the names I

* By elisions, Nerval is probably referring to the fact that of the 28 letters in the Arabic alphabet, 22 change their shape or size according to their position in a word, while a further 6 (which include 2 of the 22) can never be connected to the following letter. — N.G.

knew pertaining to this cosmogony, but for all the effect they had I might just as well have spoken in French.

She certainly had to eat something; I offered her a simple piece of bread, but of the very best quality from the Frankish district; she responded in a melancholy voice with *Mafisch!* a word I didn't know, but the sound of it troubled me. Then I remembered some poor Indian dancing-girls who had been brought to Paris some years ago; thanks to a friend of mine, I had been able to see them in a house on the Champs-Elysées. They only ate food which they had prepared themselves in brand-new vessels. A little reassured by this memory, I decided that after I had finished my own meal I would go out with the slave to clarify the matter. Despite this initial setback, I still had no intention of depending on Abdullah.

Just when I was eating the last of my koulkas I heard the tinkle of a little bell in the street; looking through the latticework I saw a young goatherd in a blue smock-frock coming our way from the Frankish district with a few of his animals. I pointed him out to the slave; she turned to me immediately and smiled, saying *Aioua!* which I interpreted as Yes.

I called out to the goatherd. About fifteen years old, sunburnt, almost swarthy, with enormous eyes and, what's more, a large nose and thick lips, like those which deck the heads of sphinxes, he was one of the purest Egyptian types. He came into the courtyard and started milking one of his goats into a clean earthenware vessel which I let the slave see before he used it. She repeated *Aioua!* and from the top of the balcony but remaining veiled this time she watched the goatherd at his work.

All that was idyllically simple and I found it quite natural that Zetnaybia should address him with these two words : *Talay bouckra,* by which I concluded that she was telling him to return on the following day. When the vessel was full the goatherd looked at me fiercely and shouted *At foulouz!* I had already encountered enough donkey-drivers to know what that meant : Give money ! When I had paid him he shouted *Bakchis!* another favourite expression of the Egyptian, who demands a tip on every possible occasion. I replied with the same words the slave had used : *Talay bouckra!* and he went away quite satisfied. Slowly but surely, that's how you begin learning a language !

Zetnaybia was quite content to drink her milk without dipping a piece of bread into it. Her meal was light, to say the least, but I was relieved to see her enjoying some nourishment, for I had begun to fear she might belong to that Javanese tribe which feeds only on a kind of oily grass. How on earth would I have found any of that in Cairo !

On my way to tell Ibrahim, the door-keeper, to fetch a couple of donkeys, I discovered him in the middle of a whispered conversation with Mustapha who immediately slunk away when I fell into his view. Sinister, I thought. Returning to the room, I saw that Zetnaybia had finished her milk; I indicated that she should put on her milayeh (an outer garment). She looked with a certain disdain at this chequered cotton tissue, although the majority of Cairo's women wear one. Unaware that we were going out, she thought that I was telling her to prepare for a rest, if not for bed.

'*An' aouss habbarah!*' (I sleep in a *habbarah*), she exclaimed.

How quickly one learns! I realized that she expected to be dressed in silk instead of cotton, to wear the clothes of noble ladies instead of those of the mere bourgeoisie.

'Lah!' I said, shaking my hand at her this time and wagging my head, 'Lah!' and I made her understand that we were about to leave the house.

11　A Domestic Revolution

I had no intention, however, of buying a *habbarah* or of going on an aimless donkey ride. We trotted towards the French reading room, where I was already known to the directress, the amiable Madame Bonhomme, who, I hoped, would now act as an interpreter for preliminary explanations with my young captive.

The reading room was crowded, but Madame Bonhomme immediately ushered us into a shop which adjoined the library; it was full of toilet-sets, cosmetics, dresses and what-have-you : in the Frankish district, every shopkeeper sells everything. Quite enraptured, the slave examined all these marvels of European luxury, while I explained my position to Madame Bonhomme, who, in her turn, also had a slave, a black girl to whom she gave various orders every now and then in Arabic.

My story interested her; graciously, and mustering all her patience, she prepared to act as an interpreter between Zetnaybia and me. First of all, I wanted to know if the slave was happy to belong to me.

Aioua! was her affirmative reply, and then she added that she would be even happier if she could dress as a European. Smiling at her wish, Madame Bonhomme selected a bobbin-net cap with ribbons and adjusted it upon Zetnaybia's head. Frankly, it didn't suit her, for it was so white that it made her complexion sallow.

'My child,' Madame Bonhomme said to her, 'you should remain as you are, you look much better in a tarboosh.'

But the slave took off the cap with such reluctance that Madame Bonhomme brought her a Greek *taktikos* festooned with gold, which suited her much better than the white cap. Evidently I was being encouraged to make a purchase, but considering the exquisite handiwork of the *taktikos*, the price was quite reasonable.

Certain now of what I can aptly term Madame Bonhomme's twofold benevolence, I asked for a detailed account of this poor girl's adventures. It reminded me of all the stories of every possible kind of slave, from Terence's Andrian to the count of Ferriol's Aissa, though I didn't suppose that I was necessarily listening to the complete truth.

Born of noble parents, the infant Zetnaybia had been kidnapped by Arabian pirates on the seashore, something quite unfeasible today in the Mediterranean, but probable enough in the South Seas. Besides, where else could she have come from? There was no doubting her Malayan origins, for subjects of the Ottoman empire cannot be sold under any pretext; anyone who isn't black or white and who is made into a slave must therefore hail from Abyssinia or the Indian archipelago.

She had been sold to a very old sheikh in the territory of Mecca; on his death, the caravan slave-merchants had carried her off and put her up for sale in Cairo. That sounded convincing enough, and I must admit that I was only too glad to believe that before she belonged to me, she had been owned by no one, in fact, except the venerable sheikh who must have been frosty with age.

'Yes,' Madame Bonhomme confirmed, 'she's only eighteen years old, but she's strongly built; you would have had to pay much more for her if it wasn't for her race. The Turks are a people of habit, they want Abyssinians or Negresses. You can be sure that the caravan merchants must have paraded her up and down the streets without being able to get rid of her.'

'So,' said I, 'fate ordained that I should meet her the very next day at Abd-el-Kerim's. I had been reserved to decide what would lie ahead for her.'

This way of looking at the situation, which was in keeping with Oriental fatalism, was conveyed to the slave and won her smiling assent.

I then asked why she hadn't wanted to eat at supper. Did she belong to the Hindu religion?

'No, not at all,' Madame Bonhomme told me, after consulting Zetnaybia again, 'she's a Muslim. There's a fast today, but it will be over at sunset, so you can be sure that any minute now she'll be only too ready for a meal.'

I was disappointed to learn that she did not belong to the Brahminical cult, I have always had a certain partiality for it; as for her language, she spoke the purest Arabic, and all she remembered of her native tongue was a few songs or *pantoums*, which I would encourage her to sing one day.

'And how will you manage to converse with her from now on?' Madame Bonhomme asked me.

'Madame,' I replied, 'I already know a word which signifies that you're satisfied with everything; tell me another word which signifies the exact opposite. My wits will make up for my ignorance, and I shall soon apply myself to a more thorough study of the language.'

'Have you had any objections from her yet, any refusals?' she asked me.

'I've been very close to them,' I replied, 'it's inevitable, isn't it.'

'There is one terrible word,' Madame Bonhomme whispered to me, 'which signifies every possible kind of negation, from a mild disagreement to a thunderous No . . . *Mafisch!*'

'Ah, yes,' I said, remembering the slave's response when I had offered her a piece of bread, 'I'm afraid I've already heard that terrible word.'

'In future, then,' she advised me, 'be sure that you're the only one to use it.'

Zetnaybia, who had been peering anxiously through the window for some minutes, suddenly turned round and spoke to Madame Bonhomme who then called to her black girl and gave her some instructions.

'The sun has set,' Madame Bonhomme explained, 'so I've told my girl to bring her some food.'

I thanked her for her kindness, and then she asked me about my domestic situation in general. As soon as I mentioned the name of Abdullah, she interrupted with a knowing laugh.

'That one!' she exclaimed, 'you've certainly chosen the most . . . famous dragoman in the city.'

'I didn't have much choice,' I replied. 'He fastened himself on to me on the boat which brought me to Cairo, and he hasn't left me since then. Despite his roguery, though, he has been of some help. Anyhow, since Zetnaybia's arrival, I've made him understand I don't require his services that frequently. But I don't trust my door-keeper

very much, he's one of Abdullah's protégés, and I think he's up to
something with the cook my dragoman brought from Monsieur
Jean's.'

'That old rascal! He was one of the first here to make his money
by selling wine in public. One thing seems clear enough, my good
man, you're living in the midst of bandits. I don't advise you to leave
your girl alone in the house with that particular crew!'

'Exactly . . . but how can I change things for the better?'

'We'll see to that right now,' Madame Bonhomme assured me,
once she had checked that Zetnaybia had finished eating.

This time, she had more than finished, she hadn't left even a morsel
behind on the plate.

Madame Bonhomme, who looked quite striking on her donkey, led
us to the house of an old Copt, Mansour, who lived a most respectable
but poverty-stricken life alone with his wife. They were, Madame
Bonhomme told me, the most trustworthy couple that she had ever
met in Cairo, and indeed they welcomed us most courteously. The
house was in a dilapidated state : the ceiling sagged down to such a
degree that it threatened the inhabitants' heads; the splintered
wooden framework of the windows looked like torn and ragged lace;
the chairs were tattered, and the rest of the furniture wasn't fit for a
Paris flea-market. Dust and sun added no less gloom to these surroundings than rain and mud when they penetrate the poorest hovels
of our European cities. My heart grew heavy when I thought of how
the majority of Cairo's population lived; even the rats had long ago
decided that houses such as this one were too insecure for permanent
residence.

Mansour, however, was a cheerful soul, and he at once inspired my
trust. He had been a mameluke, he told me, but one of the mame-
lukes in the French army. The latter were mainly composed of Copts
who had followed our soldiers on the retreat of Napoleon's Egyptian
expedition. When the mob rioted at Marseille they threw poor Mansour and several of his comrades into the sea for having supported
the emperor's cause on the return of the Bourbons to power.

A true child of the Nile, Mansour saved himself by swimming to a
deserted point much farther along the shore.

He and his wife were only too thankful for the employment which
I offered them at a modest net salary of eighty centimes a day. As for
me, I was delighted at the prospect of replacing my cunning tyrants
by this kind and reliable couple, to whom I could always entrust
Zetnaybia whenever I wished to go out alone. Liberty at last and a
safe and tranquil home!

12 Zetnaybia's French Lesson

As soon as Mansour and his wife arrived, early the following morning, I went to tell Mustapha and Ibrahim that I no longer required their services. In the Orient you never give your servants notice; you pay them regularly every evening, and there is a tacit understanding that they may leave whenever they wish to. Theoretically, the freedom of the employer and the employee is in no way restricted, the system working advantageously for both parties. To my surprise, however, I was unable to find either of them, and Mansour told me that as soon as Ibrahim had seen them arrive, he had gone to consult Mustapha; the two of them had no doubt summed up the situation and left at once. They were probably on their way now to regale themselves at Monsieur Jean's tavern. Advantageous? . . . certainly, when you think of the scenes which can occur with domestics in Europe.

The slave was still asleep; telling Mansour and his wife to make themselves at home, I decided that I would enjoy this initial taste of liberty at the Société Egyptienne. Many scholars gather here, and I didn't hesitate to participate in the lively and learned discussions; moreover, there is a library which specializes in ancient and modern works on Egyptian history. Stimulated by book browsing, I would gladly have spent the whole day in these surroundings, but, bachelor though I was, I still had to supervise a household.

On my return I found the old Copt and his wife busy putting everything in order; my former domestics had never dreamed of doing that! Zetnaybia was still sleeping on the divan, but Mansour assured me that she had woken up before and drunk some milk; he must have paid the goatherd himself, though he didn't mention the fact; the cocks and hens were cheerfully pecking maize in the courtyard.

When I suggested that Mansour's wife should prepare lunch, Mansour confessed that neither of them knew much about cooking; they lived themselves on boiled maize and vegetables soaked in vinegar, so they had never learned the art of making sauces or roasting meat. For my part, I wasn't worried by a limitation which could

57

always be corrected, but as soon as my slave saw them at work in the kitchen, she started shouting and overwhelmed them with insults. Deploring this trait in her character, I was about to utter a commanding *Mafisch!* but on second thoughts I decided that she should prepare the lunch herself; the sooner she learned to do so, in fact, the better, for I intended to have her accompany me on my travels. I therefore asked Mansour to tell her to set about things, but as soon as she heard these instructions, she regarded the three of us with an expression of wounded pride which quickly changed into one of offended dignity . . . she looked as though she were about to strike us with lightning.

'Inform the sidi,' she declared to Mansour, 'that I am a cadine (lady) and not an odaleuk (servant), and that if he doesn't treat me in accordance with my rank I shall write to the pasha.'

'To the pasha!' I cried. 'What has he got to do with this? I purchase a slave to wait upon me, and if I can't afford any more domestics, which happens to be the case, I don't see any reason why she shouldn't do the housework, as women do in every country.'

'Her reply,' Mansour told me, 'is that by appealing to the pasha, every slave has the right to have herself resold and thereby obtain a more suitable master. She is a Muslim and she will never lower herself to any unseemly employment.'

I respect this kind of fierce, individual pride (though I didn't have Mansour tell her so), and since she did in fact have the right, as Mansour confirmed, to appeal to the pasha, I merely said that I had been joking, but that she should apologize to the old and venerable Copt for her abusive language; from the fashion in which Mansour translated this, however, I had the impression that the apologies came from him.

For the moment, then, it seemed that I would have to try and teach Mansour and his wife how to cook Egyptian dishes; I could only hope that in time the slave would change her mind. Meanwhile, I could prepare her to be my interpreter; after all, if you have a slave, she should serve some purpose or other instead of being nothing but an expensive decoration. I told her that since she was such a distinguished person, it was only fitting that she should learn French, which would also give me the opportunity of learning Arabic.

She agreed at once, and I gave her an oral and writing exercise; I had her draw some straight strokes on paper, the way you first teach a child, and I taught her a few words. She was quite amused by this exercise, and in pronouncing French she lost that guttural intonation which is so unbecoming on the lips of Arab women. I amused myself, too, very much, by having her pronounce complete sentences which she didn't understand, for example, this one: *Je suis une petite sauvage*, which she pronounced Ze souis un bétit sovaze. Seeing me laugh, she thought that I had made her say something improper and she called to Mansour to have him translate the sentence. Finding nothing objectionable in it, she said :

'*Ana?* (me?) ... *bétit sovage?* ... *mafisch!*' and her smile was more than charming.

She soon grew bored of tracing upstrokes and downstrokes, and she made me understand that there was something she wanted to write (*ktab*) to me. I thought that she knew how to write in Arabic and I gave her a sheet of blank paper. Beneath her fingers I saw a series of bizarre hieroglyphs spring to life, they evidently belonged to the calligraphy of no known people on the surface of the globe, but I let her cover the whole page and then I had Mansour ask her what exactly she had wanted to do.

'I've written to you!' she exclaimed. 'Read it!'

'But, my dear child, it doesn't mean anything. You'd get the same kind of result if you dipped a cat's paw into the ink and ran it across the paper.'

Zetnaybia was quite astonished to hear this, for she had believed that every time you thought of something and traced your pen at random over the page, your idea would be automatically and clearly conveyed to the eyes of the reader. I explained that it was otherwise and that it would take her longer to learn French than she supposed; I then had her state in words what she had intended to write.

Her uncomplicated petition contained several clauses : in the first one she referred again to her wish to wear a *habbarah* of black taffeta, like the ladies of Cairo, so that she would no longer be mistaken for a mere fellah woman; in the second she expressed her desire for a green silk robe (*yalek*), and she concluded with a third clause in which she requested a pair of yellow ankle boots to which, as a Muslim, she had an unquestionable right.

Frankly, these boots are hideous, they often make a woman look as seductive as a palmiped, while the rest of the clothes Zetnaybia required would give her the appearance of an enormous bundle of washing; but the yellow ankle boots, in particular, are an emblem of social superiority.

I promised her that I would consider the matter.

Quite satisfied with my reply, the slave suddenly stood up and started clapping her hands.

'*El fil! El fil!*' she repeated several times.

'What does that mean?' I asked Monsour.

'The *siti* (lady),' he replied, after consulting the slave, 'would like to go and see an elephant that's on display, she's heard, at a nearby park.'

It was only fair to reward her for application to her studies, so the two of us set off on a couple of donkeys to see a white elephant which had been presented to the pasha by the British government.

Zetnaybia was transported by joy and didn't weary of gazing in admiration at this animal which reminded her of her native land; even in Egypt it is something of a curiosity. Its tusks were adorned with silver rings, which the mahoud struck when he had it perform various exercises. He managed to provoke the elephant into a state which is generally reserved for private mating rather than public amusement, but when I indicated to the slave, who was veiled but hardly blind, that we had seen enough, one of the pasha's officers approached me and said in a commanding voice:

'*Aspettate!* ... *è per ricreare le donne.*' (Wait! it's done to entertain the ladies.)

Quite a number were present, in fact, and they were not in the least scandalized; many of them simply burst into delighted laughter. I let Zetnaybia stay, then, till she was ready to return home, and on our way back she promised she would sing me some *pantoums*, for I wished to learn as much as possible from her about Malayan culture.

13 The Afrites

The following days passed quite calmly. At the Société Egyptienne I obtained a list of the other principal libraries in Cairo, and at one of them I discovered an entire section devoted to works on the history of the Druze. I was fascinated by the character of their supposed founder and Messiah, Caliph Hakim. In one particular book I found a concise document which I copied out for future reference: the Druze catechism; drawn up in the form of a question and answer dialogue between a young member of the cult and a Druze priest, it covered the essential articles of their faith in a manner which was, paradoxically enough, as clear as it was cryptic. This was the library to which I most frequently returned.

Meanwhile, at home, under my slave's gracious guidance, Mansour and his wife learned to cook in the Egyptian style, though Zetnaybia

herself didn't sully her hands by even touching a saucepan; she enjoyed playing the lady of the house, that was clear enough, but
fortunately she didn't refer again to her ambitions for a new
wardrobe.

By studying the character of one particular Oriental woman, I
realized that I might learn a lot about many others, but I was careful
not to reach any rash, general conclusions based merely on trivial
details. Imagine my surprise, however, when I entered the slave's
room, one morning, and found a garland of onions hanging across
the door, and still more onions arranged symmetrically on the wall
above the divan where she was sleeping. Believing that it was nothing but child's-play, I unfastened these ornaments which, not to
mention their pungent odour, were hardly suitable decorations for
a room, and I threw them negligently into the courtyard. Suddenly
the slave woke up; furious and broken-hearted, she rushed out of the
room in tears and gathered up all the onions; then she put them back
in their place, making a sign of adoration as she adjusted each one of
them. At the same time, she hurled a volley of curses at me; the only
word I understood was Pharaon; perhaps she was conjuring up the
shades of the Pharaohs to wreak vengeance upon me, and I could not
decide whether I should *mafisch* her, so to speak, or simply pity her.
Hearing all the noise, Mansour hastily entered the room, and after
exchanging a few words with the slave, who spoke to him at least
without raising her voice, he explained to me that I had destroyed a
spell, that I was the cause of all the disasters which would surely
descend upon her and me only too soon.

'Well,' I said to Mansour, 'we're living in a country where onions
once were gods. If I've offended them I'm quite prepared to make
atonement. There must be a means of appeasing the wrath of an
Egyptian onion!'

But the slave had no wish to listen to a translation of anything I
might have to say. Turning towards me, she repeated :
'Pharaon !'

This was not an evocation, Mansour informed me; the word meant:
An impious and tyrannical being. I was hurt by this reproach, but
very pleased to learn that the name of the country's ancient kings
had become a term of abuse. I had no cause to be angry, in fact, for
Mansour told me that the onion ceremony was celebrated in all the
houses of Cairo on a certain day of the year; it served to ward off
epidemic maladies.

The poor girl's fears were confirmed, probably because of her
powerful imagination; she fell seriously ill, but neither my entreaties
nor my orders could persuade her to touch any of the medicines
which I went to obtain from a doctor; I was obliged to take them

back. During my absence she had called to the two women living in
the house next to ours, and they had held a terrace to terrace con-
sultation; I found them gathered around her, reciting prayers and,
so Mansour informed me, exorcizing the afrites. It appeared that the
profanation of the onions had roused up these evil spirits, among
whom were two whose hostility was directly aimed at Zetnaybia and
me; one was called The Green, the other The Golden.

Realizing that Zetnaybia's illness was localized in her imagination,
I let the two women, Cartoum and Zabetta by name, go about their
business; they soon led in to assist them another much older woman,
a renowned Santoness, carrying a small stove. She placed it in the
middle of the room and started burning a stone which looked to me
like alum. The purpose of this kitchenry was to confuse and counter-
act a number of the afrites; the women saw them clearly in the
smoke and heard them begging for mercy. But the evil had to be
completely eradicated. Cartoum and Zabetta lifted up the slave, who
made no objections when they proceeded to bend her head and hold
it over the smoke. The exorcism was concluded to the tune of an
endless coughing fit, to the drawling voices of all three women singing
Arabic prayers and invocations, and the rhythmic beat of the old
woman's hand upon Zetnaybia's back.

Mansour, a Coptic Christian, was shocked by all these practises;
but if the root of Zetnaybia's illness was a moral one I could see no
harm in our letting her be treated in an analogous and thus appropriate manner. On the very next day, in fact, she was in far better
health, and within a couple of days she recovered completely.

Despite her recovery, however, or perhaps because of it, Zetnaybia
didn't want to be separated from her nurses, the two neighbours; she
installed them in her room as her personal servants. Seeing no reason
at all to increase our household, I made a point of giving them not a
single centime as a salary, but the slave offered them gifts from her
own belongings, and since they were those which Abd-el-Kerim had
left her I had no right to raise any objections; nevertheless, I had to
replace them by others, so Zetnaybia finally acquired the *habbarah*
and *yalak* for which she had always longed.

The life of a pasha might have appealed to me if I had been able
to afford it. As it was, this new situation, which would doubtless lead
in its subtle Oriental fashion to a similar but more complicated one,
began to ravage my bank account, for even though I could refuse
Zetnaybia's servants wages, I could hardly refuse them food; moreover, her new wardrobe had proved as costly as it was 'noble' . . . in
short, I realized that my funds would soon be exhausted and I saw
my plans for future travels dwindling to a mirage : it was time to
make another decision.

'My dear child,' I said to the slave, one day, after explaining my circumstances and intentions to her, 'if you wish to remain in Cairo, you are absolutely free to do so.'

I expected an outburst of gratitude.

'Free !' she exclaimed. 'And what do you expect me to do? Where shall I go? You'd better sell me back to Abd-el-Kerim !'

'But, my child, a European doesn't sell a woman. That would be the most shameful way of obtaining money.'

'Well,' she said, breaking into tears, 'how can I earn my livelihood? ... is there anything I can do?'

'Can't you enter the household of a lady of your religion?'

'And become a servant ... never ! Sell me back to Abd-el-Kerim. I'll be bought by a sheikh, by a pasha, perhaps, and then I'll really be a noble lady. You want to leave me ... all right, then, take me back to the bazaar !'

I understood her point of view, singular though it appeared at first; I already knew enough about the true state of Muslim society to realize that her situation as a slave was certainly superior to that of the poor Egyptian women with hard, disagreeable jobs and harsh or poverty-stricken husbands. In giving Zetnaybia her freedom I would condemn her to the most miserable circumstances, to disgrace, perhaps, and I finally acknowledged that I was responsible for her fate.

'Since you don't want to remain behind in Cairo,' I said to her, 'you'll have to accompany me on my travels. And I'm ready to leave ... now !'

'*Ana enti sava-sava!*' (You and me, we'll go together !) she exclaimed with a happy smile.

To tell the truth, I was delighted by her decision.

14 Departure

I went at once to the port of Boulac to reserve a cangia for the journey down the Nile to Damiette, from where I intended to embark upon a ship bound for Beirut; at Boulac I learnt that the *Santa-Barbara*, under its Greek captain, would be ready to set sail for Beirut within a matter of days.

I had certainly chosen the most appropriate moment for departure; the khasmin was about to envelop Cairo, and from morning onwards the air would be scorching and laden with dust. Only when a fresh breeze rises from the sea, no earlier than 3 p.m., can you safely leave your house during the fifty days that the khasmin lasts.

Returning from the port, I didn't forget to pay a last visit to the French reading room in order to bid a warm goodbye to the providential Madame Bonhomme, who wasn't in the least surprised to hear that I was about to leave along with Zetnaybia.

'Just be prepared for the unexpected,' she said.

'I am,' I assured her, 'believe me, I am!'

'*Mafisch?* . . .'

'Worse,' I replied, 'afrites.'

'Oh,' she said, 'you'll soon get used to them.'

She took me aside into her shop where there was something she claimed I required; she showed me a huge collection of flags, representing nearly every nation.

'Go ahead and choose one.'

'But I'm not leaving for the war.'

'You're going down the Nile, you must have a tricoloured flag fixed to the back of your cangia,' she explained, 'so that you'll be respected by the fellahs. You can choose any one you like. The majority of . . . messieurs prefer an English flag, it's supposed to offer the most security.'

'Alas!' said I, 'I'm afraid I'm not one of those Parisian messieurs.'

'I didn't suspect for a moment you were,' she said with a smile, 'but I thought I should tell you the facts.'

The flag which really appealed to me was the Sardinian one, but unfortunately you only have the right to it if you're making a pilgrimage to Jerusalem. Finally, then, I settled for a French flag, and that was the last purchase I ever made in Cairo.

What troubled me was having to announce my sudden departure to Mansour, but although he was a Copt he responded with a Muslim's resignation; moreover, he insisted on helping me dismantle the house. The cangia was going to carry much more than the slave and me. There was Zetnaybia's green trunk, containing the remains of her first lot of belongings, and another trunk, full of the robes I had been obliged to buy her myself; she insisted that the contents of the two trunks remain separate, even though everything could have been put into just one of them without excessive squeezing. A third trunk concealed my French wardrobe, last *encas* of misfortune, like the herdsman's attire, referred to in one of La Fontaine's *Fables*, which an emperor had preserved to remind himself of his former condition. Next, all the kitchen utensils, which now aroused Zetnaybia's acute interest for the first time; she wouldn't permit me to leave behind even the smallest and most useless implements; for my part, I claimed that our only essentials were the jugs and vessels, which were suitable for keeping water cool and fresh, and I managed to win my point by convincing her that I would be grossly inconsiderate if I didn't offer a number of household items to Mansour and his wife. Finally, there was no small amount of furniture and bric-à-brac — not to mention my books and notes — pipes, narghiles, straw mats, cotton cushions, and palm-wood cages (cafas) which could serve as divans, beds or tables; they had the further advantage of being the most appropriate means to secure our assortment of fowl and pigeons. . . . By the time we were ready to depart, I felt that I had already undergone the fifty days of the khasmin, for the house was thick with dust from ceiling to floor and littered with feathers and maize. I was longing for the breeze, the salt spray, the smack of the sea and the collision of waves!

15 Mutiny

Whatever the circumstances, a long voyage by sea inevitably proves monotonous; it provokes a special kind of ennui, in which a growing nostalgia for the land you have left behind is entangled with an obscure fear that you will never glimpse the shores to which you are now heading.

I was disturbed from reflections such as these on our fourth day aboard the *Santa-Barbara*. After lunch, the Greek captain, Nicholas, generally had his cabin-boy bring him an enormous pitcher brimming with Cyprian wine, and he would invite an Armenian passenger and me to share it with him, for the three of us were the only Christians on the ship; as for the sailors, interpreting the Prophet's law in their own fashion, they drank only a kind of aniseed brandy. On this particular day, then, when we were gathered in the captain's cabin, Nicholas whispered a few words to the Armenian.

'He wants to make you a proposition,' the Armenian told me in French.

'Let him go ahead,' I replied.

'It's rather delicate and he hopes you won't be offended even if you happen to disagree.'

'There's really no need for such beating about the bush,' I assured him.

'Well, he'd like to know if you'd exchange your slave-girl for his *walad* (little boy).'

I was about to burst into laughter, but I was disconcerted by the quite resolute expressions on the faces of both these Levantines. I concluded that this was the kind of vulgar joke which Orientals dare to make only when a Frank finds himself in a position where it would be difficult to make them regret it, and that was exactly what I told the Armenian.

'But not at all!' he exclaimed in astonishment. 'He's speaking seriously, believe me. The little boy's skin is perfectly white, while your woman's is rather tawny, and frankly,' he added conscientiously, 'I'd think about it if I were you, for the little boy is certainly worth the woman.'

On the whole, I don't give way to astonishment easily; besides, in this part of the world you learn soon enough not to be surprised by anything. I merely replied that such an exchange didn't suit me, but I must have betrayed a spark of anger, for the captain apologized for his indiscretion, assuring me that he had only wished to cater to my pleasures. I would have dismissed this insinuation as a courteous formula or as an interpreter's licence from the Armenian, had it not been for the captain's ironic tone of voice; I insisted now on a clear explanation from this wily Greek.

'Well,' the Armenian said, 'he claims that you addressed his *walad* in very complimentary terms this morning, at least that's what the boy told him.'

'Complimentary terms! On the contrary, I was furious with him . . . he was washing his hands in our drinking water! I controlled myself, however, and simply called him a *habiby*, and you told me yourself, the other evening when you translated the refrain my slave kept singing, that the word meant little rascal.'

From the Armenian's bewilderment, I realized that the root of this discussion was one of those absurd philological quid pro quos which often crop up between people who have only a limited knowledge of a language. It transpired that the real meaning of *habiby* was little darling, which the Armenian thought was the same as little rascal. No wonder Captain Nicholas believed I was enamoured of his little Corydon! We dissolved the whole misunderstanding merrily enough with another generous draught of the captain's excellent wine, and the three of us sang Zetnaybia's refrain:

> 'Ya habiby, sakel no!
> Ya makmouby! ya sidi!'

The Armenian agreed that a correct translation would be : O my
little darling, my beloved, my brother, my master! And once again
we sang it :

> 'Ya habiby! sakel no!
> Ya makmouby! ya sidi! . . .'

From then on the Armenian and I remained the best of friends;
his company diverted me from my melancholy preoccupations and
I was glad that his gaiety, his inexhaustible chatter, his observations
and his stories offered Zetnaybia the opportunity, highly appreciated
by the women of these regions, to express her own ideas with that
volley of nasal and guttural consonants which made it so difficult for
me not only to grasp the meaning, but to distinguish the very sound
of her words.

A few sailors happened to be sitting on a sack of rice close by, and
with a European's magnanimity I even permitted one or another of
them to engage her in conversation. The common people are generally unrestrained, yet polite, for among Orientals the sentiment of
equality is more sincerely ingrained than among Europeans; moreover, a kind of innate courtesy prevails through all the different social
classes. As for education, everybody is usually at the same level; their
learning is summary but widespread, which is why a man from
humble origins doesn't have to undergo any radical change in order
to become the favourite of a noble, and he can ascend to the highest
rank without ever appearing out of place.

A certain Turk from Anatolia joined the sailors gathered around
us; he spoke to the slave more frequently and for much longer than
any of the others. The Armenian told me they were discussing
religion, and I therefore raised no objections. On the contrary, I
was only too willing to encourage them, especially when I heard that
this particular Turk, who conducted morning and evening prayers
for the crew, was a *hadji*, a pilgrim returning home from Mecca.
Zetnaybia always adhered strictly to Muslim rituals; when she was
ill in Cairo she paid no attention to my advice that it was dangerous
for her at such a time to persist in dipping her hands and feet into
cold water during her morning and evening prayer recitals.

I looked at her now : her hair had grown again over her forehead
to join her long, flowing side-tresses which jostled with silken braids,
glittered with gold-plated sequins and fell, in the Levantine style, all
the way down from her neck to her heels. The gold festooned *taktikos*
was charmingly tilted over her left ear, while the strings of silver-
plated copper bracelets, which dangled on her arms, were gaudily
embellished with blue and red . . . an exclusively Egyptian style. Still

more rings jingled around her ankles, despite the Koran's interdiction, for the jewels which adorn a woman's feet are not supposed to provoke any sound.

I couldn't help but admire her . . . how graceful she was! with her blue *milayeh* draped over her silk striped robe, with her perfect resemblance to an antique statue, which so many Oriental women possess without being in the least aware of it. I was struck, at moments, but not at all disturbed, by the sudden liveliness of her gestures and by an unusual expression which marked her features; after all, the Turkish sailor who was talking to her was old enough to be her grandfather, and besides, he made no attempt to conceal his words from his comrades.

'Do you know what's happening?' the Armenian remarked to me after awhile. 'They've all decided that the woman who's with you doesn't belong to you.'

'They're mistaken,' I said, 'you can inform them that she was sold to me in Cairo by Abd-el-Kerim for about 625 francs. I have the receipt in my wallet . . . anyhow, it's none of their business!'

'They say the merchant didn't have the right to sell a Muslim woman to a Christian.'

'I'm quite indifferent to what they say. The inhabitants of Cairo are more qualified to discuss this subject; all the Franks have slaves there who are either Christian or Muslim.'

'Negroes, yes, or Abyssinians, but they can't make a slave of anyone who belongs to the white race.'

'Does this woman look so white to you?'

'Not really,' the Armenian acknowledged.

'Listen,' I told him, 'I don't have any doubts about my rights, for I made all the necessary enquiries beforehand. Now kindly tell the captain that I don't approve of his sailors talking to her.'

'According to the captain,' the Armenian said, after consulting him, 'you should have been able to stop her yourself at the very beginning.'

'I didn't want to deprive her of the pleasure of talking her own language,' I replied, 'nor did I wish to prevent her from attending prayers. Besides, considering how this ship is built without any barriers, conversation was bound to occur.'

Captain Nicholas didn't appear too well disposed in my favour; now that the effects of his Cyprian wine had worn off he probably still felt a certain resentment against me for having rejected his proposition. Nevertheless, he called to the *hadji* sailor, whom I pointed out as the most malevolent among the group, and spoke to him quietly but firmly. As for me, I didn't say anything to the slave, for fear that I would be regarded as an odious and domineering master. The sailor replied with a proud, almost insolent air, and the captain then had the Armenian tell me that I had no cause for further worry : the Turk was a *medjnoun*, a kind of exalted saint, respected by his comrades because of his piety; nobody, however, would attach the least importance to his opinions anywhere else.

Although the sailor didn't converse any more with the slave, he did speak to his disciples in a very loud voice in front of her, and I clearly understood that his persistent topic was the Muslim and the Roman. Refusing to support this method of insinuation, I had the Armenian bring the slave to me, and away from the *hadji* and his comrades we held our own conversation. She repeated what the Armenian had already summarized for me.

'And do you think it's true?' I asked her.

'Allah knows all !' she replied.

'Those men are mistaken,' I told her, 'and you're not to speak to them again.'

'It will be as you say,' she conceded.

I asked the Armenian to entertain her. My friend had become very useful; he always spoke to her in that fluty, charming tone which enlivens and captivates a child.

'*Ked ya siti?* . . . (Come, lady, what is the matter?),' he began. 'Why aren't we laughing? Should I tell you about the adventures of The Baked Head?'

Then he told her an old Constantinople story about a tailor, who, believing that he had received the clothes of a sultan which needed repairing, opened the parcel only to discover the head of an aga which had been delivered to him by mistake. Eager to get rid of this unexpected honour, he puts the head in an earthenware vase and has it sent to a Greek pastry-cook, instructing him to bake it. The Greek bakes it, then he carefully replaces his own wig with the aga's head and goes to a Frankish barber; the barber cuts and arranges it in the latest style, then the Greek jumps up from his seat, places the head in the hands of the astonished barber and runs out of the shop. The Frank now takes the head somewhere else, and a multitude of comic misunderstandings and complications follow. . . . . This is the very best style of Turkish buffoonery.

During evening prayers, I discreetly went to the fore-deck, and there I watched the stars appear and made my own prayers too, which are those of dreamers and poets who are full of admiration for nature and carried away by enthusiasm for things of the past. So pure was the Oriental air at this hour that it seemed to harmonize with man's idea of the heavens, and I beheld them, then, in their diverse and sacred forms, those god-stars which the Divinity has cast forth one after the other like the masks of the eternal Isis. . . . Astarte,

Saturn, Jupiter, for me you will always represent the transformations of the humble beliefs of our ancestors! They who in their millions furrowed through these seas and assumed no doubt that the radiance was the flame, the throne the god. But who indeed would not worship in the stars of the firmament the very proofs of eternal power, and, in their regular course, the vigilant activity of a hidden mind! . . .

When I returned to the main deck, I saw the slave and the old *hadji* sailor together in a corner at the foot of the longboat; here they had resumed their religious discussions despite my prohibition.

This time I resorted to direct action; grabbing hold of the slave's arm, I dragged her violently away; she fell down, without any hurt, upon a sack of rice.

'*Giaour!*' she shouted.

I understood the word and I remained inflexible.

'*Enti giaour!*' I replied, though I wasn't too sure whether this was also the feminine form of the noun. 'It's you who are the infidel, and as for him,' I added, pointing to the *hadji*, 'he's a *kelb* (dog)!'

I didn't know what angered me the most : the fact that I was despised because I was a Christian, or the ingratitude of this woman whom I had always treated as an equal. The *hadji*, hearing himself described as a dog, took a threatening step towards me, but he turned back to join his comrades with that typical cowardice of Arabs who belong to the lower classes, for, after all, he would never dare attack a Frank unless he were supported by some of his kind. Three or four of them now advanced, hurling abuse, and I instinctively whipped out one of the pistols from under my belt, quite forgetting that these weapons, with their glittering butt-ends, which I had purchased in Cairo to add a finishing touch to my costume, generally proved fatal only to the person whose finger pulled the trigger. Moreover, I have to admit that not one of them was even loaded.

'Calm yourself,' the Armenian said, taking hold of my arm. 'He's a madman, but for them he's a saint. Just let them shout, they won't do anything, let the captain deal with them.'

The slave was pretending to cry, as though I had gravely wounded her, and she would not budge from the sack of rice. The captain appeared.

'What do you expect,' he said to me without concern, 'they're savages!' And he addressed them without raising his voice.

'Add this,' I told the Armenian, 'that as soon as we land, I shall go and see the pasha, and they'll receive more than a few baton strokes for their behaviour.'

The Armenian translated my words in such a moderate tone, however, that they sounded almost like compliments. The sailors said nothing more, but their silence was menacing, and I felt that my position was ambiguous, to say the least. I remembered, by chance, that I possessed a letter of introduction to the pasha of Acre which a friend of mine had given me in Paris; abruptly I took my wallet out of my jacket pocket, thereby provoking a general alarm. The pistol, had it been loaded, would have only served to stun me, especially since it was of Arabic manufacture; but the lower classes in the Orient still believe that Europeans are endowed with magic powers enabling them, at a crucial moment, to take from their pocket some mysterious item or other which could annihilate an entire army. The sailors quietened down, however, when they saw that I had only extracted a letter from my wallet; but it was written in perfect Arabic, and on the following day, in fact, we would put into port at Acre, as everybody knew, in order to replenish our supplies of fresh water.

As is the custom with letters of official introduction, the envelope wasn't sealed; I handed it to the Armenian, who first touched his head with the envelope as a sign of respect, and then withdrew the letter; while the captain looked over his shoulder, he ceremoniously read out this document to the crew, upon whom it produced the effect of Neptune's *quos ego* in the first book of the *Aeneid*. The *hadji* and his fellow rogues bowed low their heads, realizing the promised baton strokes were no longer an idle threat. The captain explained to me that his own conduct was guided by his fear of offending their religious ideas, for he himself was only a poor subject under the sultan, having no authority beyond his limited scope as captain of the *Santa-Barbara*.

'As for the woman,' he said, 'if you're a friend of the pasha's, she certainly belongs to you. Who would dare to contest the favours bestowed by the great?'

Although she had clearly understood the contents of the letter, the slave still hadn't budged from the sack of rice. She could have no doubts about her present situation, for in a Turkish country a pasha's protection is worth more than a questionable right. Nevertheless, I wanted to prove to everybody that my right was far in fact from being questionable.

'Weren't you born,' I had the Armenian ask her, 'in a country which doesn't belong to the Turkish sultan?'

'That's true,' she replied, 'I'm *Hindi* (Indian).'

'So a Frank has as much right to you as he does to Abyssinian women. They're also copper-coloured like you, but probably much more dependable!'

'*Aioua!*' she said, as though she were convinced, '*ana memlouk enti* (I am your slave).'

'But remember,' I added, 'before leaving Cairo I offered you your liberty. You told me you wouldn't know where to go.'

'That's true,' she said, 'you'd better resell me when we land.'

'You've followed me, have you, because you want to reach another country and then take leave of me! Well, since you're so ungrateful you'll remain a slave for ever. You won't be a lady either, you'll be a servant! From now on you'll keep your veil up and you'll stay on the fore-deck in the little cabin with crickets in it. And you won't speak another word to anyone!'

She adjusted her veil and, without replying, walked towards the fore-deck cabin which I dramatically pointed out to her, even though it was the only one there.

A European's surest way to triumph in the Orient — perhaps, indeed, his only way — is to deploy every possible theatrical device; the most imposing actor on stage subdues not only the audience, but also the rest of the cast.

Yet I have to confess that where Zetnaybia alone was concerned, she had in fact aroused my anger by her behaviour; however extravagantly I had reacted in my intent to impress the crew, my personal resentment was by no means simulated.

As soon as we put in at Acre, early the following morning, the *hadji* and his two most fervent disciples were the first to jump ashore; the Armenian and I watched them scurry through the crowds, and he assured me, correctly enough, that we would not be seeing them again; evidently, my performance the previous evening had proved more effective than a dozen baton strokes! For my own part, I did not particularly wish to visit the pasha; it was some years, in fact, since he had entertained my Parisian friend, and I could not be sure that he would welcome me on the strength of a former acquaintanceship which he might well have forgotten by now. Besides, my former ennui had returned and I felt its weight even more heavily than before; I doubted whether further attempts at sociability would ever relieve me of it. What I required was not exactly solitude, but the opportunity to roam around freely, meeting people when I wished and taking leave of them when I wished : the space and heights of Lebanon called to me, promising appeasement and adventure. How confining, after all, is the world of a ship!

I still wasn't sure, however, as to what future role Zetnaybia would play in my life; at all events, I couldn't expect her to accompany me on a dangerous exploration of the Lebanese countryside where several tribes are reputed to be far from trustworthy. I briefly explained my dilemma to the Armenian; he suggested that on reaching Beirut I should deposit the slave at a well-known French school for young girls which was owned by a lady from Marseille, a certain

Madame Carlès who had a reputation for honesty and kindness. Was providence leading me to another Madame Bonhomme?

The rest of the voyage passed without further incidents; Captain Nicholas treated me with special deference, even though I was responsible for the 'loss' of three of his crew. Speaking to my Armenian friend, I had the opportunity to mention my interest in the Druze. He told me that a famous Druze sheikh, Saide-Eshayrazy, was in prison at Beirut; the Turks had put him there because he hadn't paid his taxes for the last three or four years.

'But nobody is sent to prison for anything as trivial as that,' the Armenian added. 'The fact is he refuses to acknowledge the present government, and on more than one occasion he played a leading part in local seditions. You will find him highly qualified in all matters concerning the Druze, for he is a most pious and learned man.

I promised myself that I would visit him, and I thanked the Armenian for all his help and advice. Soon we would land, and I saw no reason to release the slave until then; besides, she had settled down cheerfully enough among the crickets in her private cabin.

16 Farewell

A tall building in the Italian style, the French school of Beirut had formerly been the French consulate; you could still see several *fleur-de-lis* coats of arms upon the pediments, though the gold had apparently disappeared with the consul and his staff. The interior gallery encircled a large space, one half of which was a terrace, the other a courtyard, while the fluttering shade of a streaked *tendido* protected the whole of the area. Planted in round holes made between the courtyard flagstones, orange-trees and pomegranate-trees added some cheer to the place, for it was completely cut off from exterior nature. Notched by the friezes and occasionally traversed by pigeons from a nearby mosque, a patch of blue sky was the only horizon in sight for the poor schoolgirls.

The slave and I walked along a first-floor gallery towards the humming recital of lessons in one of the suites of rooms. At the entrance I saw a group of young girls squatting in a circle, in the

Turkish manner, upon an Indian mat; they were presided over by Madame Carlès who was seated close to them upon a divan.

She greeted me without a trace of surprise at my costume, which suddenly struck me, at least, as too flamboyant in these surroundings; she took me aside so that I could explain my circumstances to her, while of her own accord Zetnaybia sat down among the girls and immediately started chatting. Naturally, I didn't tell Madame Carlès the whole of my story; I simply asked if she could conveniently house my slave, as I wished to travel alone for awhile. She could indeed, she assured me; for the very modest fee of three Turkish piastres a day Zetnaybia would receive regular meals and instruction. I decided to leave her at the school for a trial week, at the end of which I would return, hoping for a good report, so that I could prepare for my expedition.

'There's always the possibility of converting her,' Madame Carlès said in a strong Provençal accent. 'This is the way I go about it : "Listen, my girl, all the good gods of every country are really the same one God. Now, Mohammed was a wonderful man, but there's a lot to be said, too, for Jesus Christ. . . ." '

I was highly impressed by this most tolerant and gentle method of leading up to conversion, but knowing my slave, I advised Madame Carlès not to force her in any way at all.

'In fact,' I added, 'she can't be persuaded to do anything she doesn't want to do, and trying to find out why she doesn't want to is always another problem. . . .'

'Hush !' Madame Carlès interrupted, 'listen . . . yes, she's just told one of the monitresses that she wants to go with them all to mass on Sunday. Now, the best thing for you to do is tiptoe away without saying goodbye to her, and come back, as you said, in a week's time.'

I could certainly leave Zetnaybia in no better hands than those of Madame Carlès who would teach her at least the rudiments of the Christian religion and the French of . . . Marseille.

I spent the following days reading through what I had already written in my travel journal and making the kind of only too hasty corrections which one inevitably does while the travelling still continues. I paid more careful attention, however, to the notes which I had amassed at the Société Egyptienne and at my favourite Cairo library, for I intended to visit the Druze sheikh before starting out on my Lebanese adventures; even though I hoped to learn a lot from him I didn't wish to introduce myself as a kind of confused ignoramus. On the other hand, I already knew that the Druze were highly secretive; even if Saide-Eshayrazy did find me well informed, there was still the risk that he would consent only to a general discussion and reveal nothing of fundamental importance.

Returning to the school when the week of trial was over, I decided that I would behave as a spy for a few moments, so that I could form my own initial impressions about my slave's conduct and well-being, before listening to Madame Carlès' report ... how zealous a master I was! I spied Zetnaybia, then, cheerfully sitting in the ring of girls upon the Indian mat; she looked quite at home, in fact, like a pupil of long standing, though she appeared to be watching the lesson rather than taking part in it.

As soon as I entered the room she leapt up to greet me with a cry of joy. Telling a monitress — not the same girl who had encouraged Zetnaybia to attend mass on Sunday — to take charge of the class, Madame Carlès led us both to her private apartment. Evidently this particular deputy wasn't Christian, for she quickly lifted a book to her face and kept herself veiled, as it were, while I remained in sight, a gesture no Christian girl would have made inside a house or outside. I glimpsed no more than an apparition, then, but an exceptionally graceful one whose abundant tresses were entwined with silken braids. I was struck, above all, by her hands which, with tapering fingers and long nails, were signs of noble lineage.

As soon as the three of us were alone Zetnaybia let flow a warm stream of tears and squeezed my hand against her forehead. I was deeply affected, but I wasn't yet sure whether this demonstration was the preface to one complaint or another, or whether she had come to miss me, even appreciate me, during a week of separation. I asked her if she was happy in this house and she responded by throwing her arms around her mistress' neck.

'*Ima!* (Mother!)' she exclaimed, 'she is my mother.'

'She's a good girl,' Madame Carlès told me in her heavy Provençal accent, which she seemed to have developed rather than dropped since her departure from Marseille, 'but she doesn't want to do anything except chat a little in French with the younger girls. She won't learn how to write or sew. "I can't punish you," I told her. "When your master comes back he'll decide what's to be done."'

I was vexed to hear this news, for I had hoped that by leaving Zetnaybia at the school I would solve the problem of her future; the curriculum would prepare her for a suitable position and eventually enable her to take care of herself. I now felt like a father who sees his projects overturned by the ill-will or laziness of his child. Adopting the most severe tone possible, I had the following conversation with the slave; Madame Carlès interpreted and added helpful comments of her own.

'Why don't you want to learn how to sew?'

'Because as soon as people see me doing a servant's work they'll make me into a servant.'

'A Christian's wife isn't a servant, but she still works.'

'I'll never marry a Christian! It's a husband's duty to give his wife a servant.'

I was about to reply that as a slave she was already less than a servant, but I remembered the fine distinction she had drawn between her own position as a *cadine* (lady) and that of an *odaleuk* (domestic). In front of Madame Carlès I could hardly refer to the judgment I had pronounced upon her on the ship; besides, now that the situation had changed the judgment was no longer valid . . . such are the ways of the Orient!

'Why don't you want to learn to write?' I asked her. 'Next you'd be taught to sing and dance.'

'All that's for an alma, for a buffoon,' she said. 'I prefer to remain as I am.'

We know how strong are the prejudices of European women, but I have to admit that bolstered as they are by an ancient tradition the ignorance and customs of Oriental women render their prejudices quite indestructible. They would even abandon their belief more readily than any idea which involves their self-respect.

'Don't worry,' Madame Carlès reassured me, as though she had read my thoughts, 'as soon as she becomes a Christian she'll see clearly enough that the women of our religion can work without losing their dignity, and then she'll learn whatever we wish to teach her. On Sunday, at mass at the Capuchin convent, the Superior was quite struck by her piety, and your girl has already told me more than once that she's looking forward to going there again.'

'But that doesn't prove anything,' I said to Madame Carlès. 'In Cairo I saw Santons and Dervishes entering the churches, either out of curiosity, or to listen to the music, and they, too, behaved in a very devout manner.' On the table near to us was a copy of the New Testament in French; I opened it haphazardly at a page with a picture of Jesus Christ and — in the background — Mary. The slave put her finger on the first picture.

'*Aisse!* (Jesus!),' she said, then, putting her finger on the second one, '*Myriam!* (Mary!).'

Smiling, and keeping the book open at this page, I put it close to her lips, but she stepped back in fright.

'Mafisch!' she exclaimed.

'But,' said I, 'in your religion don't you worship Aisse as a prophet and Myriam as one of the three holy women?'

'Yes,' she replied, 'but it is written: "Thou shalt adore no images." '

'Well,' I said to Madame Carlès, 'you can see how near she got to conversion last Sunday.'

'Wait,' Madame Carlès said, 'wait awhile.'

Ill at ease and irresolute I started walking up and down the room; I had felt like an angry father before, but now I felt myself moved by a more truly paternal emotion for this poor girl who had no other prop but me. There you have the main, even praiseworthy, aspect of slavery as it is practised in the Orient. Of prime importance when material objects and animals are concerned, does the idea of possession become insignificant or ignoble when applied to one's fellows? I'm not, of course, referring to the unfortunate Negro slaves in Christian countries, but to the slaves owned by the Muslims, for in this case ownership conforms and is answerable to custom, law, and religion.

I took Zetnaybia's hand in mine, and I looked at her with such tenderness that Madame Carlès reached a hasty conclusion :

'That's just what I've been telling her,' she said. ' "Listen, my girl, if you become a Christian your master will marry you, perhaps, and take you back to his own country." '

'Madame Carlès!' I exclaimed with a laugh, 'you argue better than a Jesuit.'

Here was a solution I hadn't thought of yet. When I'm ready to return to Europe it will certainly be a nuisance, to say the least, if I still haven't managed to arrange some kind of future for a slave I've purchased in the Orient . . . but to marry her? . . . no! that would be too Christian.

'Think a moment, Madame Carlès,' I said, 'this woman is already eighteen years old, that's almost middle age in this part of the world. She'll be beautiful for another ten years, and me, I'll still be young then, the young husband of a yellow woman who has suns tattooed on her forehead and . . . elsewhere, who has a buttonhole in her nose for a ring she used to wear. . . . Think a moment, Madame Carlès . . . she's lovely enough in Levantine costume, but she's hideous in the dresses and whatnot of Europe. Do you see me entering a salon with a beauty who could pass for a cannibal! Nothing would be more ridiculous for her as well as for me. . . . No, my conscience doesn't push me that far, nor does my affection. This slave is dear to me, I admit it, but I'm not her first master, after all, and then, she has no education, nor any will to learn, and I doubt very much whether Europe would change her mentality . . . why, it would probably do the exact opposite . . . make her cling even more tightly to her present customs. How can such a woman become my equal? She isn't stupid at all, she isn't vulgar, but she's definitely illiterate. What disturbs me most . . . what I've finally come to understand is that it's impossible to establish much sympathy . . . to find much in common between two individuals when each belongs to a radically different race from the other. Yet I shall leave her, I know, with more than a little sorrow, and . . . you must excuse me, Madame Carlès. . . .' I stammered in embarrassment, for she had never asked me for such a confession, 'this whole situation has confused me . . . there are so many contradictory notions running through my head. . . .'

'The two of us will discuss what's to be done,' said Madame Carlès gently, 'but first I'll tell the girl to join her comrades again.'

Zetnaybia cheerfully returned to the class.

Madame Carlès' soothing voice had once again assured me that I could have complete confidence in her.

'It's best that she remains here, isn't it,' she suggested.

'Yes,' I agreed, 'it's best that she remains here.'

'And I promise you that we'll look after her until she's ready to make her own way.' She added with a touching and maternal smile, 'And if she's never ready, why, we'll still look after her.'

Thanking her with as much sincerity as relief, I then paid the modest fees for the next three months, and said that I would instruct my bank to send regular sums in the future until Madame Carlès notified them otherwise.

'I think,' she said, as we stepped into the classroom, 'that it would be wiser for you not to say goodbye.'

Zetnaybia was sitting close to the monitress; seeing me, she threw her arms around the girl's neck, so that this time the monitress could not hide her face behind a book, as she had at my arrival.

'*Ya makbouba!* (She's my friend!)' Zetnaybia cried.

I couldn't help but admire not only the European whiteness of her features, but also, and in particular, their aquiline purity, which is a sign of royalty in Asia as in Europe. Her proud expression was tempered by grace, it was also intelligent and serious. Was it only to please Zetnaybia, I wondered, that she favoured me now with a smile.

As Madame Carlès accompanied me along the gallery, I questioned her about Zetnaybia's friend.

'She's very gifted,' Madame Carlès said, 'she teaches the youngest class classical Arabic, and she's also learning Italian. If they hold a certain rank the women of her nation are encouraged to study and even to specialize in the Arts. Muslim women, on the contrary, regard this as a sign of social inferiority.'

'What nationality is she?' I asked.

'She belongs to the Druze, and. . . .'

'The Druze!' I cried.

'Why are you so surprised?'

I explained that I was fascinated by their history and religion.

'Moreover,' I added, 'I'm actually on my way to visit a Druze sheikh, Saide-Eshayrazy by name.'

'Now it's my turn to be surprised,' said Madame Carlès, 'for he is her father!'

I considered this unexpected revelation an excellent omen, and admitted as much to Madame Carlès.

'Only I don't understand how his daughter happens to be here.'

'As there are no Druze institutions in Beirut, her father sent her,' said Madame Carlès modestly, 'to the one place where she can lead a respectable and enjoyable life. Please don't tell him that you've seen his daughter, for the news may sadden him, even make him suspicious. She's allowed to visit him once a week, but he longs to see her more often.'

I promised I would be discreet, and letting Madame Carlès return to her class, I left the school, more eager than ever to meet the sheikh.

Part Two *The Tale of Caliph Hakim*

Introduction

The state prison of Beirut was surrounded by a group of towers on the east side of the city. As soon as I had handed out some tips, one of the guards went to tell the Druze sheikh that I wished to be introduced to him. Nobody was surprised by my request, for Europeans are renowned here for their curiosity. On his return, the guard said that the sheikh was prepared to welcome me, and he led me through the prison. I was expecting a dismal hovel with seeping walls and miserable cells, but I saw nothing of the kind; the building might have been a large private residence in the centre of the city. Moreover, there were only a few guards and soldiers around, and they looked more like the inmates' bodyguards than their warders.

Saide-Eshayrazy had an entire suite to himself, and he was allowed the privilege of strolling along the terraces. He received me in his parlour and had his personal slave bring us coffee and pipes. The guard withdrew immediately, telling me that I could stay as long as I liked. The sheikh, an *akkal* (holy man), did not smoke himself, but he insisted that I make a choice from the various tobaccos offered to me by the slave. I was struck at once by Saide-Eshayrazy's noble features, though I was discreet enough to refrain from telling him that I had already seen them reproduced on his daughter's lovely face. I was also surprised to see how young he was; he did not, in fact, appear to be much older than me.

We spoke to each other in Italian, which the sheikh knew perfectly. This was not the first time, he assured me in a quiet but penetrating voice, that he had received foreign visitors (Englishmen, in particular) who wanted to question him about his nation and his own position. Besides, he had become extremely patient during his imprisonment, and he looked forward to company and conversation.

I began with general questions :

'Is it true that? . . .' and I expounded all the arguments of Niebur, Volney, and Sacy.

The sheikh merely nodded his head with prudent, Oriental reserve :

'Ah,' he said, 'really? . . . interesting. . . . Are the Christians so knowledgeable? . . . I wonder how they learned all that. . . .' and other non-committal phrases.

'You doubtless know,' I persisted, 'that in our libraries we have about a hundred of your religious books; they have all been carefully studied, translated and annotated.'

'Our Lord is great,' he replied.

'I don't deny that they're full of contradictions and confusions which you could elucidate,' I continued. 'The Druze have been compared to the Pythagoreans, the Essenes and the Gnostics, while some scholars claim that the Knights-Templar exploited many of your ideas, and that the Rosicrucians and Freemasons have done the same today. Also, there's no agreement, except a negative one, about the role played by Caliph Hakim.'

Encouraged by the keener and more attentive fashion in which Saide-Eshayrazy was now looking at me, I decided to be more personal :

'I've been struck by particular points in your doctrine. There's no mention of original sin; no paradise for the righteous, no hell for the wicked; reward and atonement, if I'm not mistaken, take place upon the earth, through the transmigration of souls. Christians, Jews, Mohammedans and idolaters are regarded as distinctly inferior, but your religion is the only one, to the best of my knowledge, which doesn't condemn its enemies to everlasting torment.'

'That is correct,' the sheikh murmured.

'As for Hakim, I have to admit that he has been represented as a mixture between Nero and Heliogabalus, and I realize that from your point of view such opinions are tantamount to blasphemy.'

'Hakim,' said Saide-Eshayrazy quietly, 'is our Messiah.'

I thought he would immediately tell me more about this mysterious caliph, but he remained silent and continued watching me attentively.

'I don't want to sound presumptuous,' I said, 'but in one of the books I read in Cairo I discovered the Druze catechism.'

'Really,' the sheikh remarked ironically.

Although I had no copy of the catechism on me — and even if I had arrived armed, so to speak, in such a way I well might not have produced it for fear of angering him — I did remember clearly a certain passage which I quoted now as a response to the sheikh's incredulity.

QUESTION : What is the fundamental belief of the Druze priests?
ANSWER : The contrary of all that other tribes and nations believe. Everything which they consider impious or irreligious we ourselves believe, as it is written in *The Epistle of Illusion and Caution*.
QUESTION : But if an individual came to understand our holy cult, to believe in it and conform to it, would he then be saved?

ANSWER: Never! for the door is closed, the matter is over, the pen is blunt. After his death his soul would rejoin the souls of his original nation and religion.

Without revealing any surprise at my knowledge, Saide-Eshayrazy must have been impressed by my assiduity, at least, by this decisive proof of my seriousness, for he was willing now, he said, to disclose the whole truth about the caliph. Having ordered his slave to prepare a room for me (evidently I was going to be a prisoner myself for a few days!), he started reciting his story with stately, measured pomp. I have set it down following his own style as closely as possible and omitting none of the details. In the Orient every subject becomes a tale; nevertheless, the principal facts of the one which follows are definitely based upon authentic traditions.

I Hashish

During the fourth century of the Mohammedan era, by Christian reckoning not long after the year 1000, a small village straggled on the right bank of the Nile not far from the port of Fostat where the ruins of old Cairo lie, and quite close to mount Mokatam which towers over the new city; the majority of its inhabitants belonged to the sect of the Sabians.

From the last houses along the river there is a delightful view; the Nile splashes the island of Rodda with caressing waves and seems to hold it up, like a slave carrying a basket of flowers in his arms. Giza is visible on the opposite bank, and in the evening the gigantic triangles of the pyramids cleave the band of violet mist left behind by the setting sun. The tops of the palm-trees, sycamores and fig-trees of Pharaon stand out in black relief against this luminous background. Stretched out in the plain, like a hunting dog ready to spring, the sphinx seems to guard from afar the herds of buffaloes that descend in long files to the watering-place, while the lights of the fishermen prick the dense shadows on the sloping banks with golden stars.

The best place in the Sabian village from which to enjoy this view

was an okel; its white walls were thick and high, and it was surrounded by carob-trees. The foot of the terrace dipped into the water,
and every night, as they made their way down the Nile or up again,
the boatmen could see the flicker of the watch-lights that were floating in pools of oil.

Glancing along the arcades from a cangia in the middle of the
river, a spy could easily have made out the travellers and regular
customers in the okel seated in front of small tables on coops of palm-
tree wood or divans covered with mats; he would certainly have been
astonished by their strange behaviour. From the dazed immobility
which followed their extravagant gestures, from their crazy laughter,
from the inarticulate cries which burst intermittently out of their
lungs, he would have realized that here was one of those houses where
the infidels go, defying the law, to get drunk on wine, *bouza* (beer), or
hashish.

One evening a boat drew near, skilfully steered by an oarsman who
must have been well acquainted with the region; it landed in the
shadow cast by the terrace, right at the water-washed foot of a short
staircase. A good looking fellow, who was apparently a fisherman,
sprang out of the boat and streaked up the steps; he sat down in a
corner of the room, choosing a place which seemed to be his own.
Nobody paid any attention to his arrival, he was evidently a regular
customer.

At the very same moment a man entered from the opposite door,
that is, from the land side, wearing a black woollen tunic and a
takieh (white cap); contrary to custom, his hair was long. His sudden
appearance caused some surprise. He sat down quietly, however, in
a dark corner; the clientele succumbed again to their drunkenness,
and soon nobody paid him any further attention.

Although the newcomer was miserably dressed, his face showed
none of the restless humility of the destitute. His firmly chiselled
features recalled the stern lines of the leonine mask. Dark blue, like
sapphires, and brimming with an indefinable power, his eyes could
terrify and at the same time enchant.

When the young man, Yousouf by name, who had arrived in the
cangia noticed the unfamiliar presence of the unknown man a secret
sympathy at once arose within his heart for him. As he hadn't joined
the revellers, Yousouf approached the stranger, who was now seated
cross-legged upon a divan.

'Brother,' Yousouf greeted him, 'you look tired. You've doubtless
had a long journey. Won't you take some refreshment?'

'My journey has indeed been long,' replied the stranger. 'I came
into this okel to rest, but what refreshment can I take here where they
only serve forbidden drinks?'

'You Mohammedans only dare to moisten your lips with pure water, but we who belong to the Sabian sect may quench our thirst with the generous blood of the vine or the pale liquid of the barley without offence to our law.'

'But I don't see any fermented drink in front of you.'

'Oh, I gave up such crude means of intoxication a long time ago,' Yousouf replied, signalling to a young Negro.

The boy approached carrying two small glass cups, embossed all around with silver, and a box full of a greenish paste with an ivory spatula sticking in it. He put them on the table and withdrew.

'This box contains the paradise promised by your prophet and his believers. If you weren't so scrupulous I could soon put you into the Houris' arms without,' laughed Yousouf, 'making you pass over the bridge of Alsirat.'*

'But this paste is hashish if I'm not mistaken,' said the stranger, pushing away the cup in which Yousouf had dropped a portion of the fantastic mixture, 'and hashish is also strictly forbidden.'

'Every source of pleasure is always forbidden,' said Yousouf, swallowing his first spoonful.

The stranger fixed his sombre blue eyes upon him; his forehead contracted into such violent creases that his hair followed their undulations. For a moment it looked as though he would throw himself upon the impudent young man and tear him into shreds; but he controlled himself, his expression grew milder, and suddenly changing his mind he reached out his hand, took hold of the cup and slowly started to taste the greenish paste.

After some minutes Yousouf and the stranger felt the first effects of the hashish; through their limbs a gentle languor spread, while a faint smile hovered on their lips. Although they had passed scarcely half an hour in each other's company they fancied that they had known each other for a thousand years. As the effect of the drug grew stronger they started laughing, moving about and talking most loquaciously, in particular the stranger, who, as a strict observer of the law, had never before tasted this concoction and therefore felt the effects more acutely, as beginners generally do. He appeared to be gripped by an extraordinary exaltation; a multitude of marvellous and unprecedented thoughts shot through his mind in a whirlwind of fire, his eyes flashed as though they were lighted from within by the reflection of an unknown world, and his appearance was enhanced by a superhuman dignity. Then, as the vision died away, he lay back on the cushions and surrendered himself luxuriously to the ecstatic reveries that followed.

* In the Koran, the bridge of Alsirat is the one leading from Hell to Heaven — N.G.

'Well, my dear companion, what do you think of this honourable pistachio jam?' Yousouf asked, profiting from this break in the stranger's intoxication. 'Will you still anathematize all the good people who calmly gather together in a small room to find happiness in their own particular fashion?'

Slowly and profoundly the stranger replied, 'Hashish renders you equal to God.'

'Exactly!' Yousouf agreed enthusiastically. 'Water drinkers perceive nothing but the crude and material appearance of things, while intoxication, on the contrary, dulls the eyes of the body and brightens those of the soul. Delivered from that clumsy gaoler of a body, the spirit escapes, like a prisoner whose warder has fallen asleep, leaving the keys at the dungeon door. Free and full of joy it wanders through regions of space and light, to be startled by the unexpected and delightful revelations of the friendly genii whom it encounters. With a quick stroke of its wings it travels in less than a minute through atmospheres of indescribable bliss, but time seems eternal, for these sensations succeed each other with astonishing rapidity. . . . As for me, I have a dream that never fails to return with one variation or another. When I leave in my cangia, reeling under the splendour of my visions, I drift along, keeping my eyes closed so that I can all the more enjoy the perpetual stream of hyacinths, carbuncles, emeralds and rubies, which forms the background for the marvellous patterns of the hashish frieze. Then, in the heart of infinity, as it were, I perceive a celestial figure; fairer than all the creations of the poets, she smiles at me with piercing sweetness and even descends from the heavens to come quite close to me. . . . Is it an angel, a peri? I don't know. As she takes her place beside me in the boat, its common wood is at once transformed into mother-of-pearl and floats on a river of silver, steered by a perfume laden breeze.'

'A wonderful and singular vision,' the stranger murmured, nodding his head.

'And that's not all,' Yousouf continued. 'One night, having taken a weaker dose than usual, I awoke from my intoxication as my cangia was passing the tip of the island of Rodda. A woman like the one in my dreams cast her eyes upon me; human though they were, they did not lack celestial light. Studded with precious stones, her jacket blazed in the moonbeams through her partly open veil. Our hands touched; her soft skin was sweet and fresh like a flower petal, and the carving on her ring slightly grazed my finger. That was enough to convince me of her reality.'

'Near the island of Rodda . . . indeed,' the stranger murmured pensively to himself.

'I hadn't been dreaming,' Yousouf continued, paying no attention to the remark of his unexpected confidant, 'the hashish had only released a memory hidden in the deepest recesses of my soul; this divine face was known to me. When, for instance, had I seen her before? In what world had we already met? What former existence had brought us together now? I cannot answer those questions, but this strangest of encounters, this most bizarre adventure didn't surprise me at all; on the contrary, nothing could have seemed more natural to me than finding this woman, my ideal incarnate, in my cangia right in the middle of the Nile, as though she had soared up from the cup of one of those large flowers which rise to the surface of the waters. Without asking her for any explanation I threw myself at her feet and spoke to her, as I had to the peri of my dream, in the most ardent and sublime terms which love can invent in its exaltation. I had access to words of immeasurable significance, to expressions that concealed whole worlds of thought, to mysterious phrases that vibrated with the echo of vanished civilizations. My soul glided through past and future aeons, and I was convinced I had felt for all eternity this love to which I now gave utterance.

'As I spoke I saw her large eyes take fire and shoot forth emanations; she reached out her diaphanous hands towards me, and they tapered into rays of light. Feeling that I was wrapped within a net of flame, I fell back, despite myself, into my latest dream, and when I was at last able to shake off the delightful and almost invincible torpor that bound my limbs I found myself on the opposite shore, at Giza, resting against a palm-tree. My Negro was sleeping peacefully beside the cangia which he had hauled on to the sand. The horizon was fringed by a glimmer of rose, the day was about to break.'

'A love like that scarcely resembles earthly love,' the stranger said, without raising any objections to the impossibilities of Yousouf's story, for under the influence of hashish it is easy to believe in marvels.

'Why have I confided in you when I've never seen you before? You're the first person, in fact, to whom I've told this incredible story. That's difficult to explain. A mysterious attraction draws me towards you ... when you entered this room a voice cried out from the depths of my soul : "There he is at last!" I had been harrowed in secret for a long time by a kind of relentless anxiety which was calmed by your arrival. I didn't realize until I saw you that you were the one for whom I'd always been waiting. Ready was I and eager to welcome you to my thoughts, and I have had to tell you all the mysteries of my heart.'

'My feelings are the same as yours,' the stranger replied, 'and now I shall reveal to you something I haven't even dared fully acknowledge myself. You have an impossible passion, let us say, while

I have a monstrous one, you love a peri, while I love . . . you will shudder . . . my sister! Strange though it be, however, I cannot feel any remorse for this unlawful inclination; although I often condemn myself I am always absolved by a mysterious power which I feel within me. There is no earthly impurity in my love, sensuality doesn't drive me towards my sister, even though she is as beautiful as the phantom of my recent visions. I am moved, rather, by an attraction I cannot define, by an affection as deep as the depths of the sea and as vast as the vaults of the heavens . . . the kind of affection a god might experience. The idea of my sister uniting with a man fills me with horror and disgust; it would be a sacrilege, for through the veils of her flesh I perceive something celestial about her. Despite the name by which she is known on earth she is the bride of my divine soul, the virgin who was reserved for me when the universe was created. At times I believe I have recaptured from the ages and the darkness some tokens of our secret relationship. Scenes that occurred before the appearance of man upon the earth arise again in my memory; I see myself under Eden's golden boughs seated next to her and served by the obedient spirits. By joining myself to another woman I fear I would betray and violate the soul of the world which throbs within me. Through the condensation of our divine blood I would like to obtain an immortal race . . . and an ultimate god. A god more powerful than all those who have so far made themselves manifest under different forms and names! . . .'

While Yousouf and the stranger exchanged these long confidences the other customers yielded in their drunken excitement to extravagant contortions, crazy laughter, ecstatic swooning and convulsive dancing; but gradually, as the power of the hemp dwindled, they grew calm again and collapsed upon the divans in that state of exhaustion which generally follows such outbursts.

An individual of patriarchal bearing, whose beard was longer than his trailing robe, entered the okel and advanced to the centre of the room.

'Arise, my brothers!' he exclaimed in a resonant voice. 'I have been watching the sky. The hour is propitious for sacrificing a white cock in front of the sphinx in honour of Hermes and Agathodaemon.'

The Sabians rose steadily to their feet and prepared to follow their priest, but the stranger, on hearing this proposal, changed colour two or three times; the blue of his eyes grew black, dreadful creases furrowed his face, and a muffled roar burst from his lungs. The company trembled, as though a real lion had broken into their midst.

'Reprobates! Blasphemers!' he cried in a voice of thunder. 'Vile brutes! Idolaters!'

His explosion of anger stupefied the crowd. This unknown man had such an authoritative air and lifted the folds of his tunic with such imperious gestures that none of them dared reply to his insults. The old man, however, approached him and asked :

'Where is the harm, brother, in sacrificing a cock, according to the rites, to the good genii Hermes and Agathodaemon?'

The mere mention of these two names made the stranger grind his teeth.

'If you don't share the Sabians' beliefs why have you come here? Are you a follower of Jesus or Mohammed?'

'Mohammed and Jesus are impostors!' the stranger cried in a violent, blasphemous fury.

'You practise the religion of Zoroaster, no doubt, and venerate fire. . . .'

'Illusions! Lies! Mockery!' the man in the black tunic interrupted in a paroxysm of rage.

'Then whom do you worship?'

'He asks me whom I worship! . . . I worship nobody because I am God myself! I am the one, the true and the only God, while all the others are nothing but my shadows.'

At this extraordinary and insane assertion the Sabians hurled themselves upon the blasphemer and would have killed him if Yousouf, shielding him with his own body, hadn't managed to push him backwards, despite his fierce resistance and frantic shouts, to the terrace that was splashed by the Nile. Then, with a sharp kick at the bank, Yousouf launched his boat into the middle of the river.

'Where should I take you to?' he asked his friend when they had gained the current.

'Over there, where those lights are shining on the island of Rodda,' the stranger replied, as the night air calmed his exaltation.

Skilfully handling his oars, Yousouf soon reached the spot which his friend had indicated. Before he jumped ashore the man in the black tunic drew an ancient wrought ring from his finger and gave it to his deliverer.

'Wherever you may chance to meet me,' he said, 'you have only to show me this ring and I shall grant whatever you wish.'

Then he withdrew and disappeared among the trees which skirted the bank of the river. To recover the time which he had lost Yousouf sliced his oars more keenly now into the Nile, for he wished to be present at the sacrifice of the cock.

2 Famine

Some days after this incident the caliph left his palace as usual to go to the Mokatam observatory. Everybody was accustomed to seeing him depart, from time to time, riding on an ass and accompanied only by a young mute slave. They supposed that he spent the night examining the stars, for they saw him return in the same fashion at daybreak; his servants were not at all surprised, for his father, Aziz-Billah, and his grandfather, Moezzeldin, the founder of Cairo, had acted likewise; both of them were deeply versed in the kabbalistic sciences. Once he had observed the disposition of the stars, however, and assured himself that he was threatened by no immediate danger, the Caliph Hakim would lay aside his customary apparel and put on the clothes of his slave, who remained behind in the tower waiting for him; then, having darkened his face a little in order to pass unrecognized, he would go down into the city to mingle with the people, thereby learning many secrets which could prove valuable to a sovereign. It was in a similar disguise that he had recently visited the okel of the Sabians.

On this particular occasion Hakim made his way towards Roumelieh Square, where the inhabitants of Cairo form the liveliest groups; there they gather together in the shops and under the trees to enjoy sugared drinks, lemonades and preserved fruits, while they listen to recitals of poems and tales. The jugglers, almas and the animal showmen usually draw a crowd around them eager for entertainment after the day's work, but this evening was an exception; hostile and gloomy, the people resembled a surging, storm tossed sea. In one corner and another angry voices rose above the general uproar, and speeches charged with gall resounded in every part. Wherever he walked the caliph heard this persistent exclamation : 'The public granaries are empty !'

For some time, in fact, the population had been alarmed by a crucial shortage of bread; the hope of seeing wheat arrive soon from upper Egypt had momentarily calmed their fears, and meanwhile everyone kept a watchful eye on his own supplies. During the day, however, an exceptionally large caravan had arrived from Syria, and

92

Coffee Shop. *Lithograph by Louis Haghe*

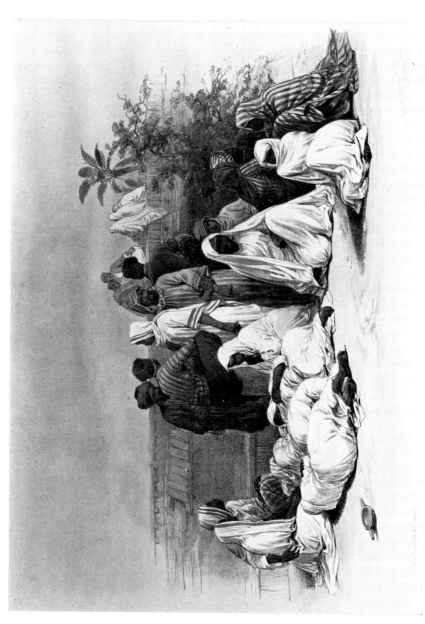

Slave Market. *Lithograph by Louise Haghe*

it had been almost impossible to find food enough for its members as well as for the population; provoked by the foreigners, a big crowd had rushed to the public granaries of old Cairo, the final resort in the worst famines. The tenth part of every harvest is piled up there within an edifice which dates from the time of Amrou; its huge enclosures are formed by high walls. On the command of the conqueror of Egypt, these granaries were left without roofing, so that the birds could take their share. This pious injunction was still respected, for it seemed to bring good fortune to the city and usually cost no more than a fraction of the reserve. But when the people in their fury demanded grain today the employees replied that innumerable flocks of birds had come down and devoured everything. At these words the population believed they were threatened by imminent disaster and they gradually succumbed to fear and consternation.

How is it I knew nothing about any of this? Hakim asked himself. Could such a phenomenon really have happened? I would have seen signs of it in the stars; there would have been a disturbance in the pentacle I drew.

He was immersed in these reflections when an old man in Syrian costume approached him and said :

'Why don't you give them bread, Lord?' Hakim lifted his head in astonishment and fixed his leonine gaze upon the stranger, believing the latter had recognized him under his disguise. The man was blind.

'You are surely mad,' said Hakim, 'to address such words to someone you cannot see, someone whose footsteps you have only heard in the dust !'

'All men are blind,' the Syrian said, 'compared to God.'

'So you are addressing God?'

'I am addressing you, Lord.'

Hakim was pensive for a moment, and his thoughts whirled again as they had under the intoxication of hashish.

'Save them,' the old man said, 'for you alone are the power, you alone are the life, you alone are the will.'

'What do you mean . . . do you think I can create wheat here on the spot?' Hakim replied, troubled by an obscure thought.

'The sun cannot shine through clouds, it disperses them slowly. The cloud that veils you at present is the body in which you have deigned to descend; it can only muster human strength. We all submit to the law of things decreed by God, while God alone obeys no law but the one he has formed himself. The world, which he created by kabbalistic art, would immediately disintegrate if he swerved from his own will.'

'It's clear enough,' the caliph said, exerting his reason, 'that you're only a beggar. Somebody must have recognized me under my disguise and told you who I was. Your flattery is too boorish . . . here, take this purse of sequins and go your way.'

'Nobody has told me who you are, Lord; I am blind, it is true, but I see with the eyes of my soul. As for gold, I am versed in alchemy and know how to make it when I need it. This purse which you have handed to me . . . I shall give it to your people. Bread is costly, but in this good city of Cairo, gold buys everything.'

A necromancer, no doubt, Hakim thought.

Snatching up the coins which the old Syrian scattered on the ground, the crowd rushed to the oven of the nearest baker. An ocque (two pounds) of bread cost as much as one gold sequin.

'Ah! that explains it,' Hakim said aloud, infuriated by the baker's extortion, 'now I understand! That old man who comes from the country of wisdom did indeed recognize me himself and he spoke to me in allegories. The caliph is the image of God, therefore, like God, I must deal out due punishment.'

He made his way at once towards the citadel, where he found the chief of the watch, Abou-Arous, who shared the secret of his disguises. Instructing this officer and his executioner to follow him, as had already been his wont on more than one occasion, for, like the majority of Oriental princes, he believed in this kind of summary justice, Hakim led them towards the house of the baker who was selling bread at the weight of gold.

'Here is a thief,' he said to the chief of the watch.

'Then his ear should be nailed to the shop shutter,' the latter replied.

'Yes,' the caliph said, 'but first his head must be cut off.'

The crowd, which was not expecting such festivities, formed a joyful circle in the street, while the baker vainly protested his innocence. Wrapped in a black *abbah* which he had put on at the citadel, the caliph appeared to perform the duties of a mere cadi, and nobody suspected who he really was. On his knees now, the baker stretched out his neck and commended his soul to the angels Monkir and Nekir.* The executioner lifted his scimitar, but at that moment a young man elbowed his way through the crowd and dashed towards Hakim, showing him an ancient wrought ring: it was Yousouf the Sabian.

'Grant me this man's life!' he cried.

Hakim remembered his promise as he recognized his friend from the banks of the Nile. He made a sign to the executioner, who immediately stepped back, and the baker rose happily to his feet again.

---

* Before judgment is pronounced upon him, a dead man is interrogated by the Angels of Death, Monkir and Nekir. — N.G.

Hearing the mutter of disappointment from the crowd, Hakim spoke quietly to the chief of the watch.

'The sentence is suspended until tomorrow at the same hour,' Abou-Arous declared in a loud voice. 'Then every baker will have to provide bread at the rate of ten ocques a sequin!'

'I realized clearly enough that you represented the law,' the Sabian said to Hakim, 'when I saw your angry reactions the other evening to the forbidden drinks. This ring likewise gives me a certain legal right which I shall exercize from time to time.'

'My brother, you have spoken the truth,' the caliph replied, embracing him. 'My duties are over now, so let's go and enjoy some hashish at the okel of the Sabians.'

3 The Lady of the Kingdom

On their arrival at the okel Yousouf took the proprietor aside, asking him to excuse the manner in which his friend had behaved during his first visit.

'Like everyone else,' Yousouf said, 'he has his own fixed idea when he's intoxicated, he believes that he is God.' The customers were quite understanding when this explanation was conveyed to them.

The two friends sat down in their former place; the Negro brought them the box which contained the inebriating paste, and each helped himself to a portion which soon produced an effect. Instead of abandoning himself to the hallucinations, however, and launching into an extravagant discourse, the caliph yielded to the iron grip of a fixed idea, but not the one for which everybody was now prepared. Suddenly he leapt to his feet; his majestic, powerfully carved features were marked by an inflexible decision.

'Brother,' he said to Yousouf in a voice of irresistible authority, 'you must take me immediately in your cangia to that place on the island of Rodda, near to the garden terraces, where you left me the other evening.'

Yousouf was unable to articulate the objections which rose to his lips at this unexpected command; he certainly judged it outrageous to leave the okel just when the raptures of hashish called for repose upon the divan in order to unfold at their leisure, but confronted by the will-power that blazed forth from the caliph's eyes, the young man had no choice but to climb down the steps in silence to his cangia. Hakim sat at the prow, while Yousouf bent over the oars. The caliph was prey to the most extraordinary exaltation during the short crossing; he jumped ashore before the boat had even landed and dismissed his friend with a royal and imperial gesture. Yousouf returned to the okel in bewilderment, while the prince took the path which led to the palace.

He entered through a postern, which he opened by touching a secret spring; passing through several gloomy corridors, he soon emerged at the centre of his private apartment. His appearance astonished his attendants, who had never seen him return before the first glimmer of day. When the eunuchs noticed his illuminated countenance, his rigid bearing, his ambiguous expression, and his strange gestures, they succumbed to a wave of dread; they imagined that something exceptional was about to occur, and, lining up against the walls, they lowered their heads, crossed their arms, and waited for the event in a state of respectful anxiety : Hakim's punishments were known to be prompt, terrible, and void of apparent motive; everyone trembled, for none felt pure.

Hakim had no heads fall, however, for he had not arrived to deal with judicial trifles; he was wholly preoccupied by a more serious subject. In blatant defiance of Muslim etiquette, he strode towards the rooms of his sister, the princess Setalmulc. Lifting the door-curtain, he entered the first hall, to the considerable alarm of the princess' eunuchs, and of her waiting women, who hastily veiled their faces.

At the back of a secluded room, Setalmulc (*sit'al mulk* means the lady of the kingdom) was seated on a pile of cushions which adorned an alcove carved out in the solid wall. The interior of this room was dazzling in its magnificence. Made up of small domes, the ceiling resembled a honey cake or a grotto of stalactites, for the ornamentation was intricate and ingenious, and shone with intermingling tints of red, green, gold and azure. Splendid slabs of tall glass mosaics embellished the walls; arcades, hollowed out in the shape of a heart, looked down gracefully upon the bevelled, turban-shaped capitals which crested small marble columns. Inscriptions in karmatic script ran along the cornices, door jambs and window-frames; their elegant letters were entwined by flowers, foliage, and scrolls of arabesque. In the middle of the room the sculptured basin of an alabaster fountain welcomed a jet of water; its crystal volley first rose right up to the ceiling, then fell back again in a fine shower with a silver-toned pattering.

At the disturbance caused by Hakim's entry, Setalmulc, troubled, stood up and moved towards the door, thereby revealing the full splendour of her majestic stature. The caliph's sister was indeed the most beautiful princess in the world. No one could look into her eyes, crowned by the perfectly symmetrical arcs of her velvety black eyebrows, for a moment longer than he could gaze at the noonday sun; the faintly aquiline curve of her delicate nose testified the royalty of her ancestry, while the golden pallor of her complexion, which was heightened at her cheeks by small white streaks of paint, offset her mouth of lustrous purple, which sparkled like a pomegranate crammed with jewels.

The opulence of Setalmulc's apparel was likewise extraordinary; a metal horn studded with diamonds held up her spangle dappled veil of gauze; her velvet gown, half green and half incarnadine, disappeared under the elaborate floral patterns of its embroidery. Centres of miraculously brilliant light, where sparks of gold and silver intermingled, appeared upon her sleeves, her elbows, and her breast. Made of meticulously engraved gold orbs and studded with enormous ruby buttons, her girdle slipped, owing to its weight, below her supple and majestic waist, to be halted by the ample contour of her hips. Thus attired, Setalmulc resembled one of those queens of vanished kingdoms who counted gods among their ancestors.

Suddenly the door-curtain was torn aside and Hakim appeared on the threshold. At the sight of her brother Setalmulc was unable to suppress a cry of astonishment; the caliph's unprecedented behaviour startled her much less than his truly extraordinary appearance. Hakim seemed to be imbued no longer with terrestrial life, for his pallid features reflected the light of another world; there was no mistaking the caliph's form, but it was illuminated by a different mind and another soul. His gestures were those of a phantom, and indeed he resembled his own ghost. Conveyed by will-power rather than by ordinary movements, he advanced towards Setalmulc and pierced her with a look which was so pensive, so acute, and so searching that the princess shivered and crossed her arms over her breast, as though an invisible hand had rent her robes.

'Setalmulc,' said Hakim, 'for a long time I have thought of giving you a husband, but no man is worthy of you. Your divine blood is not to be polluted. The treasure we have received from the past must be handed unblemished to posterity. It is I, Hakim, the caliph, lord of the heavens and earth, who will be your bridegroom. Our wedding will take place in three days' time : this is my sacred will.'

Stunned by this unexpected declaration, the princess could not even murmur a reply; fascinated, moreover, by Hakim's domination and by the authority of his words, she felt that it was impossible to raise any objections at all. Without waiting, however, for his sister's response, Hakim strode towards the door; he returned to his own rooms, and, overcome by the hashish, which had reached the height of its effect, he threw himself in a heap upon the cushions and fell asleep.

As soon as her brother had left, Setalmulc sent for the Grand Vizier, Argevan, and told him everything that had just occurred. Argevan had been regent of the kingdom during Hakim's early youth, for the latter was proclaimed caliph at the age of eleven; he had wielded unlimited power, and through force of habit he still managed the affairs of the real sovereign, while Hakim enjoyed only the honours.

It is impossible to describe the thoughts which stirred in Argevan's mind when he had heard all that Setalmulc had to tell him. Who indeed could probe the secrets of this profound and subtle soul? Were study and meditation responsible for the emaciation of his cheeks and the darkness of his austere gaze? Were determination and will-power responsible for that sign of a disastrous fate, the sinister shape of the *Tau* carved across the lines of his forehead? Did the pallor of that immobile mask, which wrinkled at moments just between his eyebrows, signify only that he came from the burnt plains of the Maghreb? Did the respect he inspired among the population of Cairo and the influence he had gained over the rich and powerful prove that everybody recognized and appreciated the wisdom and justice he exercised in his administration of the State?

Setalmulc herself had been educated by him and she regarded him as the equal of her father, the former caliph. As indignant now as the sultana, Argevan said:

'Alas! What a misfortune for the kingdom! First the heavens strike us with famine, now with another calamity; the order must be given for public prayers, for our lord has lost his sanity.'

'May God forbid it!' Setalmulc exclaimed.

'When the prince of believers wakes up,' the vizier added more calmly, 'I hope he will be in full possession of his faculties and able to preside as usual over the Great Council.'

At dawn Argevan waited for the caliph to rise, but Hakim didn't call for his slaves until much later; they informed him that the assembly hall was already crowded with doctors, notaries, lawyers and cadis. When he entered, the audience prostrated themselves according to the custom. Then the vizier scrutinized the ruler's thoughtful face.

The caliph noticed Argevan's attentive look; his minister's features, it seemed to him, were marked by glacial irony. That he had allowed excessive authority to inferiors was a constant source of regret to the prince, but every time he attempted to act alone he was astonished to meet with resistance among the ulemas, cachefs and mudirs, all of whom were devoted to Argevan. His recent use of disguise and his nocturnal walks were explained, in fact, by his intention to escape from tutelage and judge things for himself.

Since nobody mentioned anything except ordinary affairs, the caliph stopped the discussion :

'Let us talk a little about the famine,' he said in a commanding voice. 'I have decided that I shall have the heads of all the bakers cut off today.'

'Prince of believers,' said an old man, getting up from the ulemas' bench, 'didn't you have one of them pardoned last night by a cadi?' The sound of that voice wasn't unknown to the caliph.

'True,' he replied, 'but I had him pardoned on condition that bread be sold at a rate of ten ocques a sequin.'

'Remember that those unfortunate men have to pay ten sequins for an ardeb (approximately 350 lbs) of flour,' the old man said. 'Better punish those who sell it to them at such an exorbitant price.'

'And who are they?' the caliph asked.

'The moultezims, the cachefs, the mudirs and even the ulemas, they all have stacks of it in their houses.'

The members of the council and all the bystanders shivered at these words, for they were the leading citizens of Cairo to whom the ulema had just referred. The caliph held his head pensively in his hands for a few moments. Argevan was about to retort in anger to the old ulema when Hakim's voice of thunder resounded in the assembly hall :

'I shall leave my palace at Rodda this evening at the hour of prayer, and I shall cross the branch of the Nile in my cangia. The chief of the watch will be waiting for me on the shore with his executioner. I shall take the left bank of the calish and enter Cairo by the gate of Bab-el-Tahla in order to go to the Raschida mosque. At the house of every moultezim, cachef and ulema, I shall ask if there is any wheat, and, in those houses where there isn't any, I shall have the owner hanged or beheaded !'

Argevan didn't dare raise his voice in the council hall after this declaration, but seeing the caliph return to his rooms, he hurried after him.

'You will surely never do that, my lord !' he exclaimed.

'Silence !' Hakim shouted angrily. 'When I was a child, you called me the Lizard for a joke . . . remember? Well, the Lizard has now become the Dragon !'

4 The Moristan

On that very evening, then, at the hour of prayer, accompanied only by the chief of the watch and his executioner, Hakim passed through the soldiers' quarters and entered the city. He noticed that lights were shining in all the streets ahead of him. Holding candles in their hands to guide the prince on his way, the common people had gathered in groups mainly in front of every house belonging to a cachef, a notary or any other of the leading citizens mentioned in the ordinance. In each house he entered the caliph found a large stack of wheat; he immediately gave orders for it to be distributed to the crowd and wrote down the owner's name.

'According to my promise your head is spared,' he said, 'but from now on understand that you are not to hoard up wheat again. You are not to enjoy plenty in the midst of general misery or resell the wheat at the weight of gold, grasping hold of all the public wealth within a few days.'

Having visited several houses in this manner, he sent officers to the others, while he went himself to the Raschida mosque to pray, for it was Friday evening. As he entered, however, he was amazed to see the rostrum occupied and to hear himself hailed as follows:

'May the name of Hakim be glorified on earth as it is in heaven! Everlasting praise to the living God!'

However enraptured the people were by what the caliph had just accomplished, faithful believers were bound to rise in indignation at this unexpected salutation; indeed, a number of them rushed forward to throw the blasphemer off the rostrum. He rose to his full height, however, then climbed majestically down, making his would-be assailants retreat at every step. As he passed through the astonished crowd they were able to see him closely.

'He is blind!' they all cried out. 'The hand of God is upon him!'

Hakim had recognized the old Syrian from Roumelieh Square, and, just as an unprecedented affinity sometimes links an aspect of everyday life to the details of a dream which otherwise would have remained forgotten, he saw in a flash of lightning, as it were, the double existence of his life and his hashish visions as one: they joined

100

and intermingled. His reason, however, struggled to withstand this vivid impression; without staying any longer in the mosque, he mounted his horse and rode towards the palace.

Hakim wished to interview the Grand Vizier, but, strangely enough, Argevan could not be found, even though all the servants searched for him. As it was now the hour to go to mount Mokatam to consult the stars, the caliph set out towards the observatory tower; he climbed to the upper floor where he examined the twelve houses of the stars through the meticulously pierced cupola. Saturn, Hakim's planet, was pale and leaden, while Mars (Caher), which had given its name to the city of Cairo (Al Caherah), blazed gory red, predicting danger and war. Hakim climbed down to the first floor of the tower where a kabbalistic table had been installed and arranged by his grandfather Moezzeldin. The names of all the countries of the world were written in Chaldean round the circumference of a circle, in the middle of which stood the bronze statue of an armed horseman; he usually held his spear up straight, but if Egypt were threatened by an enemy, he would lower it and turn towards the country from which the attack was coming. Hakim saw that the horseman was turned towards Arabia.

'That race of the Abassides once again!' he exclaimed aloud. 'Those degenerate sons of Omar whom we defeated in their capital of Baghdad! But what do I care for those infidels now when I hold the lightning in my hand!'

Pondering the matter over, however, he realized that he was in fact no different from the man he had always been, for hallucination no longer added, to his conviction that he was a god, the assurance that he possessed superhuman strength.

'Let's go,' he said, 'and hear what advice ecstasy has to offer.' And he set out to get intoxicated once again on that marvellous paste which is the same, perhaps, as ambrosia, the food of the immortals.

The faithful Yousouf had already arrived at the okel to gaze at the mournful waters of the Nile which had ebbed to a level still predicting famine and drought.

'My friend,' Hakim greeted him, 'are you still dreaming of your love? Tell me who the mistress of your heart is, and I swear I shall make her yours, for as a cadi I enjoy the right to ask personal favours of the caliph.'

'If only I knew, alas!' Yousouf sighed. 'I haven't seen her golden cangia on the Nile since the nights grew stifling under the khasmin wind. Would I dare ask her who she is even if I saw her again? . . . At times I suspect that it was all merely an illusion of this treacherous herb which attacks my reason so drastically, perhaps, that already I can't even distinguish dreams from reality.'

'Really,' said Hakim, 'you think . . . but what does it matter.
Come !' he cried, dispelling all concern, 'let's forget this life once
more.'

When both of them were deeply intoxicated by the hashish something strange occurred : the two friends entered into a certain com-
munion of ideas and impressions. Yousouf imagined that his companion, kicking the earth which wasn't worthy of his glory, soared
up towards the heavens and, taking him by the hand, carried him off
into space amidst the whirling stars and glittering marvels of the
Milky Way. Pale but crowned by a luminous ring, Saturn increased
in size as it approached them, followed by seven moons borne along
in the wake of its rapid advance. Then . . . but who could relate what
happened when they had reached this divine home of their dreams?
Human language can only reveal experiences conforming to our
nature, and we must bear in mind that when the two friends con-
versed together in this celestial dream even the names by which they
addressed each other were no longer names which are known on
earth.

In the middle of this ecstasy, at the stage when their bodies resembled inert masses, Hakim suddenly writhed and cried out, *'Eblis!
Eblis!'*

At that very instant the okel door was broken open by *zebecks* led
by Argevan. The vizier had the room surrounded and ordered that
all the infidels be seized, for they were violators of the caliph's ordinance which forbade the use of hashish and fermented drinks.

'Demon !' the caliph cried, recovering his senses and coming to
himself. 'You've been hiding from me to save your head ! You
organized the famine and distributed the reserve of the State granary
to your creatures ! Fall to your knees before the prince of believers !
Confess now and die later !'

Argevan frowned; a cold smile creased his sombre features. Pointing scornfully at Hakim, he addressed his officers :

'Take this madman who thinks he's the caliph to the Moristan,' he
commanded them.

As for Yousouf, he had already managed to jump into his cangia,
realizing that he would be quite unable to defend his friend against
such powerful adversaries.

The Moristan, which now adjoins the Kalaoum mosque, was a
huge prison in those days, one part of it being reserved for raging
madmen. Although the Orientals respect the insane they nevertheless
lock up any who are potentially dangerous.

Waking up, then, the next day in a gloomy cell, Hakim immediately understood that he would gain nothing by an outburst of anger
or by claiming to be the caliph when he was dressed as a simple

fellah. Besides, there were already five caliphs on the premises and quite a number of gods, so this last title was no more advantageous than the first. Having made the utmost effort during the night to break his chains, Hakim was only too convinced, moreover, that his divinity, imprisoned in a feeble body, left him, like the majority of Indian Buddhas and other incarnations of the Supreme Being, abandoned to all the malice of human beings and to the physical laws of force. Above all, he thought, I must try to avoid flagellation. This wasn't easy, for in those days it was the usual cure for an intemperate imagination. When the *hekim* (physician) made his regular calls he was accompanied on this particular day by another doctor who appeared to be a foreigner. Hakim was prudent enough not to show any surprise at his visit; he merely explained that too much hashish had momentarily caused him to lose his wits and he assured the physician that he had recovered completely now. The latter consulted his colleague, speaking to him with great deference. The foreigner shook his head, saying that the insane often had moments of lucidity when they ingeniously managed to have themselves freed. There was no need, however, to prevent this inmate from walking around in the courtyard.

'Are you a physician too?' the caliph asked the other doctor.

'This is the prince of science!' the asylum physician exclaimed, 'the great Ebn-Sina (Avicenna). He arrived recently from Syria and has deigned to visit the Moristan.'

The caliph was deeply impressed to hear the renowned name of Avicenna, the learned doctor and venerated master of men's health who was also popularly considered to be a magician capable of performing the greatest miracles.

Hakim's prudence now abandoned him and he cried out, 'O you who see me here, like Aisse (Jesus) long ago, abandoned in this form and by my human impotence to the machinations of hell, disowned as caliph and as god, be prudent enough to have me freed from this wretched situation as soon as possible. If you are with me, let it be known! If you don't believe in my words, may you be damned!' Avicenna made no reply, but shaking his head, he turned towards the physician.

'You see how quickly his reason abandons him,' he said. 'Fortunately, fantasies like this do nobody any harm. I have always believed that the hemp used for hashish paste is the same herb as the one mentioned by Hippocrates; it drove the animals that chewed it into such frenzy that they hurled themselves into the sea. Hashish was already known in Solomon's times. The word *hachichot* appears in the *Song of Songs*, and the inebriating properties of this mixture....'

Hakim was unable to hear the rest of Avicenna's words, for the two physicians went into the courtyard.

He remained alone for awhile, helplessly confused, doubting whether he was god, doubting sometimes whether he was even caliph, and he was hardly able to reassemble the scattered fragments of his thoughts. Taking advantage of the relative freedom allotted to him, for thanks to Avicenna he was permitted to enter the courtyard, he approached the unfortunate people dispersed here and there in strange attitudes, and, listening to their songs and speeches, he overheard some ideas which attracted his attention.

After fumbling in a pile of rubbish, one of the madmen had managed to make himself a sort of tiara with bits of glass for stars; draped over his shoulders, he wore rags covered with glittering embroidery which he had adorned with tinselled loops.

'I am the *Kaimalzeman* (chief of the century), and I tell you the time has come!'

'You're lying,' another replied. 'You're not the real one, you belong to the race of the *dives* and you're trying to deceive us.'

'And who am I then, according to you?' the first one haughtily asked.

'You're no other than Thamurath, the last king of the rebellious genii! Don't you remember being conquered on the island of Serendib by no less a personage than Adam, that is to say, myself? Your spear and shield are still hanging as trophies upon my tomb.'

'His tomb indeed!' the Kaimalzeman said, bursting into scornful laughter. 'Why, nobody has ever been able to find it! I suggest you tell us where it is.'

'I have the right to speak of my tomb, for I have already lived six lives among mankind and died six lives as I was bound to. Magnificent tombs have been consecrated to me, but as for your tomb, that would certainly be difficult to find . . . you *dives*, you abide only in corpses!'

The general booing that followed these words was directed against the unfortunate emperor of the *dives*; he reacted in a fury, but the alleged Adam knocked off his crown with the back of his hand. The other madman now hurled himself upon him, and the struggle between the two foes was about to be renewed after five thousand years (according to their reckoning), when one of the guardians separated them with a whip, dealing out the blows quite impartially.

You will wonder what interest Hakim took in these insane conversations to which he listened with keen attention or even provoked by certain remarks. Only master of his reason in the midst of these distracted minds, he was silently absorbed again in a whole world of recollections. Strangely enough, perhaps because of his austere attitude, the madmen appeared to respect him; none of them dared confront his gaze, yet something led them to gather around him, like those plants which already turn in the last hours of the night towards the light to come.

If mortals cannot conceive by themselves what occurs in the soul of a man who suddenly feels that he is a prophet, or even a god, myth and history have enabled them at least to imagine what doubt and anguish must arise in these divine natures at that troubling hour when their intelligence is freed from the ephemeral trammels of incarnation. Hakim's doubts corresponded to those of the Son of Man in Gethsemane, but, above all, he was almost crushed by the thought that his divinity had first been revealed to him in the ecstasies of hashish. There is, then, he reasoned, something stronger than he who is all . . . but would a herb from the fields be able to create such marvels? True, a mere worm proved itself stronger than Solomon when it bored through the staff on which that prince of the genii was leaning and broke it right in the middle. But what was Solomon compared to me, if I am really Albar (The Eternal)?

5 The Fire of Cairo

A situation fraught with irony occurred one day for which only the spirit of evil could have been responsible. Following the royal custom, the sultana Setalmulc visited the Moristan to aid and console the prisoners. After passing through the criminal quarters, she wished to see the lunatic asylum. The sultana was veiled, but Hakim recognized her by her voice, and he was unable to restrain his fury on seeing her accompanied by Argevan who was doing her the honours of the place in a calm and smiling manner.

'These poor wretches,' he informed her, 'are victims of a thousand follies. One says he's the prince of the genii, another actually claims to be Adam, but the most ambitious of them all is the fellow over there who bears a striking resemblance to your brother the caliph.'

'Indeed an extraordinary resemblance,' Setalmulc agreed.

'And he owes his present misfortune precisely to that,' Argevan continued. 'Hearing so many people say he was the very image of the caliph, he came to believe that he actually was the caliph, and when that wasn't enough to satisfy him, he claimed that he was also god. He's merely a poor fellah who has damaged his wits, as so many others have, through excessive use of intoxicants . . . but it would be curious to see how he would react in the presence of the real caliph. I suppose. . . .'

'Wretch!' Hakim interrupted. 'So you found a phantom who resembled me and set him up in my place! . . .'

He stopped, realizing in time that his prudence was abandoning him and that perhaps he was exposing his life to further dangers; but his words were smothered, anyhow, by the uproar of the madmen, all of whom overwhelmed Argevan with imprecations, while the king of the *dives*, in particular, hurled terrible challenges at him.

'Just wait until I'm dead,' the latter concluded, 'we shall meet again elsewhere, as you know only too well yourself!'

Argevan shrugged his shoulders and left with the sultana.

Hakim hadn't even attempted to appeal to Setalmulc; he realized that the thread was too well woven for him to entertain any hopes of breaking it with a single blow. Either an impostor was profiting from the fact that he really was not recognized as one, or his vizier and his sister had agreed to teach him a lesson in wisdom by having him spend a few days in the Moristan. Perhaps they intended to take advantage later, from the scandal which his present situation would precipitate when it was announced to everyone, by seizing power themselves and keeping him in tutelage for ever. Something of that sort was doubtless afoot, and in fact an incident occurred which increased his suspicions. Leaving the Moristan, the sultana promised the imam of the mosque that she would donate a considerable sum to have the lunatic asylum enlarged and magnificently rebuilt. The madmen had quietened down now and Hakim was situated where he could distinctly hear her words:

'I want their residence to appear as worthy as a caliph's,' she said.

When his sister and his minister had finally departed, Hakim thought no more than: It was bound to be like this, and he resumed his way of life without renouncing any of the sweetness and patience which he had exercised before. Moreover, he held long discussions with certain companions in misfortune who had moments of lucidity and also with inmates of the other section of the Moristan, for the latter often came up to the railing, which separated the two courtyards, to be entertained by their neighbours' extravagances. Hakim welcomed them in a tone which led these unfortunates to gather around him for many hours; they looked up to him as though he were a melbous (an inspired prophet). How strange it is that the divine word should always find its first followers among the wretched!

Likewise, a thousand years ago, the Messiah's congregation was made up mainly of degenerates, toll-gatherers and publicans.

Once he had gained their confidence the caliph called them to him one after the other; he asked them to tell the stories of their lives and describe the circumstances which had led to their crimes or misdemeanours; perspicaciously, he searched for the principal causes of their confusion : ignorance and misery were what he found at the bottom of everything. He learned, too, about the mysteries of society, about the machinations of the usurers, the monopolists, the lawyers, the corporation chiefs, the tax-gatherers and the richest merchants of Cairo, how they connived, built up secret cliques, assisted and abetted each other, increasing their power and influence by means of useful inter-family marriages. Corrupters and corrupted, altering prices when it suited them and being thereby responsible for famine or plenty, for riots or war, they were the invincible oppressors of the people who were struggling for the bare necessities of existence. Such were the results of the vizier Argevan's administration during Hakim's long minority.

Ominous rumours circulated in the prison which the warders themselves did not hesitate to encourage; a foreign army was advancing upon the city, they said, and had already set up camp in the plain of Giza. Cairo would surrender to it without offering any resistance, owing to the treachery of the nobles, the ulemas and the merchants, who were unwilling to support the cost of a siege; they were prepared to open the gates and had already bribed the military chiefs of the citadel. The enemy general was actually expected to make his entry into the city the next day through the gate of Bab-el-Hadyd. The Fatimid line would be deposed and the Abassid caliphs would then reign in Cairo as well as in Baghdad, having the public prayers recited in their name.

'So that's what Argevan had arranged for me !' Hakim exclaimed. 'That's what my father's talisman announced and that's why Pharouis (Saturn) lost its splendour and turned pallid in the sky. But the moment has come to test the strength of my word and to see whether I shall let myself be conquered as the Nazarene was in former times.'

Early in the evening the prisoners gathered in the courtyards for the customary prayers. Hakim now addressed this double population of madmen and malefactors who were separated from each other by the iron railings; he told them who he was and he explained what he required of them, speaking with such authority and backing his assertions with such convincing proof that no one dared to doubt him. The interior barriers collapsed at once under the charge of a hundred men and the warders fled in terror from the gates which led to the mosque. Enraptured and reassured by the sound of Hakim's voice, those who had been his companions in misfortune now hoisted him up in triumph on to their shoulders.

'Here is the caliph!' the condemned criminals cried, as they entered the mosque. 'Here is the true prince of believers!'

'Here is Allah!' the band of madmen cried. 'He has come to judge the world!'

'Come!' cried two of them on either side of him, 'all of you, come to the assizes which our Lord Hakim will hold!'

This disturbance in the middle of prayers confounded the believers gathered in the mosque, but, tense and anxious already because of the advancing enemy, they were all prepared for an exceptional event. Some of them fled, sowing panic in the streets, while others cried:

'The last judgment is upon us today!'

And the very poor and the very infirm were gladdened by this thought:

'At last, Lord!' they cried, 'At last thy day has come!'

When Hakim appeared on the steps of the mosque a superhuman light shone around his face, while his curls tumbled over the purple mantle which his companions had draped across his shoulders, for he still kept his hair long and flowing, contrary to Muslim custom. Even the Jews and Christians, who were always numerous in the market street which intersects the bazaars, prostrated themselves, crying out:

'He is either the Messiah or the Antichrist who is to appear a thousand years after Jesus!'

Several people, however, had recognized him as the caliph, but they could not understand how he came to be in the middle of the city, for it had been officially announced that he was leading the troops against the enemy camped in the plain surrounding the pyramids.

'O you, my people!' Hakim cried, turning to the wretched around him. 'O you, my true sons, your day, not mine, has dawned. There is an era that returns every time the word of heaven loses its power over the souls of men. That era is upon us now! Virtue becomes crime, wisdom folly, glory shame, and everything evolves contrary to the ways of truth and justice. Like lightning prior to thunder, the voice from on high has never failed to illuminate human minds on these occasions. Remember how it was said each time: "Woe unto Enochia, city of the children of Cain, city of defilement and tyranny! Woe unto thee, Gomorrah! Woe unto thee, Nineveh and Babylon! And woe unto thee, Jerusalem!" This voice from on high never wearies, it resounds from age to age, always allowing time for repentance between the warning and the punishment. But from day to day the reprieve shortens . . . when the storm erupts, fire follows close upon the lightning! Let us prove that from now on the Word is armed and that the kingdom announced by the prophets is about to be established on earth! Fattened by fraud, usury, injustice, rapine, this city is yours, my children! These plundered treasures are yours, these stolen riches are yours! Today is the day of vengeance and chastisement! Destroy! Destroy this brittle luxury, these false virtues, these privileges acquired at the price of gold! Rise up in wrath against the gilded treachery that sold you to the enemy on the pretext of peace! Fire! Fire! Let there be fire throughout this city! When my grandfather founded it under the auspices of victory he didn't intend it to become the monument of your cowardice!'

Was it as a sovereign or as a god that the caliph thus addressed the population? Assuredly he spoke with that supreme reason which towers over ordinary justice, for otherwise his anger, like that of the prisoners whom he had released, would have been aimed at no particular target. Within a few moments flames had devoured the cedar-roofed bazaars and the palaces with sculptured terraces and elegant columns. The most opulent residences of Cairo delivered up their devastated interiors to the people. O night of terror . . . the sovereign power resorted to rebellion, the vengeance of heaven wielded the arms of hell!

The fire and sack of the city lasted for three days. The inhabitants of the richest neighbourhoods took up arms to defend themselves, while a squadron of Greek soldiers and Barbary troops led by Argevan fought against the prisoners and the populace who carried out the caliph's orders. The vizier claimed that Hakim was an impostor and that the real caliph was in charge of the army in the plains of Giza. Under the provocation of his words raging, fire-lit battles broke out in the public squares and gardens.

Hakim had withdrawn to the heights of Khafre, and he held his bloody assizes in the open air. Tradition tells that he was attended by angels, and that Adam stood on one side of him and Solomon on the other; the first witnessed for the men, the second for the genii. All the persons indicted by public hatred were led up there, and judgment was quickly pronounced; their heads fell to the acclamation of the crowd. Several thousands perished in those three gory days.

The fighting in the centre of the city was no less murderous. At last Argevan was struck between the shoulders by the spear of a certain Reidan who brought his head to the caliph and laid it at his feet. From then on resistance collapsed. It is said that at the very moment when the vizier fell with an appalling shriek, the inmates from the Moristan, gifted with second sight — a characteristic of the insane — cried out that they saw Eblis in the air. Emerging from Argevan's mortal remains, he summoned and rallied around him the demons released from the bodies of his partisans. The conflict which had begun on earth continued now in space. Those eternal enemies organized their ranks again, resorting to the elements for weapons in their warfare. Commemorating the event, an Arab poet has written :

Egypt! Egypt! How well you know these fearful battles of the good and evil genii, when the sultry breath of Typhon consumes both air and light, when the plague decimates your toiling population, when the annual flooding of the Nile decreases, when in a single day thick clouds of locusts strip all the vegetation from your fields.

No! No! Hell does not operate by dreadful calamities alone, for it can also people the earth with cruel and covetous souls whose human form disguises the pernicious nature of serpents and jackals!

On the fourth day, when the city was half burnt down, the shereefs assembled in the mosques, holding up their Korans and crying :

'O Hakim! O Allah!'

But their hearts were absent from their prayers. Then the old Syrian who had already proclaimed Hakim's divinity approached the prince and said :

'Lord, it is enough! In the name of your grandfather Moezzeldin, end this destruction now.'

Hakim wished to question this strange individual who appeared only on crucial occasions, but the old man had already disappeared among the jostling bystanders.

Astride his grey ass, Hakim rode through the city, uttering words of mercy and reconciliation. He profited from this opportunity to reform the severe edicts against the Jews and Christians; he exempted the former from having to wear clogs around their necks and the latter from having to carry heavy wooden crosses upon their shoulders. Showing equal tolerance to all cults, he wished to prepare the way for a new doctrine. Conferences were organized, mainly in a building which was named The House of Wisdom, while several doctors started propagating Hakim's divinity in public. The human mind, however, is so apt to resent any belief which has not been consecrated by tradition, that only about thirty thousand of Cairo's inhabitants decided to join the new sect. A certain Almoschadjar said to Hakim's followers :

'This man whom you call upon in place of God cannot create a fly, nor can he prevent one from buzzing in his face.'

Informed of these words, the caliph presented a hundred gold sequins to Almoschadjar to prove that he had no intention of forcing anybody's conscience.

'Several members of the Fatimid dynasty have entertained this illusion,' others said. 'Hakim's grandfather Moezzeldin, for example, hid himself for a few days and said that he had been taken up to the heavens. Later, he withdrew to an underground vault, and people claimed that he had disappeared from the earth without dying like other men.'

Comments such as these plunged Hakim into long hours of meditation.

6 The Two Caliphs

The caliph had returned to his palace on the banks of the Nile. Rid of his enemies now and henceforth acknowledged by everyone, he resumed his customary way of life.

One day, he visited his sister Setalmulc and told her to prepare for their marriage, which he intended to celebrate in privacy so as not to arouse public indignation; since the people were not wholly convinced yet by Hakim's claim to divinity, he didn't wish to offend them by a violation of the established laws. Only the eunuchs and slaves would serve as witnesses at the ceremony within the palace mosque. The inhabitants of Cairo would not be at all surprised by the festivities which were bound to follow; indeed, they might not even notice them, for they were quite accustomed to seeing the sheltered seraglio starlit by lanterns and to hearing sounds of music carried across the river at night by the breeze. Later, at an appropriate time, when everyone would be favourably disposed, Hakim would inform the people of this religious and mystic union.

Disguised as usual, the caliph left his palace in the evening and set off towards the Mokatam observatory to consult the stars. There were no encouraging signs, however, for Hakim in the skies : ominous conjunctions of planets and entangled clusters of stars predicted his imminent death. Conscious, like God, of his own eternity, he was not too alarmed by these celestial omens which concerned only his mortal body. Nevertheless, an acute sorrow wrenched his heart, and, renouncing his usual tour of the city, he returned to the palace in the early hours of the night.

Crossing the river in his cangia, he was astonished to see the palace gardens illuminated as though for a fête. He entered. From every tree all sorts of lanterns were hanging like fruit; they shone as brightly as rubies, sapphires and emeralds. From miniature temples on the intricately carved walks, fragile, pale blue spirals of the most precious perfumes rose up into the air, where their aromas mingled with the scents of flowers. The melodious murmurs of hidden orchestras were counterpointed by the songs of birds, for deceived by this display of light they believed that it was already time to greet the dawn. In the brilliant background every architectural detail of the palace façade stood out like a ribbon of fire.

Hakim was overwhelmed by amazement. Who, he asked himself, dares to organize a fête during my absence? Who is the unknown guest they are welcoming at such an hour? These gardens should be deserted now and silent. I certainly didn't take any hashish this evening and I am not the victim of a hallucination. As he drew nearer he saw dancers arrayed in dazzling costumes undulating in the middle of Persian carpets; their every pose and movement was emphasized by the flickering lights of lamps along the tasselled edges. At the palace gate he encountered a multitude of slaves and pages carrying golden plates, piled high with frozen fruits and confectionery, and silver bowls bubbling with sherbets. Although he moved among them, actually rubbing shoulders with them, they did not pay the slightest attention to him; indeed they did not even appear to see him. In this strange predicament Hakim fell prey to increasing anxiety; he felt that he had become a shadow, an invisible spirit, and he went his way from room to room, passing through the crowds as though he wore the magic ring of Gyges on his finger.

At the threshold of the last room he was almost blinded by a torrent of light : thousands of candles sparkled in the silver candelabra like bouquets of flames, linking their haloes to form a brilliant chain. The instruments of the musicians, who were hidden in the galleries, pealed forth in triumph. The caliph approached, staggered, and took shelter behind the heavy, thick folds of an enormous brocaded door-curtain. Then he saw a man seated next to Setalmulc on a divan at the far end of the room; he appeared to be afloat in precious stones and was, in fact, studded with diamonds which glittered in the midst of swarming fire flakes and prismatic rays : all the treasures of Haroun-al-Raschid had served, it seemed, to array this new caliph in such splendour.

Stunned and enraged, Hakim reached for the dagger at his waist, intending to hurl himself upon the usurper, but he was paralysed by an irresistible force. He interpreted this spectacle as a celestial warning, and his confusion increased all the more when he recognized, or thought he recognized, his own features in those of the individual beside his sister. He believed that he was looking at his ferouer or double, and for the Orientals there is no more ominous sign than the sight of one's own spectre; the shade compels the body to follow it within a day.

In this instance the apparition was extremely menacing, for the ferouer had anticipated Hakim's own projects. The fact that this chimerical caliph was marrying Setalmulc, as the real caliph had planned to do himself, surely concealed an enigmatic meaning; it was without a doubt a mysterious and dreadful sign. Was a jealous deity plotting to usurp the heavens by carrying off Setalmulc from her brother and thereby separating the cosmogonic and providential couple? Was the race of the *dives* attempting to disorganize the genealogy of the higher spirits and infiltrate its own impure breed? All these thoughts tormented Hakim simultaneously; in his anger he longed to produce an earthquake, a deluge, a rain of fire, or any kind of cataclysm, but he recalled once again that, restricted by his mortal clay, he could not resort to superhuman means.

Unable to reveal himself in so victorious a manner, Hakim slowly withdrew and returned to the gate which overlooked the Nile. He sat down on a stone bench and remained absorbed in contemplation, trying to unearth the significance of this strange pageant which he had just witnessed. After awhile, the postern opened again. Hakim saw two shapes emerge and managed to perceive, despite the darkness, that one of them cast a denser shadow than the other. Thanks to those faint reflections of earth, sky and water which, in the Orient, prevent the shadows from growing completely opaque, he made out the first to be a young Arab, the second a gigantic Ethiopian.

When they reached a steep point of the bank directly above the flowing waters, the young man knelt down; the Negro stood right beside him, and the flash of his scimitar pierced the shadows like a rod of lightning. To the caliph's great surprise, however, the head did not fall; the Negro bent down towards the condemned man and appeared to whisper something to him. Then the latter rose to his feet again, calmly and quietly, without any joyful haste, as though his life had never been endangered. The Ethiopian replaced his scimitar in its scabbard, while the young man went towards that very part of the river where the caliph happened to be concealed; he was probably going to retrieve the boat which had brought him there. Suddenly he found himself face to face with Hakim, who pretended that he had just woken up.

'Peace be with you, Yousouf,' he said.

'Peace be with you, too,' replied Yousouf to his friend without any surprise at finding him stretched out upon the river bank, where

many children of the Nile fall asleep during the burning summer
nights.

Then Yousouf helped the eccentric and adventurous cadi — for he
still had no inkling of his friend's real identity — into the cangia, and,
keeping to the east shore, they let themselves drift along with the
current. The neighbouring plain was already coloured by the reddish
tints of dawn which revealed the ruins of Heliopolis on the edge of
the desert. Pensively, Hakim scrutinized his companion's features as
they grew clearer in the growing light, and he perceived that Yousouf
bore a definite resemblance to him, which he had never noticed
before, since he had always seen him at night or under the effects
of hashish. He could no longer doubt that here was the ferouer, the
double, the apparition which he had seen awhile ago; perhaps
Yousouf was the very person who had been chosen to replace him
when Hakim was confined in the Moristan. These explanations were
reasonable, but the caliph was nevertheless astonished.

'We resemble each other like brothers,' he said to Yousouf. 'Perhaps we come from the same region, for that often explains a chance
resemblance. Where exactly is your birthplace, my friend?'

'I was born at the foot of the Atlas,' Yousouf replied, 'at Ketama
in the Maghreb where there were many Kabyles and Berbers. My
father's name was Dawas, but that is all I can tell you about him, for
he was killed in a battle shortly after my birth. My grandfather lived
a very long life, and he was a sheikh in that region which is now
submerged in the sands.'

'My ancestors also came from there,' said Hakim. 'Perhaps we are
descendants of the same tribe . . . but what does it matter . . . we do
not need the bonds of blood to make our friendship lasting and sincere. Tell me why I haven't seen you for some days.'

'Ah,' said Yousouf, 'now I really have a tale to tell you. These
days . . . or rather, these nights, for I have devoted my days to sleep,
have passed like exquisite dreams, and every moment of them has
been a marvel. Since we were surprised by the officers at the okel and
separated . . . but . . . but I've often asked myself why you didn't tell
them you were a cadi. . . .'

Hakim murmured a deliberately inaudible reply which made his
companion understand that he should pry no further into his official
affairs.

'Since then,' Yousouf resumed, 'I have come across that wonderful
vision again on the Nile, and I can no longer question her reality.
Many a time she has put her hand over my eyes, so that I would not
recognize the gate, and led me into magnificent gardens, into rooms
of radiant splendour . . . their architecture was so elegant, so sublime,
that it even surpassed those amazing edifices that are raised in the

clouds when we succumb to the visions of hashish. How strange indeed that I should enjoy more dreams when I am awake than when I am asleep! Nobody appeared to be surprised by my presence in this palace; in fact, everyone bowed to me respectfully whenever I passed. Then this strange and wonderful lady invited me to sit at her feet, where I remained completely spellbound. Every time she lifted her eyelids, which were fringed by long lashes, a new paradise appeared to open before me. The modulations of her melodious voice threw me into ineffable rapture. Soothed by this enchanting melody, my soul dissolved in sheer delight. Slaves approached with delicious refreshments, rose preserves, snow sherbets, but she barely touched them with her lips, for a being as perfect and celestial as she must surely live only on precious perfumes, morning dews and rays of light. On one occasion, pronouncing a magic formula to move a stone slab covered with mysterious seals, she led me down into the vaults where her treasures are stored. She showed me every one of them and even calculated their value, promising that all would belong to me if I furnished proof of my courage and love. I'll swear the wonders there exceed those that are buried in the mountain of Kaf where the treasures of the genii are hidden. Birds made of precious stones, beating their wings upon the boughs of golden trees, rock-crystal elephants, peacocks whose tails, fanning out in the form of a wheel, were studded with suns and diamonds, melon shaped blocks of camphor encased in filigree network, velvet and brocaded tents with poles of solid silver. And in every cistern which I saw, scattered like grain in a silo, were heaps of gold and silver coins and piles of carbuncles and pearls.

Hakim had listened most attentively to this description and now he said to his friend Yousouf, 'Do you know, brother, that you have seen the treasures of Haroun-al-Raschid? They were seized by the Fatimids and stored in the secret, underground vaults of the caliph's palace!'

'No,' Yousouf replied, 'I didn't know that, but judging from the beauty and wealth of my unknown guide I had already assumed that she must be of the very highest rank. A distant relation of the caliph, perhaps, or the wife or daughter of an eminent noble. But what need have I to learn her name? She loves me . . . that is more than enough! This evening, when I arrived at our usual meeting place, I was greeted by slaves who bathed me, perfumed me, and dressed me in such magnificent robes that even Caliph Hakim would not have disdained to wear them. The garden was illuminated and everyone looked happy, perhaps in anticipation of a marriage. The lady I loved permitted me to sit beside her on the divan, where she placed her hand in mine and pierced me with a look of voluptuous languor.

Suddenly, however, she turned pale, as though a fatal apparition, a sinister phantom which she alone could see, had arrived to darken the festivities. Dismissing the slaves abruptly, she said in a choking voice : "I am lost! Behind the door-curtain . . . I saw them glitter, those azure eyes . . . he will never forgive me! Do you love me . . . do you love me enough to die?" I assured her of my infinite devotion. "From now on, then," she continued, "let us presume that you have never existed, for no trace will remain of your passage upon this earth. You must be utterly destroyed, your body must be pulverized into invisible atoms, otherwise my . . . my master will quickly devise such torments for me that even the *dives* would envy his ingenuity, torments that would make the damned in the depths of hell shudder with terror. Follow this Negro . . . he is your executioner." Outside the postern, the Negro told me to kneel down, and as he swung his scimitar to and fro I waited for its deadly cut. Then, seeing how resigned and resolute I was, he told me I had undergone a test, an ordeal, for the princess wanted to learn if I was really as courageous and devoted as I claimed to be. "Be sure to go to Cairo tomorrow evening," he said, before he returned to the garden. "Wait at the fountain, where all the lovers go. Another rendezvous will be arranged for you." '

Yousouf's disclosures left Hakim without any further doubts regarding the circumstances which had undermined his plans. Much to his surprise, however, he felt no resentment at all; he was incensed neither by Setalmulc's treachery, nor by the fact that she, the caliph's sister, had been smitten by love for a man of common lineage.

After so many bloody executions, had he grown weary of punishing, or conscious of his divinity, had he now been inspired by the overwhelming paternal affection which a god is bound to harbour for his creatures? Pitiless in dealing with evil, he felt himself succumb to the invincible charms of youth and love. Prejudiced against a union which she considered criminal, was Setalmulc guilty for having rejected it? And where was Yousouf's fault in loving a woman whose exact rank was unknown to him? The caliph decided that he, too, would come in the evening to the new rendezvous arranged for Yousouf; but he would pardon, then bless, his marriage with Setalmulc. His spirit was still overcast, but it was the question of his own destiny which troubled him now. Events turn against me, he reflected, and even my will-power no longer upholds me.

Taking leave of Yousouf, he said, 'I miss our delightful evenings at the okel. We shall go there again, for the caliph has recently annulled the laws against hashish and fermented drinks. We shall see each other soon, my friend.'

On his return to the palace Hakim summoned Abou-Arous, who

commanded the night-watch with a regiment of 1000 men; he re-inforced the procedure which had been interrupted during the disturbances : all the gates of Cairo were to be closed at the hour when Hakim went to the observatory; one particular gate would re-open at a prearranged signal when he decided to return.

That evening, he was escorted to the end of the street called Derb-al-Siba where he mounted the ass which his attendants saddled at the hut of the gate-keeper, the eunuch Nessim. Then he rode across the open country, followed only by a footman and the young mute slave who accompanied him as usual. Having clambered up the mountain, he lifted his eyes towards the stars before he had even entered the tower.

Clapping his hands together, he cried out, 'O ominous sign, I behold you!'

Meeting some Arab horsemen who recognized him and asked for assistance, he told his footman to take them to Nessim's hut where their requirements would be attended to. And now, instead of going into the tower, he took the route which led to the necropolis on the west of Makotam; soon he approached the tomb of Fokkai, near Maksaba, which owed its name to the rushes growing in the region. There, three men armed with daggers hurled themselves upon him, but no sooner had they stabbed him than one of them, recognizing his features in the moonlight, abruptly turned against the other two and fought with them until he was struck down himself beside the caliph, crying out before he died, 'O my brother!'

Such, at least, was the account given, through signs and gestures, to Abou-Arous by the young slave who escaped the massacre and fled back to Cairo. But when the guards arrived at the scene of the assassination they found nothing except blood-stained garments and the caliph's grey ass, Kamar, whose legs had been broken.

Conclusion

Having reached the end of his tale, Saide-Eshayrazy said no more but plunged into a deep and reverential silence. I was extremely moved myself by the account of Hakim's Passion; it was less sorrowful than Golgotha, no doubt, but in this instance I retained a vivid memory of its setting, for during my stay in Cairo I had often climbed up mount Mokatam where the ruins of the observatory are preserved. God or man, I told myself, the caliph had certainly attempted to bring about the reign of reason and justice; he far from deserved the calumny heaped upon him by Coptic and Muslim historians. Seeing now in another light all the events described by El-Macin, Makrisi, Novairi and other authors whom I had read in Cairo, I deplored the fact that prophets, reformers and Messiahs, whoever they may be, are condemned by fate first to a violent death and then to human ingratitude. Rousing the sheikh from his meditation, I asked him who exactly were responsible for Hakim's assassination.

'You have read the historians,' he replied, 'don't you know that when Yousouf, son of Dawas, arrived at the fountain in Cairo he was met by slaves who took him to a certain house? . . .'

'No, I didn't find those details.'

'The sultana Setalmulc had come there in disguise to wait for him,' Saide-Eshayrazy explained. 'Telling him that the caliph planned to put her to death, she made him swear to kill Hakim. She promised Yousouf that she would marry him afterwards. History has preserved her final words at their last encounter. "Go to the mountain. He is sure to remain there alone, keeping none but a mute slave with him. He will descend into the valley. Run after him then and kill him. Kill the slave, too, and the footman if he is with him." She gave him one of those daggers with a spear point, they are called *yafours*, and she also armed two of her slaves, commanding them to assist him, but to kill him if he should break his oath. Having struck the first blow at the caliph, Yousouf recognized him as the companion of his nocturnal adventures. Horrified by what he had done, he turned against the two slaves, but he was overpowered by them.'

'And what became of the two corpses which, according to your

118

account, disappeared, for nothing was found there except Hakim's donkey and . . . I remember reading . . . his seven tunics with their buttons undone?'

'Did I speak of corpses? There is no mention of them in our tradition. We don't know what became of Yousouf's body, but the stars foretold that Hakim would live until he was eighty if he escaped the dangerous night of 27 schawal, 411, of our hegira (Thursday, 27 February, A.D. 1021). For sixteen years after he vanished, the people of Cairo still claimed that he was alive.'

'I have read such reports,' I said, 'but Hakim's frequent appearances were attributed to impostors, like Scherout, Sikkin, and others, who bore a certain resemblance to him and played his role. This often happens when the lives of extraordinary sovereigns become the subject of popular legends. The Copts claim that Jesus Christ appeared to Hakim, who asked pardon then for his impiety and spent years of penitence in the desert.'

'According to our books,' Saide-Eshayrazy said conclusively, 'the blows which Hakim suffered did not kill him. Found by an old man who healed and sheltered him, he did in fact survive the fatal night of the assassination ordered by his sister. Weary of the throne, however, he withdrew into the desert of Ammon where he formulated his doctrine which was published later by his disciple Hamza. His followers, who were expelled from Cairo after his death, withdrew to Lebanon, where they founded the nation of the Druze.'

It was time for me to bid the sheikh farewell, but I hesitated for a moment, tempted to break the promise I had made to Madame Carlès by telling him I had seen his beautiful daughter. Saide-Eshayrazy was looking at me attentively; his benevolent expression was marked by a kind of prophetic grief. Before I could make a decision he spoke himself in a low, measured tone which time will not easily erase from my memory.

'And can you still remember the passage from our catechism which you quoted when you arrived?'

'No,' I replied, taken aback by his question, 'no, I can't remember it any longer.'

With his eyes upon me, he intoned, 'But if an individual came to understand our holy cult, to believe in it and conform to it, would he then be saved?'

'Never!' I exclaimed, recalling part of the answer, 'for the door is closed, the matter is over, the pen is blunt.'

Then, as I shook hands with the venerable sheikh and thanked him for his hospitality, I felt a calm and tacit understanding arise between us.

Part Three   *The Tale of the Queen of the Morning and Soliman the Prince of the Genii*

Introduction

To ignore the wonderful tales that are told or declaimed by professional storytellers in the principal cafés of Istanbul would lead to an
incomplete picture of the city's attractions and nocturnal enchant-
ments during the month of Ramadan. A translation of one of these
tales should enrich our understanding of the scholarly though popular
literature that wittily adjusts religious traditions and legends to the
Islamic point of view.

Considering me a *taleb* (scholar), the Persians who had taken me
under their protection led me to the cafés behind the Beyazid mosque
where once the opium smokers gathered. This pastime is forbidden
nowadays, but through force of habit the foreign merchants in
Turkey still frequent the neighbourhood, for it is far away from the
tumult of the city centre.

You sit down, ask for a narghile or a chibouk, then listen to the
tales which are drawn out for as long as possible, like today's serials,
to the profit of the storyteller and the proprietor.

Although I was very young when I began studying Oriental
languages, I know only the most indispensable words; nevertheless,
I was immediately affected by the lively, exciting tone of the tale
and thanks to my friends in the caravanserai I managed to understand the subject at least. The traditional genius of the Orientals
revels in a narrative full of imagery and I trust that I am able to
recreate one of them now.

I should mention that the café where we were gathered is in the
working-class district of Constantinople, near to the bazaars. The
surrounding streets are a cluster of workshops belonging to iron and
copper craftsmen, and to the smelters, carvers and engravers who
manufacture or repair the ornate weapons on show at the *besestain*;
several other crafts are also practised in connection with the various
wares displayed in the numerous partitions of the main bazaar. The
company, then, might well have appeared somewhat vulgar to a man
of the world, though a few elegant costumes were conspicuous here
and there upon the benches and platforms.

The storyteller whom we were about to hear appeared to be quite

famous. Besides the customers inside the café there was a crowd outside jostling for a good position. The proprietor requested silence. A
pale young man approached and sat down on a stool in a space about
five feet square which was lined on all sides by the central benches.
His features were extremely delicate, his eyes sparkled, and his long
hair flowed down like a Santon's from under his cap, which was
different from a tarboosh or a fez. A young boy, his personal assistant,
served him coffee. Everybody prepared to listen attentively, for,
according to custom, each part of the story would last for half an
hour. These professional storytellers are rhapsodists, as it were, rather
than poets; they arrange and elaborate a subject which has already
been handled in many fashions, or one which is based on ancient
legends. The adventures of Antar, Abou-Zeyd or Medjnoun, are
thereby always brought to life again with a thousand additions or
variations. But the theme of the story chosen on this occasion was the
glory of those ancient guilds of workmen which originated in the
Orient.

'Praise be to Allah,' the storyteller said, 'and to his favourite,
Ahmad, whose dark eyes shine with so gentle a light. He is the only
apostle of the truth.'

'Amen!' the audience replied.

I Adoniram

Over the last ten years, as he carried out the designs of the great king
Soliman* ben Daoud (Solomon son of David), Adoniram, his servant,
had reduced his sleeping hours to a minimum and renounced all

---

* I have kept to Nerval's spelling, Soliman, although Soolayman would
give a better idea of the Arabic pronunciation; the French for Solomon is
Salomon.

The queen of Saba is, of course, the Bible's queen of Sheba, but I have kept
to Nerval's spelling for various reasons: *sabah* is Arabic for morning (hence
the queen of the morning); Nerval worked out a special ancestry for her, which
partly originates in Genesis 10, and thereby distinguished her from the more
popular queen of Sheba; also, Saba leads more naturally than Sheba to
Sabeans, who, incidentally, are in no way related to the Sabians of the
previous Tale.

Throughout this Tale, as in the original, king and prince are interchange-
able, as are queen and princess. — N.G.

Mosque of Sultan Hassan. *Lithograph by Louis Haghe*

Hacine. *Drawing by Gérard de Nerval*

pleasures and the mirth of banquets. In charge of the legions of work-men who co-operated in building those hives of gold, cedar, marble and bronze, master Adoniram passed his nights poring over the plans and his days moulding the colossal figures destined to enhance the edifice intended for Adonai, while it would also reflect the personal grandeur of the king of Jerusalem.

Not far from the unfinished temple he had set up forges, which ceaselessly rang with the sound of hammers, and subterranean foundries, where the bronze liquid, flowing through a hundred sand canals, assumed the form of lions, tigers, winged dragons, cherubim, or even of those fantastic, vanquished genii from former ages which have almost passed from the memory of man.

Subject to Adoniram were over 100,000 artisans, who carried out his extraordinary conceptions : the smelters numbered 30,000, the masons and stone-cutters formed an army of 90,000 strong, while 10,060 labourers were responsible for the transport of materials. Divided into numerous battalions, the carpenters were dispersed in the mountains, felling the century-old pines that stretched up to the Scythian desert and the cedars in the plains of Lebanon. With the aid of 3,300 officers, Adoniram maintained discipline and order among this population of workmen.

Adoniram himself, however, presided with a troubled soul and a certain disdain over this immense operation. To accomplish one of the seven wonders of the world struck him as a paltry task. The further the work advanced, the more aware he grew of the weakness of the human race, the more he lamented the restricted means of his contemporaries. Fervent in his conceptions, even more fervent in action, Adoniram dreamed of colossal constructions; sublime mon-strosities were engendered in the boiling furnace of his brain. And while the prince of the Hebrews was astonished by his art, he alone regarded with pity and condescension the work to which he found himself reduced.

Adoniram was a sombre and mysterious individual who had been offered to Soliman by the king of Tyre, his former patron. What was his country? Nobody knew. His birthplace? A mystery. Nor did any-one know where he had mastered the branches of a science that was at once so practical, so profound, so multiform. He seemed to create everything, predict everything, and do everything. The most care-fully guarded secret of all was the circumstances of his birth and the race to which he belonged; he tolerated no questions at all upon that subject. His misanthropy made him a solitary stranger amidst the descendants of Adam; his remarkable and audacious genius placed him above all men and outside any feeling of brotherhood. He emanated the spirit of light no less than the power of darkness!

Unresponsive to women, who would gaze at him furtively but never converse with him, despising men, who avoided his fierce regard, he was totally indifferent both to the terror inspired by his imposing demeanour, by his tall, sturdy, robust stature, and to the effect created by his strange and fascinating beauty. His heart was closed. Nothing but his activity as an artist animated his hands, which were made to mould the world, and weighed down his shoulders, which were made to support it.

Although he had no friends, he did have devoted slaves, and he cherished one companion, one alone, who was almost a child, a young artist sprung from those Phoenician families that had recently brought their sensual gods to the eastern shores of Asia Minor. A meticulous artist, a docile lover of nature, the pale and slender Benoni had passed his childhood in several schools and his youth on those fertile banks of the Euphrates beyond Syria. It is still a modest river where only shepherds gather and softly sing in the shade of the bay-trees that are all aglow with roses.

One day, at the hour when the sun begins to incline towards the sea, a day when Benoni was delicately moulding a heifer out of a block of wax, studiously reproducing the elastic mobility of its muscles, master Adoniram approached and, frowning, contemplated the almost finished figure for a long while.

'Wretched work!' he suddenly exclaimed. 'It reeks of patience, good taste, puerility! There's no spark of genius here, no sign of will! I see nothing but decay. Separatism, diversity, contradiction and insubordination, those eternal instruments of waste among your tumultuous nations, already paralyse their feeble imaginations. Where are my workmen, my smelters, my furnace heaters, my blacksmiths? Scattered! At this hour the bellows should be fanning these cold furnaces until the flames rise up and roar. The impressions of those models moulded by my own hands should have been stamped upon the earth. A thousand bodies should be sweating at the furnaces . . . but here we are . . . alone!'

'Master,' Benoni sweetly replied, 'the genius which devours you doesn't even sustain these common men who are in need of rest, while the art which captivates us doesn't occupy their minds at all. Besides, the wise Soliman himself has ordered them to take a day's leave, for Jerusalem is preparing for a festival.'

'A festival! What does that mean to me? Rest? Why, I have never known it! The very thought of sloth disheartens me. What are we building? A goldsmith's temple, a palace for pride and voluptuousness, pretty jewels which a fire-brand could reduce to ashes. They call that creating for eternity! One day, allured by the bait of vulgar gain, conquering hordes will rise up in conspiracy against this soft, enfeebled people, they will batter down this fragile edifice, and nothing will remain but its traces. Our models will melt in the glimmer of torch light, like the snows of Lebanon at the approach of summer, and posterity, surveying these deserted hills, will exclaim: "The Hebrew race . . . what a weak, insignificant nation it was ! . . ." '

'What !' Benoni exclaimed, 'such a magnificent palace, master, and a temple which is the richest, the greatest, the strongest. . . .'

'Vanity !' Adoniram interrupted. 'Vanity ! as the lord Soliman says himself in his own vanity. Do you know what the children of Enoch built long ago? A stupendous work which frightened the Creator himself. Why, they almost turned the earth upside down ! They made it shudder and they built Babylon from the scattered materials . . . a nice enough city where you can drive ten chariots abreast along the ramparts. Do you know what a real monument is? Do you know the pyramids? They will last until the day when the mountains of Kaf which encircle the world collapse into the abyss. O no ! those weren't erected by the children of Adam !'

'But they claim. . . .'

'They lie ! The deluge has left its mark on their peaks. Listen, two miles from here, north of the Kedron, there is a block of rock six hundred cubits square. Give me a hundred thousand rough-casters with hammers and chisels in their hands and I shall carve the monstrous head of a sphinx in that block. Smiling, it will fix its implacable gaze upon the sky, and from above the clouds Jehovah will see it and tremble in consternation. That's a monument for you ! A hundred thousand years would pass and the children of men would still acclaim : "A great people has marked its passage here !" '

Lord, the trembling Benoni said to himself, from what race has this rebellious genius sprung? . . .

'These hills,' Adoniram pursued, 'which they call mountains, fill me with pity. But if we worked to arrange them into stepping-stones one on top of the other, carving collosal figures at the angles, yes, that would be worth-while. Below the foundations we would hollow out a cavern vast enough to hold a legion of priests. There they would put their ark with its golden cherubim and their pebbles which they call altars. Then Jerusalem would have a real temple, but as it is, we are going to lodge God like a rich Memphis banker !'

'You always dream of achieving the impossible, master.'

'We were born too late. The world is old, and old age is feeble . . . yes, you are right, Benoni. Decadence and downfall ! . . . You yourself are coldly copying nature,' Adoniram pointed to Benoni's heifer, 'you go about it like a housewife who weaves a linen veil. Your dazed and torpid mind is enslaved by a cow, then by a lion, a horse or a tiger. You merely compete, through imitation, with one animal after another. Granted, these figures realize your limited conceptions, they even transmit life into form. But child, that is not art at all! Art is creation. When you sketch one of those ornaments which meander along the friezes, do you restrict yourself to copying the flowers and foliage which creep over the soil? No! you invent, you let the stylet run according to your imagination, and the most weird fantasies thereby intermingle. Well then, besides man and the known animals, why don't you also seek out unknown forms, unnamed beings, incarnations which long ago made men flinch and withdraw, awe inspiring couplings, figures which are bound to command respect, gaiety, astonishment, dread? . . . Remember the ancient Egyptians, the bold and ingenuous artists of Assyria. Didn't they wrest from the entrails of granite those sphinxes, those cynocephali, those basaltic divinities whose aspect revolted old David's Jehovah? As generation after generation look upon those formidable symbols they always acknowledge that long ago there were audacious geniuses. Those artists, did they bother about form? They scoffed at it, and, mighty in their inventions, they could exclaim to the one who created everything : "You do not understand these granite beings and you would not dare to quicken them with life!" But as for you, the multiple God of nature has bent you all beneath his yoke. You are bridled by nature, your degenerate genius succumbs to the vulgarity of form, and art, alas! is lost.'

Where does this Adoniram come from? Benoni asked himself. His spirit takes no account of humanity.

'Come, let us return now to toys which are within king Soliman's limited range,' Adoniram said, passing his hand over his large forehead to sweep back a tangle of black curly hair. 'There you have forty-eight fairly large bronze oxen, the same number of lions, birds, palm-trees, cherubim . . . they are all somewhat more expressive than nature. According to my intentions, they will support a ten cubit molten sea of bronze which will be melted and solidified in a single operation. It will be five cubits deep and skirted by a thirty cubit border embellished by carvings. But I have not finished all my models yet. The basin mould is ready and I'm afraid it may crack in the heat of the day. So, just when we have to hurry, the workmen abandon me, as you see, my friend, for their festival! What festival, tell me. Why is there a festival today?'

The storyteller stopped, for half an hour had passed. Then everyone was free to ask for coffee, sherbets or tobacco. Some discussed the merit of the details, others looked forward to enjoying the rest of the narration. One of the Persians who was close to me remarked that in his opinion this tale was borrowed from the *Soliman-Nameh*.

During the pause, as the narrator's rest is called, while each completed performance is called a sequence, the young boy whom the storyteller had brought along with him went up and down the crowded rows, holding out a small wooden bowl to each member of the audience in turn; when it was full he carried it back to his master and laid it at his feet. Then the storyteller resumed the dialogue with Benoni's reply to Adoniram.

2 Balkis

'Many centuries before the captivity of the Hebrews in Egypt, Saba, the illustrious descendant of Abraham and Keturah, came to settle in that prosperous region which we call the Yemen; there he founded a city which was named after him in those times, but which is known today as Mareb. Saba had a brother called Iarab, who bequeathed his name to the stony Arabia. His descendants carry their tents here and there, while Saba's descendants continue to reign in the Yemen, a rich empire which is now ruled by queen Balkis, the direct descendant of Saba, of Joktan, and of the patriarch Eber whose great-great-grandfather was Shem, the common father of the Hebrews and Arabs. . . .'

'What an introduction!' Adoniram exclaimed impatiently. 'It sounds like an Egyptian book and you adopt the monotonous tone of Moussa ben Amran (Moses), that verbose liberator of the race of the Hebrews. Men of words take the place of men of action.'

'As the masters of maxims replace the sacred poets. In a word, then, master, the queen of the South, the princess of Yemen, the divine Balkis, has come to test the wisdom of Soliman and admire the marvels of our craft. She actually enters Solyme (Jerusalem) today. Following the king's retinue, our workmen have rushed to greet her and the countryside is swarming with people. That is why our worshops are empty. I was one of the first to run there; I saw her suite and then I returned to be close to you.'

'Speak to them of masters, and they scurry off like slaves. Idleness . . . servitude. . . .'

'Curiosity, above all, master, and you would understand why if. . . . The stars, I tell you, the stars in the sky are less numerous than the warriors who follow the queen. There are sixty elephants behind her laden with towers glittering with gold and silk. A thousand Sabeans, their skins golden from the sun, advance, leading the camels whose knees are bent beneath the weight of the princess' belongings and gifts. They, in turn, are followed by the lightly armed Abyssinians whose ruddy complexion resembles wrought copper. Obedient and watchful, a host of ebony black Ethiopians circulate here and there, leading the horses and chariots. Then . . . but what is the point of my continuing? You don't even deign to listen.'

'The queen of the Sabeans,' Adoniram remarked thoughtfully. 'A degenerate race, but their origins are pure and unpolluted. And what has she come to do at this court?'

'Haven't I just told you, Adoniram! She has come to see a great king and test his wisdom. There are rumours that she considers marrying Soliman ben Daoud, for she hopes to procure heirs worthy of her race. . . .'

'From a slave's blood . . . madness!' the artist exclaimed vehemently. 'From the blood of such abject creatures, and Soliman's veins are full of it. Does the lioness intend to unite with a tame mongrel dog? For centuries now, this people perform their sacrifices on the high places and abandon themselves to foreign women. As a result, these corrupt generations have lost the strength and vigour of their ancestors. What is he, this pacific Soliman? The child of a warrior girl and the old shepherd Daoud, while Daoud himself sprang from Ruth, who ran away a long time ago from the country of Moab to fall at the feet of a farmer in Ephrata (Bethlehem). You admire this great nation, my child . . . why, it has dwindled to a shadow, and the warrior race is extinct. At its zenith, it now approaches its decline. Peace has softened the people, luxury and sensuality make them prefer gold to iron, while those crafty disciples of a subtle and voluptuous king are only good now for hawking wares around or spreading usury throughout the world. And Balkis chooses to step down into this heap of ignominy, Balkis, the daughter of the patriarchs! And tell me, Benoni, she is coming, isn't she? . . . This very evening she enters the gates of Jerusalem. . . .'

'Tomorrow is the Sabbath,' Benoni replied. 'Conforming to her faith, she has refused to enter the foreign city at sunset and has had her tents pitched on the banks of the Kedron. Despite the king's persuasions, for he visited her there in magnificent pomp, she intends to pass the night in the countryside.'

'Praise to her prudence! Is she still young?' Adoniram asked.

'She has barely reached the age when a woman has to remind herself that she is young. And her beauty is dazzling. I glanced at her as you glance towards the rising sun which soon will burn you and oblige you to lower your eyes. Everyone fell prostrate at the sight of her, and I did likewise. When I stood up and moved away I carried her image with me. But Adoniram! it is already night and I can hear the workmen coming back to collect their wages, for tomorrow is the Sabbath, remember.'

Then the various foremen of the artisans arrived. Adoniram placed guards at the entrance of the workshops, and, opening his huge coffers, he began paying the workmen. They presented themselves one by one, whispering a mysterious word in his ear, for they were so numerous that it would have been difficult to figure out the salary due to each individual.

On the day they were enrolled they were given a password and warned that they would lose their lives if they revealed it to anybody else; they made a solemn oath to keep it secret. The master workmen had their password, likewise the journeymen and the apprentices.

Thus, passing in front of Adoniram and his stewards, they murmured the sacramental word, and Adoniram distributed a different salary to each of them, according to the hierarchy of their functions.

When this ceremony was completed by the flickering light of resin tapers, Adoniram, determined to spend the night working in privacy, dismissed the young Benoni, put out his torch, and, reaching his own subterranean workshops, disappeared from the sight of man.

Early the following day, Balkis, the queen of the morning, entered Jerusalem through the east gate with the first rays of the rising sun. Awoken by the clamour of her retinue, the Hebrews rushed to their doors, while the workmen followed her attendants with loud acclamations. Never had they seen so many horses, so many camels, so great a number of white elephants led by so huge a multitude of black Ethiopians.

Delayed by the endless details of court etiquette, the great king Soliman was putting the final touches to his magnificent apparel and at the same time trying to tear himself away from the hands of his wardrobe officers, when Balkis, dismounting at the gates of the palace, crossed the threshold, after saluting the sun, which was already rising in radiance over the mountains of Galilee.

Wearing tall, conical caps and carrying long golden canes, chamberlains welcomed the queen and soon ushered her into the hall where Soliman ben Daoud was now seated, in the midst of his court, upon a raised throne from which he hastened to descend, with dignity, to approach his august visitor.

The two sovereigns exchanged bows with all the veneration which monarchs profess and delight in practising towards fellow royalty, then they sat down beside each other, while slaves came forth laden with gifts from the queen of Saba : gold, cinnamon, myrrh and, above all, incense, one of the Yemen's principal sources of commerce; next, elephants' teeth, sacks of aromatics, bags of precious stones, and finally, a modest, personal present of a hundred talents of fine gold.

Soliman was already well past middle age, but happiness, preserving his features in perpetual serenity, had removed from his face the marks and wrinkles wrought by profound suffering; his shining lips, his flower-petal eyes, separated by a nose like an ivory tower, as he had declaimed himself through the mouth of the Shulamite in the *Song of Songs*, and his forehead, calm as Serapis', all bore witness to the immutable peace and ineffable tranquility of a sovereign who basked content in his own grandeur. Soliman resembled a gold statue whose mask and hands were made of ivory.

Golden were his crown and his apparel : the purple of his mantle, a gift from Hiram, prince of Tyre, was woven upon a chain of golden thread; gold glittered on his girdle and shone upon the hilt of his sword; his golden foot-wear rested on a gold trimmed rug, while his throne was made of gilded cedar.

Seated beside him, the white queen of the morning, wrapped in a haze of linen tissue and diaphanous gauze, resembled a lily lost in a bunch of jonquils. Calculated coquetry! which she even emphasized with an excuse for her artless morning costume :

'My simplicity of dress,' she said, 'befits your opulence and becomes your grandeur.'

'It is most right,' Soliman replied, 'that divine beauty relies upon its power, and that man, confronting his own weakness, neglects nothing.'

'Charming modesty!' Balkis exclaimed. 'It enhances the renown attached to the invincible Soliman . . . the Ecclesiast, the sage, the arbitrator of kings, the immortal author of the aphorisms in the *Sir-Hasirim (Song of Songs)*, that canticle of such tender love, and of so many other flowers of poetry.'

'O beautiful queen,' Soliman replied with a blush of pleasure, 'you actually deigned to cast a glance at those insignificant scribblings!'

'You are a great poet,' the queen of Saba insisted.

Soliman puffed up his gold covered chest, raised his gold covered arm, and complacently ran his hand through his ebony beard, which was divided into several tresses and entwined with golden threads.

'A great poet,' Balkis repeated, 'and for this reason we pardon with a smile the errors which you commit as a moralist.'

The lines on Soliman's august countenance stood out at this hardly expected conclusion.

A ripple of agitation passed over the nearest courtiers : Zabud, the prince's favourite, aglow with precious stones; Zadok, the high priest, next to his son Azariah the major-domo, who was extremely arrogant with his inferiors; then Ahiah, Elihoreph the Lord Chancellor, and Jehoshaphat the master of the archives, who was slightly deaf. Standing up, sombrely dressed, was Ahijah the Shilonite, a man of integrity and a cold, taciturn scoffer, feared because of his prophetic genius. Closest to the sovereign, squatting on three cushions piled one on top of the other, was Benaiah, the pacific general of the placid Soliman's peaceful armies. Rigged out in gold chains and sun-shaped precious stones, weighed down by honours, Benaiah was the demi-god of war. Formerly, the king had ordered him to assassinate Joab and the high priest Abiathar; Benaiah had stabbed them to death. From that day on Soliman considered him worthy of the greatest trust and ordered him next to kill his younger brother, prince Adonijah, king Daoud's son; Benaiah cut the throat of the wise Soliman's brother.

Now, benumbed by glory, heavy with years, the almost idiot Benaiah follows the court everywhere, no longer hearing or understanding anything; he rekindles the ashes of a decaying life by warming his heart under the dazzling light of his sovereign's occasional smiles. His colourless eyes beg incessantly for the royal regard : in his old age the former lynx has become a dog.

When Balkis' adorable lips had uttered those piquant words which overwhelmed the court, Benaiah, who had understood nothing but nevertheless followed up every word of the king and his visitor with a cry of admiration, Benaiah alone, in the midst of the disturbing silence, exclaimed with a benign smile, 'Charming ! Divine !'

'You idiot !' Soliman exclaimed, biting his lips.

'Memorable words indeed !' Benaiah applauded, seeing that his master had spoken.

And the queen of Saba burst into laughter.

Then, most aptly, as everybody could not help but realize, she chose that very moment to challenge the widely renowned wisdom of Soliman with three enigmas one after the other. The king was the most expert of mortals in the art of solving riddles and unravelling charades, for such was the custom at the time : the courts had completely renounced the learning which used to inspire them, and the solving of puzzles was now an affair of State. On that, a prince or sage was judged. Balkis had covered 650 miles to have Soliman undergo such an examination.

Soliman interpreted the three enigmas without stumbling, thanks to the high priest Zadok who, the day before, had paid the high priest of the Sabeans in cash for the solutions.

'Wisdom speaks through . . . your mouth,' the queen said with the merest hint of irony.

'That, at least, is what several people suppose.'

'Nevertheless, noble Soliman, one does not cultivate the tree of wisdom without a certain peril; ultimately, there is the risk that one grows enamoured of praise, that one seeks to flatter men in order to please them, and that one yields to materialism in order to win the approbation of the crowd.'

'Have you perhaps noticed that in my works? . . .'

'Ah! my lord, I have read your works with keen attention, and because I wish to improve my understanding I now intend to question you on certain obscurities, certain contradictions, certain sophisms — for so I consider them, through my ignorance, no doubt. Indeed, I already had this intention when I prepared myself for so long a voyage.'

'We shall do our best,' Soliman said distinctly, and not without conceit, to buoy himself up in front of such a formidable opponent. In truth, he would have liked nothing better at that moment than to leave the court and take a walk all alone under the sycamores at his residence at Millo.

Attracted by such a piquant spectacle, the courtiers craned their necks forward and opened wide their eyes. What could be worse for Soliman than failing to prove himself infallible in front of his subjects? Zadok appeared alarmed, the prophet Ahijah the Shilonite barely managed to conceal a faint, cold smile, while Benaiah, toying with his decorations, expressed a moronic gaiety which already cast ridicule upon the king. As for Balkis' retinue, they were mute and imperturbable : sphinxes.

To the advantages of the queen of Saba add the majesty of a goddess and the attractions of the most intoxicating beauty : a profile of exquisite purity, so well carved, so elongated, that it always appears directly opposite to whoever is stunned by the sight of it, while her large dark pupils sparkle like a gazelle's; a mouth which opens with a smile one moment and puckers into voluptuousness the next; supple limbs whose splendour is not completely hidden by the folds of gauze; imagine, too, that artful manner of expression, haughty, mocking and lively, which is invariably cultivated by individuals of great lineage who are accustomed to dominion, and then you will understand the embarrassment of king Soliman who was confounded and at the same time enchanted, eager to conquer with his mind, while his heart was already half conquered. Those huge glittering eyes, mysterious and gentle, penetrating and calm, at play on a fervent face as bright as newly molten bronze, troubled him despite himself. He saw rising to life beside him the ideal and mystic figure of the goddess Isis.

'Do you not advocate, then,' the queen began, 'egoism and hardness of heart when you say : "Make no friendship with an angry man; and with a furious man thou shalt not go : lest thou learn his ways, and get a snare to his soul."? You never suggest attempts at reconciliation. In another proverb you praise the power and value of gold. . . .'

'But elsewhere I extol poverty.'

'Contradiction : the Ecclesiast encourages man to work and reproaches the slothful, while further on, he declaims : ". . . What profit hath he that hath laboured for the wind? . . . It is good and comely for one to eat and to drink." In *Proverbs*, you condemn debauchery, while you praise it in *Ecclesiastes*.'

'You're exaggerating, surely.'

'No, I'm quoting : "As he came forth of his mother's womb, naked shall he return to go as he came, and shall take nothing of his labour, which he may carry away in his hand. . . . Behold that which I have seen : it is good and comely for one to eat and to drink. . . . And how dieth the wise man? . . . as the fool." That is your philosophy, O sage !'

'Those are figures of speech, while the basis of my doctrine. . . .'

'Is — I can tell you — and others alas ! had already discovered it : "Live joyfully with the wife whom thou lovest all the days of the life of thy vanity, which he hath given you under the sun; for that is thy portion in this life, and in thy labour which thou takest under the sun." You often return to this theme. I therefore concluded that it suits you to attach your people to the things of the earth so that you will be more sure of governing them as slaves.'

To justify himself, Soliman was obliged to resort to arguments he far from wished to disclose in front of his people, and he writhed impatiently upon his throne.

'And then,' Balkis pursued with a ravishing smile and a languid glance, 'and then you are cruel to our sex. Where is the woman who would dare love the severe Soliman?'

'O queen ! in the Song of Songs I have laid my heart out bare like spring-time dew over the tender passion-flowers !'

'An exception which glorifies the Shulamite indeed, but you have grown severe as the years take their toll of you.'

Soliman concealed a sullen enough grimace.

'I anticipate some polite and courteous phrases,' the queen said, 'but take care ! The Ecclesiast will hear you, and you know in advance what he has to say : "Give not thy strength unto women, nor thy ways to that which destroyeth kings." How could you set down such austere maxims! Apparently, it was only to slander the daughters of Zion that you wished to receive from the heavens that beauty whom you nevertheless described in terms such as these: "I am the rose of Sharon, and the lily of the valleys." '

'Queen, once again, it was a figure of speech.'

'O king! I have expressed my opinion. Deign to consider the objections I have raised and illuminate the obscurity of my judgment, for it is I who am at fault, while you have rejoiced that wisdom abides within you. "Where the word of a king is, there is power: and who may say unto him, What doest thou?" you have written. Great king, I have already responded to some of these truths; your mind enchants me, your bearing impresses me, and I do not doubt that you can read upon my face the token of my admiration. I await your words; not only shall I listen attentively, but during your discourse your servant will place her hand over her mouth.'

'Lady,' said Soliman with a deep sigh, 'what does the sage become in your presence? Now that he has listened to you, the Ecclesiast would no longer dare uphold a single one of his thoughts; he resents their weight: "Vanity of vanities, saith the Preacher; all is vanity." '

The court admired the king's reply.

A pedant, the queen decided, a pedant indeed! But if one could cure him of his mania to be an author, he would certainly be gentle, affable, and quite well preserved.

As for Soliman, having deferred his answers, he endeavoured to choose a subject which, for once, would not involve him personally.

'Your serenity,' he said to queen Balkis, 'has a most beautiful bird there; its species is quite unknown to me.'

Now, grouped at the queen's feet and dressed in scarlet, six young Negroes were appointed to take care of this bird which never left the side of its mistress. One of these pages held it on his wrist, and the queen of Saba often glanced at it.

'We call her Hud-Hud,' she replied. 'It is said that her great-great-grandfather, who lived for a long time, was brought back by the Malayans from a distant country which they alone glimpsed and which we no longer know. She is of great service when diverse messages are to be conveyed to the denizens and spirits of the air.'

Soliman, who did not fully grasp so simple an explanation, bowed, however, like a monarch who must have understood everything perfectly, and stretched forth his thumb and index-finger to play with Hud-Hud; but the bird, although it responded to his attention, did not give way to his attempt to take it in his hand.

'Hud-Hud is a poetess,' the queen said, 'and therefore worthy of your sympathy. All the same, she is a trifle severe, like me, and she often moralizes, too. To tell you the truth, she has expressed her doubts as to the sincerity of your passion for the Shulamite.'

'Divine bird, you astonish me !' Soliman replied.

' "That poem, the Song of Songs, is certainly most tender," Hud-Hud said one day as she nibbled at a golden scarab, "but the great king who addressed such plaintive elegies to his wife, the daughter of Pharaoh, would he not have demonstrated a greater love by living with her, instead of compelling her to reside far from him in the city of Daoud where she was reduced to whiling away her forlorn youth with stanzas, though they are, in truth, the most beautiful in the world ?" '

'You make me remember so much sorrow ! Alas ! that daughter of the night followed the cult of Isis. How could I, without committing a crime, open the gates of the holy city to her, bring her within reach of the ark of Adonai, and lead her into the precincts of the temple I am raising to the God of my fathers ?'

'A delicate subject,' Balkis remarked discreetly. 'Kindly excuse Hud-Hud, for birds are sometimes thoughtless. Mine considers herself quite a connoisseur, of poetry, in particular.'

'Really,' Soliman ben Daoud replied, 'I would be most curious to learn. . . .'

'Mischievous quibbles, my lord, mischievous, I swear ! Hud-Hud ventures to criticize you for comparing the beauty of your beloved to a company of horses in Pharaoh's chariots, her hair to a herd of goats, her teeth to shorn and pregnant sheep, her temples to a piece of pomegranate, her breasts to two young roes, her head to mount Carmel, her navel to a round goblet which wanteth not liquor, her belly to a heap of wheat, and her nose to the tower of Lebanon which looketh toward Damascus !' Offended and discouraged, Soliman let his gold covered arms fall on to those of his arm-chair, which were golden, too.

'My reply to your bird, which serves so well your own inclination for raillery, is that the Oriental style permits these licences, that true poetry pursues images, that my people find my verses excellent and prefer to savour the richest metaphors rather than. . . .'

'Nothing is more dangerous for the nations than the metaphors of kings,' the queen of Saba retorted. 'Outcome of a majestic style, these figures of speech, which are perhaps too daring, will find more imitators than critics, and your sublime fancies may threaten the style of poets for thousands of years. Following your example, the Shulamite might well compare your hair to palm-tree branches, your lips to lilies dropping myrrh, your height to that of the cedar, your legs to marble columns, and your cheeks, my lord, to little beds of fragrant flowers planted by perfumers. As a result, I would be obliged to

imagine king Soliman as a peristyle with a botanical garden suspended over an entablature shaded by palm-trees!'

Soliman smiled wryly; he would have gladly strangled the hoopoe
which was pecking now with strange persistence at his chest, precisely
where the heart is placed.

'Hud-Hud is striving to point out the true source of poetry to you,'
the queen explained.

'I have felt it only too well,' the king replied, 'ever since I first
enjoyed the opportunity of gazing upon you. Come, let us abandon
this discourse. Will my queen honour her unworthy servant by a tour
of Jerusalem to see my palace and, above all, the temple I am raising
to Jehovah on the mountain of Zion?'

'The whole world has heard of these wonders. I am eager to give
way to my impatience which already competes with their splendour.
We should certainly postpone no longer the enjoyment which I have
promised myself.'

Leading the procession, which slowly passed through the streets of
Jerusalem, were forty-two dulcimers, rumbling like thunder; they
were followed by the musicians who were dressed in white robes and
conducted by Asaph and Idithmus : fifty cymbalists, forty flutists,
thirty psaltery-players; there were also ancient citherns, and let us
not forget the trumpets, that instrument which Joshua had brought
into fashion long ago under the walls of Jericho. Next came three
rows of incense-bearers who, advancing backwards, swung their
thuribles to and fro, lulling the air with the perfumes of Yemen. As
for Soliman and Balkis, they could strut about as they wished in an
enormous palanquin which was borne by seventy Philistines who had
been taken captive in the war.

The sequence was over. We broke up into groups, chatting about the
many vicissitudes in the tale, and we arranged a rendezvous for the
following evening, when the storyteller continued as follows.

3 The Temple

Newly rebuilt by the magnificent Soliman, the city followed an only too faultless plan; the streets were impeccably straight, the houses rigidly square and all alike, veritable hives of monotony.

'In these wide and lovely streets,' said the queen, 'the cold north wind coming from the sea must sweep the passers-by off their feet. Moreover, no measure has been taken to prevent the sun from penetrating the houses during the heatwaves and turning them into furnaces. Now, in Mareb the streets are narrow; sheets of fabric stretch from one house to another across the public highway, they summon a breeze and scatter shadows over the ground, thereby creating lots of fresh air.'

'To the detriment of symmetry,' Soliman retorted. 'Here we are at the peristyle of my new palace which took thirteen years to build.'

They visited the palace and it won the queen of Saba's appraisal; she found it opulent, comfortable, original, and in exquisite taste.

'The plan is indeed sublime,' she said, 'and the arrangement admirable. I must admit there is not even an echo of this boldness and elegance in the palace of my ancestors, the Hamathites, built in the Indian style with square columns topped by figures that serve as capitals. Your architect is a great artist.'

'It is I who am responsible for everything, including the workmen's wages!' the king proudly exclaimed.

'But who estimated the cost? Who drew up the plans? Who is the genius who carried out your intentions in so splendid, so honourable a fashion?'

'A certain Adoniram, a strange enough individual, almost a savage. My friend the king of Tyre sent him to me.'

'Shall I not see him at all, my lord?'

'He shuns society and scorns praise. But what will you say, your serenity, when you have examined the temple of Adonai? That is not the work of an artisan. I myself dictated the plans and decided what materials should be used. Adoniram's views were not allowed to conflict with my own poetic conceptions. They have already been working on it for five years and it will be another two before the project is realized in its ultimate perfection.'

139

'It will take you seven years, then, to house your God in a manner worthy of him, while it took as many as thirteen years to house his servant suitably.'

'Time is of no importance in matters such as these,' Soliman objected.

Balkis criticized the temple as much as she had admired the palace.

'You were too ambitious,' she said, 'you have attempted far too much, and the artist was not allowed sufficient liberty. The ensemble is rather heavy, although the details do stand out; there is too much wood . . . cedar everywhere, too many protruding beams, and the wooden flooring of the side wings appears to support the upper courses of stone. As a result, the eye is offended by a certain lack of solidity and stability.'

'My exact aim,' Soliman explained, 'was to prepare the eye, by a striking contrast, for the splendours of the interior.'

'Great God!' the queen cried, moving forward. 'What sculptures! These statues are marvellous . . . what strange animals! They command attention. Who cast them, who chiselled these wonders?'

'Adoniram, his main talent happens to be for statuary.'

'His genius is universal. Only, those cherubim are much too heavy, too golden and too big for this hall, they overwhelm it.'

'That is exactly how I wished it to be . . . each of them cost a hundred and twenty talents. You will see for yourself, O queen! that everything here is in gold, and no material is more precious than gold. The cherubim are in gold; the cedar columns, a gift from my friend king Hiram, are covered with gold leaf; there is gold over all the partitions; there will be golden palm-tree branches and a solid gold frieze of pomegranates upon these golden walls, and I shall have two hundred shields of pure gold carefully attached along the gilded wainscot. The altars, the tables, the candlesticks, the vessels, the floors and ceilings, all will be covered in gold leaf. . . .'

'A little too much gold, perhaps,' the queen suggested.

'Can anything be too splendid for the King of men!' Soliman replied. 'I intend to astonish posterity — but come, let us enter the sanctuary. Although the roof has yet to be built, the altar foundations are already placed, opposite my throne which is nearly finished. As you see, there are six steps and the ivory seat is supported by two lions with twelve cubs crouching at their feet. The gilding has yet to be burnished and the canopy raised. Deign, noble princess, to be the first to sit upon this virgin throne from where you will see everything in perspective. Only, you will be exposed to the shafts of the sun, for the sanctuary is still uncovered.'

The princess smiled and put Hud-Hud upon her wrist. The courtiers gazed at the bird with intense curiosity.

Now throughout the Orient no bird is more renowned than Hud-Hud or more respected. Neither her delicate black beak, nor her scarlet cheeks, nor her sweet hazel-nut eyes, nor her superb crest of fragile golden feathers, crowning her lovely head, nor her splendid green wings, enriched by golden streaks and fringes, nor her soft pink spurs, nor her crimson feet, no, none of these details explain why the sprightly Hud-Hud proved such a favourite among the queen and her subjects : beautiful without being self-conscious, ever faithful to her mistress, kind to all who loved her, the hoopoe emanated utter grace but never attempted to dazzle or impress. And the queen, as we have seen, consulted this bird whenever difficult circumstances arose. She now appeared to whisper certain instructions to her. Quick as an arrow, Hud-Hud flew away and disappeared into the azure. Then the queen sat down.

All the courtiers grouped themselves around her and started chatting. Balkis invited the king of Jerusalem to sit beside her. He told the princess about the sea of bronze project which had been conceived by Adoniram. Full of admiration, the queen of Saba insisted that he be presented to her. The king ordered a number of courtiers to search everywhere for the gloomy Adoniram, and they immediately ran to the forges and looked around the site. Balkis then asked Soliman how the canopy of his throne would be decorated.

'It will be decorated like everything else,' he replied.

'Does it never occur to you that by your exclusive preference for gold you disparage the other materials created by Adonai? And do you really think that nothing in the world is more beautiful than this metal? Permit me to add some variety to your plan . . . you alone will judge its value.'

Darkness suddenly falls and the sky is muffled by black specks which grow bigger as they approach; flocks of birds tumble into the temple, divide into groups, form circles, jostle together, arranging themselves finally into a sumptuous, shimmering foliage, while their wings unfold into opulent bouquets of green, scarlet, jet-black and azure. This living canopy is deployed under the skilful direction of the hoopoe; she hovers over the feathered flock, which is raised now like a delightful tree, each bird being a leaf, above the heads of the two sovereigns. Overcome by enchantment, Soliman finds himself protected from the sun under this animated, quivering roof which is upheld by the beating of wings and projects a dense shadow upon the throne, which, in turn, echoes the melodious concert of bird songs. Then the hoopoe, against whom the king still bears a certain grudge, comes down at last submissively to the feet of the queen.

'And what does my lord think?' Balkis asked.

'Wonderful!' exclaimed Soliman, making every effort to attract

Hud-Hud, but the bird continued to avoid him, a fact which the queen noticed with keen attention.

'If this fantasy pleases you,' the queen replied, 'then I am only too willing to offer you this little canopy of birds, on condition that you do not oblige me to change them into gold. Whenever you wish to summon them, all you have to do is turn the gem set within this ring towards the sun. This ring is precious,' Balkis emphasized, handing it to the king. 'I inherited it from my forefathers, and Sarahil, my nurse, will scold me for having given it to you.'

'Ah! noble queen,' Soliman exclaimed, kneeling down before her, 'you are indeed worthy to command men, kings, and the very elements. May the heavens and your kindness grant that you accept one half of a throne where at your feet you will find only the most submissive of all your subjects!'

'Your proposition pleases me,' Balkis said, 'and we shall discuss it later.' Soliman rose to his feet again, and both the sovereigns now moved away from the throne, accompanied by their retinue of birds which followed them, as a canopy, tracing a variety of ornamental figures over their heads.

When they reached the altar foundations the queen noticed the huge trunk of a vine which had been torn up from its roots and thrown aside. She started with surprise and grew pensive, while the hoopoe uttered the most woeful cries and the flock of birds at once took wing and flew away. Balkis' expression grew stern, her majestic stature appeared to increase.

'How ignorant are men! How negligent indeed!' she exclaimed in a solemn and prophetic voice. 'O vanity and pride! Thou hast erected thy glory upon the tomb of thy forefathers. This trunk of vine, this venerable wood. . . .'

'But, my queen, it was an obstacle. We removed it to make room for the altar of porphyr and olive wood which will be offset by four golden seraphim.'

'Thou hast profaned and destroyed the first vine. This tree was planted long ago by the hand of the father of the race of Shem, by the patriarch Noah himself!'

'Is it possible? . . .' Soliman replied, deeply humiliated. 'How did you discover this?'

'I have never believed that grandeur was the source of knowledge, O king! I have always upheld the contrary, and I devoted myself to study with religious fervour. Listen to me attentively, thou who hast been blinded by thy fruitless splendour. Dost thou know what fate the immortal powers have reserved for this wood which thy impiety condemns to destruction?'

'Tell me.'

'It is to be the instrument of agony upon which the last prince of thy race will be nailed.'

'Then let it be sawed into fragments! this accursed wood . . . let it be reduced to ashes!'

'Madman! Who can erase what is written in the book of God? And what would thy wisdom achieve, tell me, if it replaced the divine will! Prostrate thyself before the decrees which so far fail to penetrate thy material spirit, for it is this instrument alone which will save thy name from oblivion and lead the radiant light of immortal glory to shine upon thy house!'

While the great Soliman strove in vain to conceal his misgivings under a jovial, scoffing mien, attendants arrived to announce that they had at last found the sculptor Adoniram.

Heralded by the clamour of the crowd, Adoniram soon appeared at the entrance of the temple. Benoni accompanied his master and friend who stepped forward, his eyes burning, his expression thoughtful, his clothes in utter disorder, like an artist who has been brusquely torn away from his inspiration and work to bother about one trivial matter or another. No trace of curiosity weakened his powerful, noble features. He commanded attention not so much by his exceptional stature, but by the grave, audacious and dominating character stamped across his beautiful countenance. Proud and self-assured, but without familiarity or disdain, he halted a few paces in front of Balkis who could not help but reveal a certain timidity and confusion when she confronted his incisive, eagle gaze. She quickly overcame her embarrassment, however, as she considered the real circumstances of this master-workman standing before her with his bare arms and his bare chest, and she even smiled at the effect which he had had upon her. Almost delighted to have felt quite so young, she deigned to address the artisan. But when he replied, his voice struck the queen like the echo of a fleeting memory, although she did not know him and had never seen him before. Such is the power of genius, such is the sway of spiritual beauty: two souls fasten to each other and cannot be separated, for genius welds them together. Her conversation with Adoniram led the princess of the Sabeans to forget everything surrounding her, and while the artist pointed out particular details of the incompleted buildings, Balkis followed him automatically and impulsively, just as the king and his courtiers followed the footsteps of the divine princess, though Soliman made special haste to overtake the two of them.

Balkis did not weary of questioning Adoniram about his work, his country and his birth.

'Lady,' he replied, looking at her piercingly after a hesitant pause, 'I have travelled through many countries and wherever the sun shines I find my home ! My early years were spent all around those vast slopes of Lebanon, from where Damascus can be made out in the plain. Nature and men, too, have carved those mountainous regions which bristle with menacing boulders and ruins.'

'But,' the queen remarked, 'it is not in those deserts that one learns the secrets of the arts in which you excel.'

'It is there at least that thought grows truly animated, that imagination is aroused, and that meditation leads to the creative process. My first master was solitude. During the voyages I have made since then I have profited much from its lessons. I have turned my gaze towards the remnants of the past, I have contemplated monuments and fled from human society.'

'And why, master?'

'The company of one's fellow-men offers little pleasure . . . and I felt alone.' Touched by this mixture of nobility and sadness, the queen lowered her eyes and grew reflective.

'As you see,' Adoniram pursued, 'my apprenticeship was hardly a problem, so I don't deserve much praise for practising these arts. As for my models, I came upon them in the desert, and I reproduce the impressions made upon me by those neglected ruins and awesome, grandiose figures of the gods of the ancient world.'

'More than once,' Soliman interrupted, firmly weighing his words, 'more than once, master Adoniram, I have had occasion to curb what I would term your idolatrous tendencies : this fervent veneration of the monuments belonging to an impure theogony. Keep your thoughts to yourself and do not let the king read any trace of them in your works of bronze and stone.' Adoniram bowed and concealed a bitter smile.

'Lord,' the queen said to console him, 'the master's thoughts rise, I am sure, beyond the kind of reflections which might trouble the conscience of the levites. In his soul, the soul of an artist, he tells himself that whatever is beautiful glorifies God, and he seeks the beautiful with simple piety.'

'Moreover,' said Adoniram, 'do I not know myself what they were in their time, those gods who were exterminated and petrified by the genii of old? Who would be worried by them today? When Soliman, the king of kings, demanded prodigies from me, I could not help but recall how the ancestors of the world have left us marvels which have not been demolished.'

'If your work is beautiful and sublime,' the queen added enthusiastically, 'it will be orthodox, and to be orthodox in its turn, posterity will copy your example.'

'Noble queen !' Adoniram exclaimed, 'truly noble, your intelligence is as pure as your beauty, and. . . .'

'These ruins,' Balkis hastily interrupted, 'these ruins . . . were there many of them upon the slopes of Lebanon?'

'Entire cities wrapped in a shroud of sand which the wind would lift up one minute and press down the next. I found hypogea there of superhuman workmanship and they are known to none but me. Working for the birds of the air and the stars of the sky, I merely roamed around, sketching figures on the rocks and carving them out on the spot with mighty blows. One day . . . but I must be straining your majesty's patience?'

'No,' said Balkis. 'This account of your experiences fascinates me.'

'Shaken by my hammer,' Adoniram at once continued, 'which drove the chisel deep into the bowels of the rock, the earth suddenly sounded resonant and hollow beneath my feet. Armed with a lever, I managed to roll away the rock which had concealed, I discovered, the entrance to a cavern. I leaped inside. It was carved in sheer stone and supported by enormous columns which were loaded with mouldings and weird designs; these capitals served as roots for the ribs of the most highly daring vaults. Dispersed throughout this forest of stone stood a host of diverse and colossal figures which had remained there, immobile and smiling, for millions of years. I was gripped by a kind of intoxicating terror at the mere sight of them . . . men, giants who have disappeared from our world, symbolic animals belonging to a vanished species . . . in a word, every marvel, every magnificence which the flights of a delirious imagination would scarcely dare conceive! There I lived for many months, for years, examining these spectres of an extinct species, and it is there that I received the tradition of my art, among those splendours of primitive genius.'

'The fame of these nameless works has spread in fact as far as here,' Soliman said pensively. 'It is said that there, in the accursed regions, the ruins of the impious city which was submerged in the waters of the deluge loom up quite distinctly. The remains of the infamous Enochia built by the gigantic descendants of Tubal: the city of the children of Cain. Anathema upon this art of blasphemy and darkness! Our new temple reflects the clear light of the sun. Its lines are pure and modest, while the order and unity of the plan transmit the integrity of our faith into the most minute details of style for this abode I am raising to the Eternal. Such is our will! And it is the will of Adonai who conveyed it to my father!'

'King,' Adoniram fiercely exclaimed, 'not a single detail of your plans has been overlooked. God will acknowledge your submission to his will. But neither have I overlooked your own grandeur, and the world will recognize it, too, in the majesty of this temple.'

'Subtle and ingenious man, thou shalt not tempt the lord thy king.

Such was thy purpose in casting those monsters which inspire admiration and dread, those giant idols which rebel against the models sanctioned by the Hebrew rites. Take care ! The might of Adonai is with me, and should my power be challenged, I shall grind Baal into dust !'

'Be lenient, O king,' the queen of Saba gently advised, 'towards the artisan who builds the monument of your glory. One age gives way to another. Human destiny proceeds according to the Creator's wish. Does Adoniram disregard God's intentions by interpreting and transmitting his works in a more noble fashion? Must we eternally reproduce the cold immobility of the hieratic figures handed down by the Egyptians? Must we follow their example and leave a statue half buried in a granite sepulchre from which it can't break loose? And must we depict slavish genii trapped in stone? . . . Noble prince, the idolatry of routine implies a dangerous negation of the Creator's wishes, a negation we should beware of.'

Offended by this contradiction, but captivated by a charming smile from the queen, Soliman let her warmly congratulate the man of genius whom he admired himself, despite his caution and resentment. Usually indifferent to praise, Adoniram listened now in rapture to the queen's compliments.

The three great personages had reached the exterior peristyle which stood upon a raised, quadrangular platform from where the view was one of huge tracts of rough and hilly countryside. A dense crowd covered the whole of the neighbouring area of the city built by Daoud. In order to see the queen of Saba, from nearby or afar, whole multitudes had invaded the main approaches to the palace and the temple. The masons had left their quarries in Gilead, the carpenters had deserted their distant timber-yards, the miners had climbed up again to the surface of the earth. As the news of the renowned queen's arrival spread through the surrounding regions, it aroused this population of workmen and made them hasten towards the centre of their site. There they were, then, pell-mell, women, children, soldiers, tradesmen, labourers, slaves, peaceful citizens of Jerusalem . . . and the spacious plains and valleys appeared to belittle this immense throng. The queen's astonished eye ranged for more than a mile over a mosaic of human heads which sloped up into an amphitheatre on the horizon. Here and there, a few clouds intercepted the radiant sun, casting tufts of shade over this living ocean.

'Your people,' said queen Balkis in amazement, 'are more numerous than the grains of sand upon the shore !'

'They come from every country,' Soliman replied, 'they have rushed to see you. I am only astonished that the entire world does not besiege Jerusalem today ! Because of you, the countryside is

deserted and the city abandoned . . . all master Adoniram's indefatigable workmen are present.'

'Workmen such as Adoniram's,' the queen of Saba said, seeking to
honour the artist, 'would be masters themselves anywhere else. They
are his soldiers and he is the leader of this artisan militia. Master
Adoniram,' she declared, turning towards him, 'we wish to see your
workmen assembled so that we may congratulate them and compli-
ment you in their presence.'

Astounded by this request, the wise Soliman raised his hands high
above his head. 'Impossible! noble queen,' he exclaimed. 'Assemble
the temple workmen! scattered as they are in the fête . . . wandering
in the hills and mingling with the crowd. Why, they are innumerable,
as well as being dispersed. It would take endless hours to form so
many men into their respective groups. Coming as they do from
different countries, each has his own language, from the Sanskrit
dialect of the Himalayas to the unintelligible gibberish of savage
Libya. I regret, but. . . .'

'That presents no difficulty at all,' Adoniram interrupted quietly.
'The queen would never ask the impossible, and her request will be
fulfilled within a few minutes.'

Then, leaning against the exterior portico and using a block of
granite as a pedestal, Adoniram turns towards the multitude and
fixes his gaze upon them. He makes a sign. Every wave of this ocean
grows pale, for all have lifted their faces towards him. The crowd is
curious now and attentive. Adoniram raises his right arm and traces
a horizontal line in the air with his open hand, then he draws a
vertical line down the middle of it, thereby depicting two straight
lines at right angles, like a plumb-line hanging from a ruler: the
sign by which the Syrians draw the letter T. It was transmitted to
the Phoenicians by the inhabitants of India who had named it *tha*
and since then it has likewise been transmitted to the Greeks who call
it *tau*. Signifying in those ancient languages, because of its hiero-
glyphical analogy, certain tools of the masonic profession, the figure
T was a sign to rally.

As soon as Adoniram has traced it, this human sea surges backwards and forwards, as though it has suddenly been struck by a storm,
then it begins moving in distinct and decisive directions. At first, there
is only general confusion as everyone barges against each other, but
groups are soon formed, grow bigger and break up, while definite
spaces are arranged and particular groups draw up into square units
which drive part of the multitude into the background. Thousands
of men, following the orders of unknown leaders, fall into rank,
like an army divided into three principal regiments, and subdivided into cohorts which, dense and deep though they are, re-

main distinct and separate. While Soliman seeks to understand Adoniram's magic power, the company moves. Alined within a few moments, over a hundred thousand men now advance uniformly and in silence from three directions, and their heavy, regular footsteps resound throughout the countryside. The masons and all who work with stone can be made out in the centre; the masters in the first row, next the journeymen, behind them the apprentices. On their right, following the same hierarchy, come the carpenters, the joiners, the sawyers and the planers. On the left, the founders, the carvers, the blacksmiths, the miners and all those who apply themselves to one branch or another of metallurgy. Like huge waves ready to overflow a river bank, this army of artisans draws nearer and nearer. Troubled, Soliman retreats two or three paces. He turns round and sees behind him only the puny, glittering retinue of his priests and courtiers. But calm and serene, Adoniram stands upright on the pedestal, close to the two monarchs. He stretches forth his arm : the militia halts. Then master Adoniram bows humbly before the queen :

'Your orders are executed.'

Balkis could hardly refrain from prostrating herself before this awesome and occult power, for in his might and simplicity, Adoniram truly appeared sublime to her. She controlled herself, however, and saluted the army of assembled guilds. Next, unfastening a magnificent pearl necklace, on which hung a mysterious sun of gems framed in a golden triangle, she first held it out in homage to the company of artisans, and then she approached Adoniram who, leaning forward, trembled as he felt this precious gift fall over his shoulders and bare, broad chest. The whole crowd immediately responded to the queen of Saba's generous act by an overwhelming acclamation. While the artist's head remained close to the princess's radiant face and palpitating breast, she said to him softly :

'Master, take care of yourself . . . be prudent !'

Adoniram raised his large, dazzling eyes towards her, and Balkis was astonished by the piercing sweetness of his proud and lofty gaze.

Who exactly is he? Soliman asked himself pensively, this mortal who commands men as the queen commands the denizens of the air? With a single sign of his hand, he creates an army. My people belong to him, while my own dominion is reduced to a wretched herd of courtiers and priests. Why, he would only have to move his eyebrows to make himself king of Israel ! These preoccupations prevented him from noticing Balkis' countenance as her eyes followed the nation's real leader, the king of intelligence and genius, the pacific and patient arbiter over the destiny of the Lord's elect.

The monarchs returned in silence to the palace. The solid existence of the people had just been revealed to the wise Soliman who had

believed that he knew everything while, in fact, he had suspected
nothing as concrete at this. Defeated in the dispute about his doctrines, conquered by the queen of Saba who governed the birds of the
air, conquered by an artisan who governed men, the Ecclesiast, foreseeing the future, meditated on the destiny of kings. These priests, he
realized, my former tutors, my present advisers, the very ones who
should have informed me of everything, have, in fact, deliberately
concealed everything from me and failed to disclose my own ignorance to me. O blind confidence of kings! O vanity of wisdom!
Vanity! Vanity!

While the queen, too, indulged in her reveries, Adoniram returned
to his workshop, leaning familiarly on his friend and pupil, Benoni,
who, elated with joy, did not cease from praising the grace, the
favours, and the peerless mind of the queen of Saba. But, more
taciturn than ever, the master remained silent. Pale and panting, he
beat his chest with his clenched fists, one moment, and hugged it in
his arms, the next. Entering the sanctuary of his workshop, he locked
himself in alone; he glanced at a rough-cast statue, examined it and,
finding it faulty, broke it into fragments. Then he fell back upon an
oak bench, hid his face in his hands and cried out in a choking voice:

'Adorable and fatal goddess! Alas! why did my eyes have to behold
this pearl of Arabia!'

During the first pause in this sequence everyone admitted how
affected he had been by the story. One of the audience, however,
whose blue stained arms identified him as a dyer, did not appear to
participate in the general enthusiasm which the preceding scene had
won. He approached the storyteller and said:

'Brother, you announced that all the orders of workmen would be
involved in this tale, but up to now it's all to the glory of the metal-
workers, the carpenters, and the stone-cutters. If it's not going to be
of any further interest to me, I shan't come back to this café, and the
same applies to several others here, believe me!' The proprietor
frowned and looked reproachfully at his storyteller.

'Brother,' the latter replied, 'the dyers will be included, too, for we
shall have occasion to speak of the good Hiram of Tyre who pro-
moted such beautiful purple fabrics throughout the world. And
remember, he was Adoniram's former patron.' Reassured, the dyer
sat down again, and the tale continued as follows.

4 Millo

King Soliman had decided to entertain the queen of Saba in his villa at Millo, perched on the summit of a hill overlooking the whole of the wide valley of Joshaphat. What a cordial welcome the fields offer! Cool waters, splendid gardens, kind shadows of sycamores, tamarind-trees, bay-trees, cypress-trees, acacias and terebinths . . . they are bound to awaken tender feelings in the heart. Moreover, Soliman was delighted to honour his country residence by the queen's visit; as a rule, in fact, sovereigns prefer to keep their equals aside in privacy, rather than expose themselves with their rivals to the gossip of the crowds in the capital.

The two monarchs were standing side by side, looking at the first slopes of the valley, where pine-trees and palm-trees protected a cemetery of white tombs.

'A worthy subject indeed for a king's meditation,' said Soliman, 'this spectacle of our common end. Here, close to you, pleasure and even a promise of happiness. Over there, nothingness and oblivion.'

'We find repose from the hardship and weariness of life,' Balkis replied, 'in our contemplation of death.'

'At this moment, lady, I dread it. Death separates. . . . No! let me not discover its consolations too soon.' Glancing furtively at Soliman, Balkis saw how deeply moved he was; framed by the evening light he appeared beautiful to her.

Before they entered the banquet hall these august visitors examined the twilit house, as they breathed in the voluptuous fragrance of the orange-trees which anointed the oncoming night. This airy dwelling was built in the Syrian style. Supported by a forest of small, slender columns, it traced across the sky the silhouette of its turrets and cedar pavilions, covered with magnificent wainscotting. The open doors revealed purple curtains from Tyre, silken divans woven in India, rose-windows inlaid with coloured stones, citron-tree and sandalwood furniture, Thebaic vessels and vases, basins in porphyry or lapis lazuli laden with flowers, silver tripods fuming with aloes, myrrh and benjamin, lianas that hugged the pillars and gambolled across the walls. The whole of this charming abode might well be reserved for love, but Balkis was prudent and wise; her reason strengthened her against the enchanted and alluring dwelling of Millo.

'I confess I look at this little palace now with a certain reserve,' Soliman said. 'Honoured by your presence, it appears somewhat shabby. The villas of the Hamathites are more opulent, no doubt.'

'More opulent? . . . no, but in our country even the smallest and most fragile columns, the meticulous mouldings, the statuettes and notched bell-towers are all made of marble. We execute in stone what you cut out only in wood. Our ancestors did not depend on frivolous fantasies for their glory; they accomplished a work which will make their memory eternally blessed.'

'Tell me about this work; the account of lofty undertakings exalts our thoughts.'

'First, I must admit that the prosperous and fertile region of the Yemen was formerly arid and sterile. The heavens endowed it with neither rivers nor streams. My forefathers triumphed over nature and created an Eden in the midst of a desert.'

'And how did they accomplish this?' Soliman asked attentively.

'In the heart of the high mountain ranges, rising up in the east of my dominions, on whose slope the city of Mareb stands, brooks meandered here and there, streams evaporated in the air or disappeared into the chasms in the depths of the valley before they could ever reach the plains. Working for two centuries, our ancient kings were able to direct all these fruitless water courses towards a wide plateau where they excavated the basin of a lake. We sail upon it today as if it were a sheltered bay. They had to cut into mountains buttressed by granite slabs higher than the pyramids of Giza and supported, in their turn, by cyclopean vaults. Armies of horsemen and elephants can manoeuvre upon them easily enough today. From this immense and inexhaustible reservoir silver cascades shoot forth into aqueducts, into large canals which are subdivided into several reaches and thereby carry the waters across the plain and irrigate half of our dominions. To this amazing work I owe our abundant agriculture, our flourishing industries, our numerous meadows, our age-old trees and our deep forests, all of which contribute to the wealth and charm of the sweet country of Yemen. That, lord, is our sea of bronze, though I by no means undervalue yours, for it is an excellent contrivance.'

'What a noble conception indeed!' Soliman exclaimed, 'and how proud I would be to copy it, if God, in his mercy, had not offered us the plenteous and blessed waters of the Jordan.'

'I remember fording it yesterday,' Balkis remarked, 'why, the waters almost reached up to . . . my camel's knees.'

'It is dangerous to overturn the order of nature,' the sage declared, 'and create, in spite of Jehovah, an artificial civilization with its commerce and industries. For how long, after all, will these works of man last? Your population is at their mercy. Our Judea is arid, but it has no more inhabitants than it can feed, and they depend upon the regular produce of the soil and the climate alone. Should your lake, that basin chiselled in the mountains, disintegrate, should those cyclopean constructions collapse, then indeed you will face calamity. Your people, robbed of water, will shrivel to death in the sun, they will be decimated by famine in the midst of those artificial plains.' Impressed by the apparent profundity of this observation, Balkis grew thoughtful.

'Already,' the king pursued, 'already I am certain of what I say. The tributary streams of the mountain hollow out ravines and struggle to break loose from their stone prisons, that is the nature of things. Bear in mind, too, that earthquakes occur, that time uproots rocks, that water infiltrates and glides away like a grass snake. Moreover, it would be impossible to repair your magnificent reservoir which you managed to construct in arid ground, for it holds such a huge amount of water. O queen! your ancestors have reserved for your people a future which depends upon a stone structure. Barrenness would have made them industrious; as it is, they have taken advantage of the very ground on which they will perish, idle and dismayed, with the first leaves of the trees on the day the canals no longer revive their roots. One should not tempt God or correct his works. What He does is good.'

'That maxim,' Balkis retorted, 'originates in your religion which is enfeebled by the over-cautious doctrines of the priests. They lead to utter stagnation, they keep society in swaddling-clothes and hold human independence in check. Did God plough and sow the fields? Did God found cities and build palaces? Did God put iron into our hands, gold, copper, and all those metals which glitter in Soliman's temple? No! He has communicated genius and activity to His creatures. He may smile at our efforts, but in our limited creations He recognizes the light of His own soul with which He has illuminated ours. Believing that God is jealous, you question His omnipotence, you deify your faculties and disparage His. O king! the prejudices of your cult will ultimately impede the progress of the sciences and the impetus of genius. And when men are turned into dwarfs, they will reduce God to their size and end by denying His existence.'

'Subtle,' Soliman said with a bitter smile, 'subtle but specious. . . .'

'But I hear you sigh,' said Balkis, 'I hear you sigh when my finger touches your secret wound. You are alone in this kingdom and you suffer. Your own views are noble, audacious, but the hierarchic organization of this nation weighs heavily upon your shoulders. You tell yourself only too exactly : I shall leave posterity the statue of a king who was too great for such a little people ! As far as my nation is concerned, it is quite the contrary. My forefathers kept themselves in the background in order to exalt their subjects. Thirty-eight monarchs in succession have reinforced the lake and the aqueducts of Mareb with stone. Future generations will forget their names, but this work will continue to glorify the Sabeans, and should it ever collapse, should the greedy earth reclaim her streams and rivers, then our native soil, which has been fertilized by a thousand years of cultivation, will still produce the tall trees which shade our plains, they will retain moisture, maintain coolness, protect pools, springs, and the Yemen, the Yemen which long ago subdued the desert, will guard to the end of time the sweet name of Blessed Arabia. If you had only been freer, lord, you would have contributed much more to the glory of your people and to the happiness of men.'

'You summon my soul to such aspirations . . . alas ! it is too late. My people are rich; conquest or gold procures them what Judea itself fails to provide, and as for timber, I have been prudent enough to conclude an agreement with the king of Tyre; my timber-yards are stocked with cedar and pine-wood from Lebanon, and our ships at sea compete with those of the Phoenicians.'

'You seek for consolation from your grandeur in the paternal solicitude of your administration,' the queen said with touching sadness. A long moment of silence ensued. The dark shadows concealed the emotions stamped on Soliman's features. Then he murmured softly :

'My soul has passed into yours and my heart follows in its wake.'

Confused, Balkis glanced furtively in all directions, but she could no longer see a single courtier. Over the heads of the monarchs, the stars shone through the foliage, sprinkling golden flowers upon it; laden with the scent of lilies, tuberoses, wistarias and mandragoras, the night breeze sang in the tufted boughs of the myrtle-trees; the flowers whispered their fragrance; the breath of the wind rocked with perfume; pigeons cooed in the distance; the sound of the waters counterpointed this concert, while gleaming flies and blazing butterflies shot like green rays through the warm air which grew charged with voluptuous emotions. Balkis felt herself overcome by an intoxicating languor. Soliman's tender voice had pierced her heart and it continued to enchant her with its echo.

Did Soliman please her, or was she merely dreaming it was so, as if she already loved him? Having rendered him modest, she had grown interested in him. But mingled with gentle pity and taking the place of a woman's victory, this sympathy, born in the calm of reason, was neither animated nor spontaneous. Mistress of herself, as she had been mistress of her host's thoughts and feelings, she approached love — if in fact she really thought of it — through friendship, and that indeed is the longest route!

As for Soliman, captivated, dazzled, swaying between resentment and admiration, discouragement and hope, anger and desire, he had already been wounded more than once; moreover, when a man loves too soon, he risks loving alone.

The queen of Saba was reserved and cautious. Everybody, including the magnificent Soliman, had all the time been dominated by her influence. The sculptor Adoniram, however, was the only one who had momentarily commanded her attention, in him she had glimpsed a mystery which she could not fathom; but keen as it had been, her curiosity had no doubt disappeared by now. Nevertheless, at the sight of him this strong-minded woman had said to herself for the first time : Here indeed is a man! It is conceivable, then, that owing to this forgotten, though recent, vision, she was less swayed than she might otherwise have been by king Soliman's prestige; this was proved, in fact, more than once, for whenever she prepared to speak about the artist she hesitated and chose another topic.

Be that as it may, the son of Daoud was immediately inflamed. This was the effect she had on everybody, as he had already told her. Soliman, however, knew how to express himself most gracefully; the moment was favourable now, he realized, Balkis was mature enough to love, and thanks to the atmosphere and surroundings she was curious, and softened by affection. . . .

Torches suddenly projected their red beams on to the bushes to announce supper. What an inopportune interruption! the king thought.

What an appropriate distraction! the queen thought.

The banquet had been prepared in a pavilion built in the lively and whimsical style of the people who dwell on the banks of the Ganges. The octagonal hall was illuminated by coloured tapers and lamps burning with perfume-mingled naphtha, the shaded light darted here and there among bouquets of flowers. When they arrived at the threshold Soliman offered queen Balkis his hand, for the hall was covered by a sheet of water which reflected every detail of the tables, divans and candles.

'But why do you hesitate?' the king asked his guest in surprise. To show how fearless she was, Balkis lifted her gown with a charming movement and courageously plunged into the water . . . but her foot encountered a solid surface!

'O queen,' said the sage, 'now you understand that even the most prudent make mistakes by judging on appearances alone. I wished to startle you and I have at last succeeded . . . you are walking on a floor of the purest crystal.' Balkis smiled and shrugged her shoulders more gracefully than admiringly, regretting, perhaps, that different means had not been devised to startle her.

The king was courteous and attentive during the banquet; he presided over the courtiers around him with such incomparable majesty that the queen was overcome by respect. Strict and ceremonial etiquette was observed at Soliman's table.

The dishes were exquisite and varied, but all were heavily salted and spiced. Never having seen so much salt, Balkis assumed that the Hebrews must have a particular taste for it. She was all the more amazed, then, to notice that these people who braved such stinging condiments abstained from drinking. Not a single cup-bearer in sight, not a drop of wine or mead, and the table itself was bare of goblets. The queen's lips were burning, her palate was parched, but since the king did not drink, she dared not ask for any refreshment herself, for Soliman's dignity held her in awe.

When the meal was over the courtiers gradually dispersed and disappeared into the recesses of a dimly lit gallery. The beautiful queen of the Sabeans soon found herself alone with Soliman, who was now more courteous than ever; his eyes were tender and affectionate, though his polite attentions grew almost pressing. Smiling and lowering her eyes to overcome her embarrassment, the queen rose and announced that she was ready to withdraw.

'What !' Soliman exclaimed, 'you will leave your humble slave like this, without a word, without a hope, without a pledge of your compassion? This union I've dreamed of, this happiness I crave, this ardent and submissive love which begs for a reward — will you trample all beneath your feet?'

He seized hold of her hand, which she surrendered to him and then removed without a struggle, although Soliman was tempted to prevent her. Balkis had thought of this alliance more than once herself, but she wished to retain her liberty and power. She insisted therefore on withdrawing, and Soliman realized that he would be obliged to yield.

'So be it,' he said, 'take leave of me, but here are two conditions before I permit you to retire.'

'I am listening,' Balkis replied.

'The night is enchanting, indeed, but your voice is even more enchanting. You will surely grant me an hour of conversation.'

'Granted,' Balkis agreed.

'Second condition : when you leave this hall, you will not take away with you anything that belongs to me.'

'I agree with all my heart!' Balkis replied, bursting into laughter.

'Laugh! my queen, but the richest people have been known to give way to the most trivial temptations.'

'Admirable! How ingeniously you preserve your self-respect. No feints, then, but a treaty.'

'No treaty, but a truce, for I still have hopes,' the king retorted.

They resumed conversation, and in a lordly manner, Soliman persistently encouraged the queen to speak. A jet of water at the end of the hall babbled an accompaniment to her voice.

Now, if one can ever speak too much at night, assuredly it is after having eaten without a drink every dish of a highly spiced supper which nothing but courtesy has obliged one to endure. The lovely queen of Saba was dying of thirst; she would have surrendered one of her provinces for a patera of fresh water, but still she did not dare give way to her overwhelming desire. And the fountain, clear, fresh, silver and bantering, did not cease its patter, casting up its pearls, which fell back into the basin with a merry ring. Soon the queen could no longer support the pain of her thirst. She continued speaking, but, seeing that Soliman appeared inattentive, even weary, she started walking around the hall and more than once she passed, panting, close to the fountain . . . but still she did not dare. Her thirst grew intolerable, and, walking more slowly, she returned to the fountain. She mustered her courage, hollowed her pretty hand and plunged it into the basin, then, turning round, she quickly swallowed this mouthful of pure water.

Soliman rises, approaches, takes hold of the queen's shining wet hand: 'A queen keeps to her promise,' he said in a playful but resolute voice, 'and according to yours, you now belong to me.'

'What do you mean?' Balkis asked in astonishment.

'You have pilfered my water, and, as you judiciously remarked yourself, water is extremely scarce in my dominions.'

'Ah! lord, that is a snare, and I certainly do not wish to have such a crafty husband!'

'Then it only remains for him to prove that he is in fact more generous than crafty. If he restores you to your liberty, if, despite this formal commitment. . . .'

'Lord,' Balkis interrupted, lowering her head, 'it is our duty to set our subjects an example of loyalty.'

'Lady,' Soliman replied, falling to his knees, 'the most courteous prince of past and future ages may surely consider those words a pledge.' He rose quickly to his feet and rang a bell. Twenty servants, accompanied by courtiers, hurried into the hall carrying a variety of refreshing drinks. Majestically, Soliman pronounced the following words:

'Step forth and serve your queen!'

The courtiers at once fell prostrate before the queen of Saba and worshipped her. But, palpitating and confused, Balkis was afraid of finding herself committed before she had reached her own decision.

During the pause which followed this part of the tale an odd enough incident diverted the audience. A young Abyssinian rushed forward into the middle of the circle and started dancing a sort of *bamboula* and singing a song in faulty Arabic, stressing those repetitions of drawn-out syllables which are a speciality of Arabs from the South. I can remember only the refrain, which was quite a volley of words :

Yaman! Yaman! Yamani! ... Salem-Aleik Belkiss-Makayda! ... Yaman! Yaman! Yamani! (Yemen! O country of Yemen! Greetings to thee, most noble Balkis! Yemen! O country of Yemen!)'

This sudden note of nostalgia could be explained only by the intimacy which formerly existed between the Sabeans and the Abyssinians, who, dwelling on the western shore of the Red Sea, also formed part of the Hamathite empire. The enthusiasm of this listener, who had been silent until then, no doubt sprang from the recital of the last part of the tale which was traditional in his country. Perhaps he was happy, too, to learn that the noble queen had been able to escape from the snare set by the wise king Soliman.

This song grew monotonous, however, and annoyed the customers. Some of them shouted that he was mad and they gently pulled him towards the door. Anxious to claim the five or six paras (six centimes) owed to him, the proprietor hurried outside to pursue the poor fellow. But we did not have to wait too long before a reverential silence was restored, and the storyteller continued then as follows.

5   The Sea of Bronze

Working ceaselessly day and night, master Adoniram had completed his models and hollowed out in the sand the moulds for his colossal figures. Deeply excavated and skilfully bored, the plateau of Zion was marked now by the impression of the sea of bronze, destined to be cast on the spot. Its banks were already firmly buttressed by stonework, which Adoniram's lions and gigantic sphinxes would eventually

replace. Dispersed here and there were bars of solid gold, for it defies
fusion with bronze; they served as the supporting underlayer for the
mould of this enormous basin. The casting liquid would run through
several trenches into the empty space between the two planes and
thereby confine these golden pegs, encompass these precious, refrac-
tory landmarks.

Seven times had the sun turned round the earth since the ore had
started boiling in the furnace, covered by a massive, high brick tower,
topped, sixty cubits above ground-level, by an open cone-shaped
construction from which poured forth whirlwinds of red smoke and
blue flames spangled with sparks. An excavation, contrived between
the moulds and the bank of the furnace, would serve as a bed for the
river of fire when the moment came to open the bowels of the volcano
with iron bars.

The crucial task of releasing the ore was scheduled for night, when
the operation could be carefully observed and followed with attention; the luminous, white bronze would light up its own course, and
if the brilliant metal prepared a trap, leaked through a crack or bored
a mine in one spot or another, it would then be revealed by the
shadows.

The whole of Jerusalem's population quaked with anticipation as
they waited for the solemn ordeal which would immortalize or dis-
credit the name of Adoniram. Abandoning their activities, the workmen had hastened from every corner of the realm towards the major
site, and, as the sun set on the evening prior to the fateful night, the
surrounding hills and mountains were covered by avidly curious
onlookers.

Acting independently and in spite of all impediments, no founder
had ever confronted so formidable a challenge. The casting apparatus
aroused everybody's interest; when important pieces were being
moulded, king Soliman himself had often deigned to pass the night
at the forges, attended by courtiers who wrangled for the honour of
accompanying him. Now, the casting of the sea of bronze was a
gigantic undertaking. A single genius defied human prejudice, nature,
and the opinions of the greatest experts all of whom had declared
that success was impossible.

Thus it was that people of every age and from every country were
drawn to the scene of this contest and early invaded the hill of Zion
whose main approaches were guarded by armies of workmen. Silent
patrols surveyed the crowd to maintain discipline and prevent noise;
this was hardly a difficult job, however, for on the king's instructions,
a horn had been blown to command the most absolute silence. Whoever disobeyed would be put to death : an indispensable precaution
to guarantee the orders being transmitted with certitude and alacrity.

The evening star was already sinking over the sea; cushioned with red clouds from the furnace, the dark night announced that the moment was at hand. Followed by the chief workmen, who carried torches, Adoniram checked the preparations for the last time, darting from one spot to another. In the huge shed, close to the furnace, the blacksmiths could be made out, wearing leather helmets with wide turn-down brims and dressed in long white gowns with short sleeves. They used long hooks to pull out from the gaping mouth of the furnace half vitrified, clammy lumps of scum, scoria, which they dragged far away from the site, while others, at the very top of the construction, perched on platforms supported by massive framework, flung in baskets of coal which roared in the violent breath of the ventilators. On all sides, swarms of journeymen moved around with pickaxes, stakes and tongs, casting long, shadowy trails behind them. They were nearly nude, wearing striped sashes round their waists, while their heads were wrapped in woollen hoods and their legs protected by wooden leglets and leather thongs. Although black from coal dust, many of them stood out vividly red, like demons or phantoms, in the glow of the live coals.

A sudden fanfare announced the arrival of the court. Soliman approached with the queen of Saba to be welcomed by Adoniram, who led them to a special throne built for his noble visitors. The artist had buckled on a buff leather breastplate; a white woollen apron reached down to his knees; his muscular legs were protected by tiger-skin gaiters, but his feet were bare, for he alone could tread upon the burning metal with impunity.

'You stand before me in all your power, like the god of fire,' Balkis said to the king of the workmen. 'If your enterprise succeeds, no one tonight will be able to consider himself greater than master Adoniram!' Despite his preoccupations, the artist was about to reply, when Soliman, always wise and sometimes jealous, prevented him.

'Master,' he said in an imperious manner, 'do not waste precious time. Return to your work, lest we be held responsible for any accident which might occur owing to your presence here.' The queen made a quick, almost imperceptible bow to Adoniram before he disappeared.

If he accomplishes his task, Soliman reflected, he will indeed honour the temple of Adonai with a magnificent monument . . . but he will also increase his own tremendous influence!

A few moments afterwards the monarchs saw Adoniram in front of the furnace. Standing in the glow of the burning coals, he grew in stature and his shadow scaled the wall to which a solid sheet of bronze was hooked. The master sounded twenty blows upon it with an iron hammer, the vibrations travelled far and the silence grew even more profound than before.

Suddenly, armed with levers and pickaxes, ten phantom shapes jumped into the excavation contrived below the furnace grate, which was opposite the nearby throne. The hiss of the bellows died down to be replaced by nothing but the muffled noise of the iron points piercing the calcined clay which luted the aperture through which the liquid metal would soon shoot forth. This part of the excavation grew violet, turned from purple to crimson, then grew red, shone with a brighter light and finally grew orange. A white spot appeared in the centre, and all but two of the workmen withdrew. Under the anxious eye of master Adoniram, the latter carefully hacked away the crust around the luminous spot without making a hole in it.

During this initial phase of the operation, Adoniram's faithful companion, the young Benoni who was so deeply devoted to him, went among the groups of workmen, testing the zeal of each one, checking that the orders were carried out and reaching his own conclusions about everything he examined.

All of a sudden Benoni rushed towards Soliman in terror and threw himself at the king's feet :

'Lord !' he gasped, 'postpone the casting . . . all is lost . . . we have been betrayed ! . . .'

It was strictly contrary to custom that anyone should approach the prince in such a manner, lacking any authorization at all, and the guards were already advancing upon this reckless young individual, but Soliman raised his hand as a signal for them to withdraw. Leaning towards the prostrate Benoni, he said to him quietly :

'Explain what has happened.'

'I was inspecting the site. . . . I saw a man behind the wall, looking around impatiently. Another arrived. "Nehmamiah !" he said in a low voice. "Eliael !" the first replied. A third arrived and he too pronounced "Nehmamiah !" The first replied as before with "Eliael !" and then exclaimed :

' "He has subjected the carpenters to the miners."

'The second : "He has subordinated the masons to the miners."

'The third : "He wanted to rule over the miners."

'The first resumed : "He gives authority to foreigners."

'The second : "He has no country of his own."

'The third added : "There is truth in that."

'The first resumed : "The journeymen are brothers. . . ."

'The second followed up his words with : ". . . And the guilds have equal rights."

'The third concluded : "There is truth in that." I realized,' Benoni continued, 'that the first was a mason, because next he said : "I have mixed limestone into the bricks and it will crumble into powder." The second was a carpenter, for he said : "I have lengthened the cross-pieces of the beams so that the flames will reach them." As for the third, he is evidently a metal-worker : "I took bituminous and sulphurous lava," he declared, "from the poisonous lake of Gomorrah and I mixed them into the casting liquid."

'A shower of sparks suddenly lit up their faces. The mason is a Syrian, his name is Phanor; the carpenter is a Phoenician, his name is Amrou; the miner is a Hebrew from the tribe of Ruben, his name is Methuselah. Great king, I have thrown myself here at your feet . . . stretch out your sceptre and stop the operation !'

'It is too late,' Soliman replied thoughtfully. 'Look, the crater is already opening. Keep silent, for you must not disturb Adoniram . . . and those three names, repeat them to me.'

'Phanor, Amrou, and Methuselah.'

'May God's will be done !'

Benoni stared fixedly at the king, then disappeared at the speed of lightning.

The terra-cotta was falling now, under the miners' repeated blows, around the muzzled mouth of the furnace, while the thin layer grew so luminous that it appeared ready to surprise and replace the sun which had already withdrawn for the night. At a sign from Adoniram, the workmen stepped aside, and, as the hammers resounded upon the bronze, the master lifted high an iron club and brought it down right through the diaphanous surface lining; he twisted it round in the wound, then violently wrenched it out. A white liquid torrent immediately shot into the canal and rushed onwards, like a golden serpent streaked with crystal and silver, up to a basin hollowed in the sand, at the outlet of which the liquid dispersed and pursued its course along several trenches.

Then a purple and blood red light shone upon the faces of the innumerable spectators on the hills and its gleams penetrated the obscurity of the shadows and reddened the ridge of the distant rocks. Jerusalem emerged out of the darkness, as though it were prey to a conflagration, while the profound silence added to this solemn spectacle the fantastic dimensions of a dream.

But as the torrent rushes onward, Adoniram glimpses a shadow fluttering around the bed which the liquid is about to invade. A man has leaped forward and, in total defiance of the master's orders, ventures to cross over this canal which is reserved for the fire. No sooner has he made his first step than the metal fusion hits him and topples him over; he disappears at once within the torrent. With eyes only for his work, Adoniram is confounded by the prospect of an imminent explosion, but he hesitates for a second, wondering whether the corpse will do no more than impede the operation for awhile by blocking the entrance to the bed . . . no! the torrent is too powerful . . . the banks would overflow at the very least . . . catastrophe is inevitable unless. . . . Risking his own life, Adoniram rushes forward now, armed with a long iron hook; he spots the bulge of the rash intruder and thrusts the hook deep into his breast; quickly and deftly he twists it round to fix it tightly in place, then hauls out the victim and with superhuman power hurls him like a lump of scoria far away on to the opposite bank where this luminous body soon dies down. And Adoniram has not had time to recognize his eternally faithful friend, Benoni.

While the streaming torrent went on its way, filling up the cavities in the sea of bronze whose vast outline was already traced out like a golden diadem upon the dark ground, swarms of workmen carrying big fire-pots, deep ladles with long iron shanks for handles, plunged them by turns into the basin of the liquid fire and, running here and there, poured the metal into the moulds reserved for the lions, oxen, palm-trees, cherubim and gigantic figures which will bolster the sea of bronze. What an abundance of fire the earth imbibes! Inclined upon the ground, the bas-reliefs retrace the distinct, vermilion silhouettes of the horses, winged bulls, cynocephali and monstrous chimeras engendered by Adoniram's brain.

'O sublime spectacle!' the queen of Saba cried. 'O the grandeur! the omnipotent genius of this mortal who subdues the elements and masters nature!'

'He has not conquered yet,' Soliman retorted bitterly. 'Adonai alone is almighty.'

And it is now that Adoniram sees the river of metal overflowing its banks. The gaping source pours out torrents and the sand collapses under the excessive load. Glancing at the sea of bronze, he sees the mould debouching, too; a crack rents open the summit and lava streams down from every side. The air is convulsed by Adoniram's dreadful cry and the mountains shudder at its echo. Convinced that the over-heated earth is vitrifying, he seizes a hose near a reservoir and directs a tremendous volley of water at the base of the tottering buttresses of the basin mould. But the running metal has gained the initiative and rushes on even down to there; the two liquids collide and lock together in a deadly struggle. A mass of metal hems in the water, gripping it into a prison. To free itself, the water vaporizes and does indeed break loose from its fetters with a resounding detonation! The river of metal spurts up twenty cubits above ground-level, a blinding shower of sparks which looks like the erupting crater of a raging volcano. And the blast is followed by lamentation and fearful howls, for this rain of stars sows death wherever it falls; every drop of liquid is a scorching dart which pierces the flesh and kills. The entire area is strewn with the dying and the dead, and an overwhelming cry of horror and dismay replaces the former reverential silence. As the terror reaches its climax, everyone flees; the very fear of danger hurls into the fire the ones whom the fire pursues. Illuminated, resplendent and crimson, the countryside re-evokes that dreadful night when Sodom and Gomorrah blazed beneath Jehovah's lightning. The distracted Adoniram runs here and there to rally his workmen to close the aperture of the inexhaustible abyss, but all he meets with is wailing and cursing; everyone has scattered to safety, while those he does encounter are already corpses.

Only the monarchs have not moved : Soliman remains impassive upon the throne with the queen sitting calmly beside him.

'Jehovah has chastised him,' Soliman says to his guest, 'and he has punished me by the death of my subjects for my weakness, my complacency, and my monstrous pride.'

'Adoniram's vanity is criminal,' the queen declares, 'for it has caused an appalling sacrifice. Lord, you could have perished during this infernal ordeal, for the bronze was falling around us.'

'And you! . . . you were here. And this vile agent of Baal has endangered so precious a life! Forgive me! I did not think . . . the spectacle overwhelmed me . . . come, my queen, let us depart at once. The danger is not over yet, but you shall no longer be exposed to it.'

Adoniram overheard these words, for he was passing by close to the monarchs as they descended from the throne. Blushing with pain and sorrow, he withdrew. He espied a group of workmen in the distance and heard them hurling reproaches and curses upon him. The Syrian Phanor, however, came up to him and said :

'You are great. Fortune has betrayed you, but she did not have the masons for accomplices.'

Amrou the Phoenician came up to him and said in his turn :

'You are great. You would have conquered if all had done their duty like the carpenters.'

And the Hebrew Methuselah said to him :

'The miners did their duty, but many foreign workmen jeopardized the enterprise through their ignorance. Courage! an even greater work will revenge us for this defeat.'

These three, Adoniram thought, are the only friends whom I have found.

It was easy for him to avoid further encounters, for everyone turned away from him, and the darkness shielded their desertion. Soon the gleams of the braziers and the river of metal, which reddened as its surface cooled down, no longer lit up any but faraway groups which gradually vanished in the shadows. Downcast, Adoniram searched in vain for Benoni.

'You, too,' he murmured sadly, 'you have abandoned me. . . . O Benoni!' And the master remained alone beside the furnace.

'Dishonoured!' he exclaimed aloud and bitterly. 'Dishonour, that is the fruit of an austere and laborious life which I dedicated to an ungrateful prince! He condemns me, my fellows disown me, and the queen, she was there, alas! she saw my disgrace and I had to suffer her contempt! . . . But where, O where is Benoni in the hour of my affliction! Alone! I am alone and accursed. The future is closed to you, Adoniram, but smile, smile at your own deliverance and seek for it in this fire, your element and your rebellious slave!'

Calm and resolute, he approached the river which still rolled forward its waves of molten metal and burning scoria, spouting and crackling here and there as it came in contact with moisture. The lava was leaping over many a corpse. Heavy whirlwinds of tawny, violet smoke broke loose in serried columns, veiling the deserted stage of this woeful adventure. And here it was that this vanquished giant collapsed upon the ground, fixing his eyes upon those blazing whirlwinds which could lean over and suffocate him at the first breath of the wind.

6 The Apparition

Certain weird, fugitive, and scintillating shapes appeared now and then amidst the dazzling but dismal frolics of the fiery vapour. Through gigantic limbs and blocks of gold, Adoniram's astonished eyes glimpsed gnomes who disappeared in smoke or disintegrated into sparks. These fantasies, however, did not help at all to alleviate his sorrow and despair, but soon they succeeded in driving his imagination towards delirium until he was almost sure that he heard a solemn and sonorous voice rising from the heart of the flames and pronouncing his name. There was nobody around him. He watched the flaming peat attentively and murmured eagerly:

'The voice of the people summons me!'

He rose up on to one knee, stretched forth his hand, and perceived in the middle of the red smoke a blurred but colossal form which seemed to grow bulkier in the flames, assemble, then separate and fade away. Everything stirred and flared around it, but this particular form settled, obscure in the luminous fumes then bright and distinct in a whirlwind of soot. Soon it stood out in sharp relief and grew even bigger as it approached Adoniram who, almost terror-stricken, wondered what this bronze could be which was endowed with life. The phantom advanced. Adoniram looked at it in amazement now. Its gigantic bust was covered by a sleeveless dalmatic; its bare arms were adorned with iron rings, and it carried a hammer in its hand. Framed by a square beard, plaited and curled into several strands, its bronze head was crowned by a vermilion mitre. Its large shining eyes looked down sweetly upon Adoniram.

'Rouse your soul,' it declared in a voice wrested from the very bowels of the bronze. 'I have seen the misfortunes of my race and I have been moved to compassion. Come, my son, follow me.'

'Spirit . . . who are you?'

'I am the shade of your forefathers' father, the grandsire of those who work and suffer. Come . . . when my hand has touched your forehead you will be able to breathe in the flames. Be as fearless as you were resolute.'

Adoniram suddenly felt himself enveloped by an acute, invigorating heat which did not harm him at all. The air he breathed was purer, and an invincible force drew him towards the brazier into which his mysterious companion had already plunged.

'Where am I? What is your name? Where are you taking me? . . .'

'To the centre of the earth, to the soul of the inhabited world. There stands the subterranean palace of Enoch our father, whom Egypt calls Hermes, whom Arabia honours with the name of Edris.'

'By the immortal powers!' Adoniram exclaimed. 'O my lord! is it true that you are. . . .'

'Your ancestor, O mortal artist, Adoniram, your master and patron . . . I was Tubal-Cain!'

The further they advanced, however, into the depths of silence and night, the more Adoniram questioned himself and the reality of his impressions. Gradually, though, as he turned his attention away from himself, he succumbed to the charm of the unknown, while his soul, firmly linked to the power that ruled him, followed its mysterious guide without any hesitation.

From regions which were cold and damp they moved into a mild and rarefied atmosphere. Tremors and peculiar humming sounds came from the interior life of the earth; steady, muffled, periodic throbbing announced the proximity of the heart of the world. Adoniram felt the growing power of its beat and he was amazed to find himself wandering among infinite spaces; he searched for a support, a rail, but he failed to find one, and, scarcely able to see it, he continued to follow the silent shade of Tubal-Cain.

After some moments, which seemed as long as a patriarch's life to him, Adoniram perceived a luminous point in the distance. This spot rapidly increased in size and grew distinct as it expanded in long perspective; there the artist glimpsed a world peopled with bustling shades engaged in occupations which he did not understand. These ambiguous lights soon died down, however, under the brilliant mitre and the dalmatic of the son of Cain.

Adoniram strove in vain to speak, his voice was stifled in his almost empty lungs; but he recovered his breath when he found himself in a huge gallery of incomparable depth; it was also exceptionally wide, for it was impossible to see the walls, and it was supported by an avenue of columns which were so high that, looking up, he lost sight of them as he did of the vault which they, in turn, supported. Suddenly he trembled as Tubal-Cain addressed him :

'Your feet are treading now upon the great emerald which serves as root and pivot for the mountain of Kaf. You have arrived at the domain of your fathers, where the offspring of Cain reign supreme. Under these granite fortresses, in the midst of these inaccessible caverns, we have at last found our liberty. Here, Adonai's jealous tyranny expires; here, without danger of death, we can nourish ourselves on the fruits of the Tree of Knowledge.' Adoniram gave vent to a long and peaceful sigh. He knew that an overwhelming load had weighed him down throughout his life, and that now, for the very first time, it had been removed from his shoulders.

There was a sudden burst of life. Through the hypogea huge crowds appeared; their work animated and excited them; the joyful din of metals reverberated, while sounds of gushing water mingled with the noise of boisterous winds. The illuminated vault stretched out like an immense sky, shooting down upon the largest and strangest of workshops torrents of an azure dappled white light which assumed all the colours of the rainbow as it reached the ground. Adoniram moved among a crowd whose busy occupations still puzzled him. Astonished by this brightness, by this celestial cupola in the bowels of the earth, he came to a halt.

'This is the sanctuary of fire,' Tubal-Cain explained to him. 'The earth's heat originates here, and without us, the earth would perish from cold. We prepare the metals and distribute them into the veins of the planet when we have liquefied their vapours. As they intermingle above our heads, the lodes of the various elements release contrasting spirits which ignite and project these fiery lights, which are too dazzling for your deficient sight. Drawn by these currents, the seven metals vaporize in the immediate environs to form those clouds of sinope, azure, purple, gold, vermilion and silver which circulate in space and reproduce the alloys found in the majority of precious stones and minerals. When the cupola cools, these condensed clouds pour down a shower of rubies, emeralds, topazes, onyxes, turquoises and diamonds, then the earth's currents carry them along with a mass of scoria which turns into granite, flint and limestone, heaving up the surface of the globe to emboss it with mountains. This matter solidifies as it approaches the domain of man and Adonai's cold sun . . . that makeshift stove which couldn't even fry an egg if it weren't for us! What would man's life be like, then, if we did not secretly deliver him the element of fire which is imprisoned in the stones like iron ready to break forth into sparks?' Although he understood these explanations, Adoniram nevertheless remained astonished. He approached the workmen . . . how could they work at these rivers of gold, silver, copper and iron, separating them, damming them, and filtering them like water?

'These elements,' said Tubal-Cain, divining his thoughts, 'are liquefied by the central heat. The temperature here is almost twice as great as that of your smelting furnaces.' Wondering how he was able to remain alive, Adoniram looked at him in amazement.

'This heat,' Tubal-Cain continued, 'is the natural temperature of souls which originate in the element of fire. Adonai placed an imperceptible spark in the centre of the mould of earth from which he ventured to make man, and this particle sufficed to heat the block, to animate it and give it consciousness, but, up above, this soul struggles against the cold, hence the narrow limits of your faculties. In time, the spark is drawn towards its central source and attraction . . . and you die.' Adoniram responded with disdain to Adonai's method of creation.

'Yes,' his guide continued, 'as a god, Adonai is subtle rather than strong, more jealous than generous. He created man from mud and ignored the genii of fire; then, alarmed by his work and by their compassion for this sad creature, he condemned men to die, turning a deaf ear to the sound of their tears. There you have the main dispute which divides us. All terrestrial life which originates in fire is drawn towards this fire burning in the centre. We had hoped that, in turn, the central fire would be attracted by the circumference and radiate outside, for this two-way interaction of the elements would lead to immortal life. But Adonai, who reigns about the worlds, walled in the earth and intercepted this exterior attraction. As a result, the earth itself will die like its inhabitants. Already it ages. The cold affects it more and more. Entire species of animals and plants have disappeared, races diminish, the duration of individual life shortens, and the earth, whose marrow congeals and withers, now receives no more than five of the seven original metals. The sun grows pale, it will expire in five or six thousand years. . . . But it is not for me alone, O my son, to reveal these mysteries to you. Come, there is more for you to learn, come and listen to others who are also numbered among your ancestors.'

7 The Subterranean Kingdom

The two of them entered a garden illuminated by the gentle gleams of a pleasant fire and thronged with unknown trees whose foliage, formed by little tongues of flame, projected, instead of shadows, livelier lights upon the emerald ground which was dappled with strangely shaped and vivaciously coloured flowers. Blossoms of the fire deep in the earth of metals, these flowers were their purest and most fluid emanations. This arborescent vegetation of flowering metal shone like precious stones and sprayed forth scents of amber, benjamin, frankincense and myrrh. Nearby, streams of naphtha meandered, fertilizing the dragon-trees, the roses of these subterranean regions.

Several giant old men were wandering around, and their stature was proportionate to this robust and exuberant nature. Under a canopy of brilliant light Adoniram perceived a row of colossi; seated one behind the other, they displayed the sacred costumes, the sublime and symmetrical dimensions, and the imposing attitudes of the figures he had glimpsed long ago in the caverns of Lebanon. He recognized the vanished dynasty of Enochia, and he saw again, crouched around them, the cynocephali, the winged lions, the griffins, the smiling and mysterious sphinxes . . . all those doomed species which had been swept away in the waters of the deluge but immortalized by the memory of man. These androgynous slaves supported the massive monumental thrones which were at once docile, inert, but animated nevertheless. As motionless as sleep, the princely sons of Adam appeared to be dreaming and waiting. Reaching the far end of the line, Adoniram moved towards an enormous square stone as white as snow. He was about to place his foot upon this incombustible asbestos rock when Tubal-Cain cried out :

'Stop! . . . we are under the mountain of Serendib — you were going to trample on the tomb of the unknown, the tomb of the earth's first-born. Adam rests beneath that shroud which protects him from the fire. He will not rise again until the very last day of the world. His captive tomb contains our ransom . . . but listen! our father is calling you.'

Rising from a painful crouching position, Cain stood up nude to reveal a superhuman beauty, despite the sadness of his eyes and the pallor of his lips. Coiled around his care-laden forehead, a golden serpent served him as a diadem. How harassed the wanderer still appeared!

'May sleep and death be with you, my son! It is I who am responsible for your suffering, O oppressed and industrious race! Eve was my mother. Eblis, the angel of light, placed within her breast the spark which animates me and which has regenerated my race. Adam, kneaded out of mud, trustee of a captive soul, Adam fed me. A child of the Elohim, I loved this rough-draft image of Adonai and I put to the service of weak and ignorant men the mind of the genii who dwell within me. I nursed my foster-father in his old age and I cradled Abel in his infancy — Abel whom they called my brother. Woe! Woe! Before introducing murder to the world, I had experienced ingratitude, injustice, bitterness, they corrupt the heart. Working ceaselessly, uprooting our food from the miserly earth, inventing for the good of men those ploughs which compel the soil to produce, reviving for them in the midst of this new abundance that Eden which they had lost, I put the whole of my life to sacrifice. But Adam, O Adam loved me not! Eve remembered that she had been banished from Paradise for having given birth to me; she closed her selfish heart against me and opened it to none but Abel. As for him, disdainful and pampered, he looked upon me as a mere household servant. And Adonai was with him, what more did he require! Moreover, while my sweat irrigated the land where he considered himself a king, idle and fondled as he was, he slept beneath the sycamores, leaving his flocks to stray and graze. I complained . . . our parents appealed to God for a decision. We offered up our sacrifices to him, and mine, sheaves of wheat which had blossomed thanks to me, the first-fruits of summer! mine was scornfully rejected. . . . And ever since that day, this jealous God has persisted in thrusting aside any inventive and fruitful genius, and he has handed power, with its right to oppress, to mediocre minds. You know what followed . . . but what you do not know is that Adonai the judge, condemning me to sterility, gave Abel a wife, Aclinia; she was our sister and it was not Abel whom she loved, but me. Herein lies the origin of the first struggle between the jinn, or children of the Elohim, born of fire, and the sons of Adonai, begotten in mud. I extinguished Abel's light. Later, Adam saw himself reborn in Seth's descendants, while I, to atone for my crime, I became the benefactor of the children of Adam. It is to our race which is superior to theirs that they owe all the arts, trades, and principles of the sciences. Worthless effort! for by educating them, we liberated them. Adonai has never forgiven me, and that is why he holds as an unpardonable crime my having broken a vessel of clay, he who drowned multitudes in the waters of the deluge! he who has set up so many tyrants to annihilate men! . . .'

Then the tomb of Adam spoke :

'It is you,' the deep voice uttered, 'it is you who gave birth to murder. God seeks in my children the blood of Eve from which you spring, the very blood which you shed! It is because of you that Jehovah set up priests who have immolated men, and kings who have slaughtered priests and soldiers. The day will dawn when he will create emperors who will crush the people, the priests, and the kings themselves. Then posterity will declare : "These are the sons of Cain !" '

The son of Eve writhed in despair.

'Never !' he exclaimed, 'never has he pardoned me.'

'Never !' the voice replied, and from the depths of the abyss it moaned, 'Abel, my son, Abel ! O what have you done to your brother Abel? . . .' Hurling himself down, Cain beat his fists upon the ground until it echoed, while the convulsions of his sorrow rent his breast. Such is the torment of Cain for having shed blood.

Overcome by respect, love, compassion and horror, Adoniram turned aside.

'And I, what had I done?' the venerable Enoch exclaimed. 'Men rambled around like lost herds. I taught them to carve statues, to construct buildings, to gather in towns. I was the first to teach them the nature and benefits of communal living. I had brought together a mass of brutes, but I left behind a nation in the city which I founded, and the ruins of Enochia still amaze the degenerate races. It is thanks to me that Soliman raises a temple to Adonai, but this temple will cause his downfall, for the God of the Hebrews has recognized my genius, O my son, in the work of your hands.'

Adoniram studied this great shade. He wore a tiara, adorned with red bands and two rows of stars, which rose to a high point shaped like a vulture's beak. Enoch's long beard was plaited; two small, fringed bands hung down his hair and tunic. He held a long sceptre in one hand and a set-square in the other. His colossal stature exceeded that of his father Cain. Close to him were Irad and Mehujael, with small, modest bands around their heads, while rings encircled their arms. The one had long ago confined the fountains, the other had hewed and squared the cedars. And near to them was Methusael who had invented written characters. Edris had since got hold of and mastered the books which he had left behind, and then he had hidden them in the ground . . . the books of *Tau*. Methusael wore a hieratic pall over his shoulders and a short sword dangling from a baldric at his waist; upon his magnificent girdle shone in fiery shafts the symbolic T which rallies the workmen sprung from the genii of fire. While Adoniram turned now to study the smiling features of Lamech whose arms were covered with folded wings from which his elongate hands emerged to rest upon the heads of two young persons seated cross-legged at his feet, Tubal-Cain left his protégé's side and assumed his place upon his throne of iron.

'You are looking at the venerable face of my father,' he said to Adoniram. 'Those whose hair he caresses are the children of Adah : Jabal, who pitched tents and learned to stitch camel hide, and Jubal, his brother, who was the first to pluck the strings of the lyre and the harp and discover how to draw true sounds from them.'

'Son of Lamech and Zillah,' Jubal replied in a voice as melodious as the evening wind, 'you are greater than us, your brothers, and you rule over your ancestors. You gave rise to the arts of war and peace, you subdued and transformed the metals, you lit the very first furnace. By giving gold, silver, copper and iron to human beings, you handed them a substitute for the Tree of Knowledge. Gold and iron will raise them to the utmost peaks of power, a power that shall prove fatal to them, thereby aiding our revenge against Adonai. Honour to Tubal-Cain !'

Clamours of acclamation rose on all sides, repeated further off by the legions of gnomes, who then resumed their work with fresh enthusiasm. The hammers resounded under the vaults of the eternal workshops, and Adoniram, a workman in this world where workmen were kings, was stirred by the deepest joy and pride.

'Child of the race of the Elohim,' Tubal-Cain addressed him, 'muster your courage again, your glory resides in servitude. Thanks to your ancestors, human work and skill inspire apprehension, and for this our race is condemned. For two thousand years it has fought, and Adonai has not been able to destroy us, for we are of immortal essence, but he has been able to conquer us, because the blood of Eve was mingled with our blood. Your ancestors, my descendants, were unharmed by the waters of the deluge, for while Jehovah prepared our destruction as he gathered the waters together in the reservoirs of the sky, I summoned fire to our assistance and precipitated rapid currents towards the surface of the globe. Following my orders, the flames dissolved the stones and hollowed out large galleries suitable for our retreat. These subterranean routes emerged in the plain of

Giza, not far from those banks where the city of Memphis has since been raised. In order to protect these galleries from invasion by the waters, I mustered the race of the giants, and together we erected with our own hands an immense pyramid which will last until the end of the world. Its stones were cemented with impenetrable bitumen and we let in no other opening than a narrow corridor, sealed off by a small door which I built myself on the last day of the ancient world.

'An abyss reached down to subterranean abodes excavated in the rock; they sloped along a low gallery leading to the regions of water which I had confined in a river abundant enough to provide for the men and flocks buried in this retreat. Beyond this river I had gathered together in a vast space lit by the interaction of contrasting metals the vegetable fruits which feed themselves on earth.

'There, in the shelter of the waters, lived the sorry remains of Cain's descendants. All the ordeals we had undergone and overcome . . . we had to undergo them anew in order to behold the light again when the waters had regained their bed. Those routes were perilous and the interior climate deathly. On our way back we lost even more companions than we had during the descent. Finally, I alone survived along with the son whom my sister Naamah had given me.

'I reopened the pyramid and glimpsed the earth. It had changed almost beyond recognition! Desert, rachitic animals, stunted plants, reptiles creeping through heaps of barren mud, while a pale and barely tepid sun mouldered in the sky.

'Suddenly, a glacial wind laden with foul miasmas penetrated my lungs and parched them. Suffocating, I vomited, but I had to inhale again in order not to die. I never learned what cold poison circulated within my veins, but my strength expired, my legs tottered, night surrounded me, and a black shiver wrenched my every limb. Not only the earth but its climate had radically changed, and the cold, damp soil no longer released enough heat to animate what it had formerly imbued with life. Like a dolphin seized from the heart of the sea and cast aside upon the sand, I writhed in agony, and I realized that my hour was upon me. . . . But an overwhelming instinct of self-preservation urged me to flee from that dismal earth with its foul climate, and, struggling back into the pyramid, I there lost consciousness. It was my tomb. My soul, released then and drawn towards the interior fire, returned to find the souls of my fathers.

'As for my son who was not yet an adult, he continued growing up, he was able to live, but he ceased to increase in stature. He became a wanderer . . . such is the fate of our race! and the wife of Ham, second son of Noah, found him more beautiful than the sons of men. He knew her, and she gave birth to Cush, the father of Nimrod who taught his brothers the art of hunting and founded Babylon. They started building the tower of Babel, then Adonai recognized the race of Cain and renewed his persecution against it. The race of Nimrod was scattered in its turn, while . . . but let the voice of my son conclude this mournful story for you.'

Pained and troubled, Adoniram looked around to find the son of Tubal-Cain.

'You cannot see him,' the prince of the genii of fire explained. 'My child's soul is invisible, for he died after the deluge, and his corporal form belongs to the earth. It is the same with his descendants, and your father, Adoniram, wanders through the burning air which you are breathing, yes, your own father.'

'Yes, your father, your father,' repeated the echo of a tender voice which passed by, touching Adoniram's forehead like a kiss.

The artist turned aside and wept.

'Console yourself,' said Tubal-Cain, 'he is happier than me. He left you in the cradle, and as your body does not yet belong to the earth, he enjoys the good fortune of seeing its form. But listen now attentively to the voice of my son.' Then a voice spoke :

'I am the only one among the mortal genii of our race who has seen the world before and after the deluge, and I have looked upon the face of Adonai. I was expecting the birth of a son, but I was harrowed by despair, for the dry, cold north wind of the old earth desiccated my lungs. One night, God appeared before me . . . I cannot describe his face.

' "Hope," he said.

'Inexperienced, isolated in an unknown world, I timidly replied :

' "Lord, I fear. . . ."

' "This fear will be your salvation. You must die, your name will be neglected by your brothers, and future ages will hear no echo of it. You will give birth to a son whom you will not see. He, in turn, will father beings who will be lost among the multitudes like the stars rambling through the firmament. I have humiliated your body, O founder of giants. Your offspring will be weaklings, their lives will be short, and solitude will be their lot. The soul of the genii will nevertheless preserve its precious spark within their breasts, but their very nobility will be their torment. Superior to men, they will be their benefactors, but remain the object of their scorn, and their tombs alone will be honoured. Unrecognized during their days on earth, they will enjoy the bleak awareness of their power while they exert it for the glory of others. Sensitive to the misfortunes of humanity, they will utter words of caution, but none will hearken unto them. They will be subjected to base and common sovereigns, to despicable tyrants whom they will fail to vanquish. Superior in soul, they will be the toys of opulence and carefree imbecility. They will establish the renown of the people of the earth, but they themselves will win no share of it during their lifetime. Giants of intelligence, torches of knowledge, organs of progress, lights of the arts and instruments of liberty, they alone will remain despised and lonely slaves. Tender of heart, they will be exposed to envy; fervent souls, they will be paralysed for the general good, and they will even disown each other."

' "God of cruelty!" I cried out. "At least their lives will be short, for their souls will break their bodies."

' "No," he asserted, "for they will nourish and sustain themselves on hope which will be for ever deceived and revived. And the more they work with the sweat of their brows, the more ungrateful will men become. They will bestow all the joys and receive all the sorrows. The burden of labour with which I have encumbered the race of Adam shall weigh heavily on their shoulders; poverty will pursue them, and their families will be their partners in hunger and grief. Complaisant or rebellious, they will be for ever degraded; they will work for all, but in vain shall they dispense their genius, the skill of their hands and the strength of their arms."

'Those last words of Jehovah rent my heart, and cursing the night on which I had become a father, I expired.'

The voice faded, leaving a trail of sighs in its wake.

'Now you fully understand,' Tubal-Cain resumed, addressing Adoniram, 'and our situation is the proof. Beneficent genii, the real creators of nearly all the intellectual conquests which have rendered men so proud, we are, in the eyes of Adonai, the damned, the demons, the spirits of evil. Son of Cain! submit to your fate, bear it imperturbably, and may the God of reprobation be dumbfounded by your perseverance. Be great in front of men and strong in front of us. I saw that you were about to succumb, my son, and I wished to restore you to yourself. The genii of fire will come to your assistance. Dare all, for you are destined to revenge us, and this temple you are raising to Adonai will cause the downfall of his faithful servant, Soliman. You will beget a founder of kings who will restore upon the earth, in the face of Jehovah, the neglected cult of fire, the sacred element. When your days on earth are over, the indefatigable and unwavering militia of workmen will rally to the sound of your name; the battalions of labourers and the myriads of thinkers will unite to rise, one day, in rebellion and reduce the blind power of kings . . . those despotic ministers of Adonai! Go, my son, fulfil your destiny. . . .'

At these words, Adoniram felt himself lifted up, the garden of metals with its sparkling flowers and glittering trees, the vast and radiant workshops of the gnomes, the brilliant streams of gold, silver, cadmium, mercury, naphtha . . . all mingled below him into a huge wake of light, a rushing river of fire. Then everything gradually grew obscure, and the realm of his ancestors looked for an instant like an immobile planet in the midst of a gloomy sky. . . . Suddenly, he felt the shock of a fresh wind upon his face, and, glancing round, he found himself stretched out upon the sand, at the edge of the mould of the sea of bronze, surrounded by the cooled lava which still, however, projected russet gleams into the haze of the night.

'A dream!' he said aloud, 'but was it a dream? . . . Misery! one thing alone is certain : my hopes are shipwrecked, my projects are ruined, and disgrace awaits me at sunrise!'

But he recalls the vision so vividly that he suspects the very doubt which has taken hold of him. In his confusion and dismay, he lifts up his eyes and sees before him the colossal shade of Tubal-Cain.

'Genie of fire!' he exclaimed, 'lead me back into the depths of the abyss, and let the earth conceal my shame.'

'Have you forgotten what I told you?' the shade sternly replied. 'Come, no more useless words. The night draws to a close and soon the blazing eye of Jehovah will range over the earth . . . we must hurry. Poor child! would I have abandoned you in such a perilous hour? Be free of fear. Your moulds are full. When the smelting metals suddenly enlarged the mouth of the furnace, whose stone walls were not sufficiently fire-proof, they caused an eruption, and the excess liquid shot out over the banks. You thought there was a fissure, lost your head, poured water all over, and the cast-iron naturally cracked.'

'And how can we get rid of the cast-iron seams which have stuck to the bank of the basin?' Adoniram asked.

'Cast-iron is porous and does not conduct heat as well as steel does. Take a block of cast-iron, heat one end of it and cool the other, then give it a thunderous blow and it will break in the middle. The same applies to clay and crystal.'

'Master, I am listening to your words.'

'By Eblis! you should anticipate them. Your basin is still burning. Now quickly cool the surplus on the banks and use a hammer to sever the seams.'

'But that requires more than superhuman strength!'

'It requires a hammer! Tubal-Cain's opened the crater of Etna to give an outlet to the scoria from our workshops.'

Adoniram heard the noise of iron falling on to the ground. He bent down and picked up a hammer. Weighty though it was, its balance was perfect. He wanted to express his gratitude, but Tubal-Cain had disappeared, and the rising dawn had started dispelling the stars.

One moment afterwards, the birds, who were tuning the preludes of their songs, took flight at the sound of Adoniram's hammer. Redoubling his blows upon the banks of the basin, he now disturbed only that profound silence which precedes the break of day.

The audience were highly impressed by this sequence, and the following evening their numbers increased. The mysteries of the mountain of Kaf had been mentioned, a subject which is still of extraordinary interest to the Orientals. As for me, I had found it as classic as Aeneas' descent into hell.

8 The Pool of Siloam

At the hour when mount Tabor protects the hilly route of Bethany with morning shade, diaphanous white clouds roam around the plains of the sky, softening the early light; the tissue of meadows is still azure under the dew and the murmuring breeze in the foliage counterpoints the songs of birds lining the path to Moriah.

On this particular morning, the linen tunics and gauze robes of a procession of women were visible in the distance; crossing a bridge over the Kedron, they soon reached the banks of a river replenished by the pool of Siloam. Eight Nubians followed them carrying a splendid palanquin and two laden camels tramped along swinging their heads.

The litter was empty. Accompanied by her attendants, the queen of Saba had left her tent at dawn — she still insisted on residing with her retinue outside the walls of Jerusalem — and now preferred to walk so that she could best appreciate the charm of the fresh and blooming countryside. Balkis' lovely young companions were heading towards the fountain to wash their mistress's linen. Balkis herself, dressed as simply as they, cheerfully preceded them with her nurse, and the two of them chatted without a pause.

'I am not convinced by your reasoning, my girl,' the nurse was saying. 'This marriage seems sheer folly to me, and if the error can be excused, it is only for the pleasure it promises.'

'How edifying!' the queen exclaimed, 'I wonder what the wise Soliman would say if he heard you.'

'At his age, is he really so wise to covet and lust after the rose of the Sabeans?'

'It is too early in the morning for such flattery, good Sarahil!'

'Take care, then, not to arouse my severity. I would say that. . . .'

'Well, go on.'

'. . . That if you love Soliman, you deserve him.'

'I don't really know whether I do,' replied the young queen with a laugh. 'I've considered the question seriously and . . . apparently I'm not indifferent to the king.'

'If that were true, you wouldn't have examined such a delicate point so methodically. No, you're planning an alliance, a political alliance, and thus you scatter flowers on the barren path of convention. Soliman has reduced your States and those surrounding him to mere tributaries of his power, and you dream of freeing yours by accepting a master whom you intend to turn into a slave — but take care!'

'Take care? I have nothing to fear, he adores me.'

'His feelings for you are limited to sensuality, for his excessive appreciation of his own noble self curtails him from any further sentiment. Nothing could be more fragile, more brittle. Soliman is calculating, ambitious and cold.'

'Is he not the greaest prince upon the earth, the noblest scion of the race of Shem from which I spring myself? Tell me, what prince in the world is as worthy as he to give successors to the Hamathite dynasty!'

'The offspring of the Hamathites, our ancestors, come from a higher source than you imagine. Do you see the children of Shem commanding the denizens of the air? No. I still hold firmly to the predictions of the oracle. Your destiny is not yet fulfilled, nor has the sign yet appeared which will lead you to recognize your future husband . . . the hoopoe has not expressed the will of the eternal powers which protect you.'

'Does my fate depend upon the will of a bird?'

'The will of a bird who is unique in the whole world, whose intelligence differs from that of any known species, whose soul, the high priest told me, originates in the element of fire. She is by no means a terrestrial animal; moreover, she raises the jinn.'

'It is true,' Balkis remarked, 'that Soliman tries in vain to win her over, offering her his shoulder or his wrist without any effect.'

'In my opinion she will never alight on any part of him. At the time when the animals were brought under subjection, and that species is now extinct, they never obeyed men created from mud;

they responded only to the *dives* or to the jinn, children of air or fire. Soliman belongs to the race which Adonai formed from clay.'

'But how do you explain, then, that the hoopoe obeys my commands? . . .' Sarahil smiled and shook her head. A princess of the Hamathite race and a relative of the last king, the queen's nurse had deeply studied the natural sciences for many years. Her prudence, however, did not fail to match her kindness :

'Queen,' she said, 'there are certain secrets which you are still too young to know, secrets which the daughters of our race do not learn until they marry. If passion entices and overcomes them, then these mysteries shall not be unveiled to them, and thus they will never be disclosed to common men. This much I shall tell you : Hud-Hud, this renowned hoopoe, will acknowledge as master only the husband who is reserved for the queen of Saba.'

'You will make me curse this feathered tyranny !'

'Who will save you perhaps from a sword-armed despot !'

'But I have given Soliman my promise, and we risk his just resentment if . . . Sarahil, the die is cast, the time is almost at hand, and this very evening. . . .'

'But great is the power of the Elohim,' Sarahil murmured.

To interrupt the conversation Balkis turned aside and started gathering hyacinths, mandragoras and cyclamens which dappled the green of the meadow, while the hoopoe, who had fluttered after her, now strutted coyly around her, as if she were asking for Balkis' pardon.

Taking advantage of this interval, the attendants were able to rejoin their sovereign. They gossiped about Adonai's temple, whose walls could be seen in the distance, and about the sea of bronze which nobody, in fact, had ceased to discuss for the last four days. Eagerly the queen took up this new topic and full of curiosity her women gathered around her. Tall sycamores, tracing verdant arabesques against an azure background, covered this charming group with transparent shadows.

'Nothing equals the astonishment which overwhelmed us yesterday evening,' Balkis was saying. 'Soliman himself was dumbfounded. Three days ago, all was lost; master Adoniram collapsed, thunderstruck, on the ruins of his work. Proved unjustified, his fame flowed away with the torrents of mutinous lava, and the artist was hurled back into nothingness. But now ! his victorious name is echoed on every hill; his workmen have set up a heap of palms at the threshold of his house, and he is more famous than ever in Israel.'

'The noise of his triumph,' said a young Sabean, 'reached right up to our tents, and, troubled by the memory of the recent catastrophe, O queen, we trembled for your life. Tell us exactly what happened, for none of us know the details.'

'Without waiting for the river of metal to cool down, Adoniram, so I have been informed, summoned his discouraged workmen early in the morning. The rebellious chiefs surrounded him, but he calmed them with a few words. For three days they applied themselves to the work and cleared away the moulds to accelerate the cooling down of the basin which they thought was broken. Their plans remained a profound mystery. On the third day, before dawn, the host of workmen heaved up the bulls and lions of bronze with levers still black from the heat of the metal. They hauled these enormous blocks into the basin and adjusted them with a truly miraculous speed. Freed of its supports, the sea of bronze broke loose to settle on its twenty-four caryatides, and while the population of Jerusalem deplored such a fruitless expense, the marvellous undertaking dazzled the astonished eyes of those who had finally accomplished it. Suddenly, pushing down the barriers set up by the workmen, the crowd rushed forward. We could hear the clamour even in the palace. Soliman suspected that a riot had broken out and hurried to the site. I accompanied him and a multitude of people followed us. We were welcomed by a hundred thousand delirious workmen crowned with green palms. Soliman was unable to believe his eyes. Everyone extolled the name of Adoniram to the very heavens.'

'A wonderful triumph!' exclaimed one of Balkis' attendants. 'How happy he must be!'

'Adoniram . . .' the queen replied, 'a weird genius, a deep and mysterious soul. Following my orders, the workmen rushed around, calling for him, searching for him, but all in vain. Indifferent to his victory, scorning it, Adoniram had hidden. Swerving away from praise, the star had eclipsed itself. I departed with Soliman who declared that the king of the people had disgraced us. As for me, leaving the battlefield of this genius, my soul was sad and I . . . I was overwhelmed by memories of this extraordinary mortal. His work had proved him great, yes, but his absence at such a moment proved him noble.'

'I saw him pass by the other day,' said a virgin of Saba, 'the flame of his eyes swept across my cheeks and I could not help but blush . . . he has the majesty of a king.'

'He is more beautiful than the children of men,' one of her companions remarked. 'His stature is commanding and his countenance dazzling . . . that is how I imagine the gods and genii.'

'I'm sure that more than one of you would like to be Adoniram's partner and share his destiny,' the queen remarked.

'O queen! what are we in the eyes of so great an individual? His soul is in the skies, his proud heart would never descend to us.'

Jasmin blossoms surrounded the pool of Siloam, while terebinths, acacias and occasional palm-trees, inclining their pale crests, towered over them. There, sweet marjorams grew, grey irises, thyme, verbena and the red roses of Sharon. Below these clumps of star-studded bushes, age-old reefs stretched out, while springs of pure water, the fountain's tributaries, babbled in their tracks. Twining around the branches, lianas decked this tranquil spot. The apios with red and fragrant bunches of grapes and the graceful, perfumed festoons of blue wistaria surged right up to the peaks of the pale and quivering ebony trees.

As the queen of Saba and her attendants walked on and gathered round the fountain, they surprised a man who was sitting on the edge, plunged in meditation, letting his hand laze in the cool shadows. He stood up, intending to retreat. Balkis was almost in front of him. He looked up at the sky and rapidly turned away. But the queen acted even more rapidly and placed herself in front of him.

'Master Adoniram,' she asked, 'why do you avoid me?'

'I have never searched for company,' the artist replied, 'and I fear the face of royalty.'

'Does it appear so frightening at this moment?' the queen asked with a piercing sweetness which confused the young man and forced him to look at her. The queen had left aside her insignia of royalty, and the woman, in the simplicity of her morning attire, was far from frightening, but she troubled Adoniram nevertheless. Her hair was arranged under the folds of a long flowing veil; her white, transparent robe, stirred by the inquisitive breeze, allowed a glimpse of her beautiful, conch-shaped breast. Thanks to this simple dress, Balkis' youth appeared more tender, more sprightly, and Adoniram's deference was no longer marked either by official admiration or, paradoxically enough, by desire. This touching, innocent grace, this child-like face, this virginal appearance, all stamped a profound and new impression upon the artist's heart.

'Why should I restrain myself?' he said bitterly. 'My power equals my misfortune. You are teasing and indifferent, your favours are capricious, you bestow them as though you were setting a trap to torment more cruelly those whom you have already captured! Farewell! You forget too quickly, lady, and you do not reveal your secret.'

Pronouncing these last words in a melancholy tone, Adoniram glanced at Balkis, who was immediately disturbed, but ready to assert herself. Quick by nature, and wilful, for she was accustomed to commanding, she did not wish to be, as it were, abandoned on the spot. She mustered all her coquetry and replied :

'Adoniram . . . you are ungrateful.'

But the more than firm Adoniram did not surrender.

'It is true,' he said, 'it would be wrong of me to forget — to forget that despair overtook me for one hour in my life and that you took advantage of it to spite me in the eyes of my master, my enemy!'

'You were there . . .' the queen murmured, shamefaced and contrite.

'I saw that your life was in danger and I ran to protect you.'

'Such care, such consideration at so perilous a moment,' the queen acknowledged, 'and for what a miserable reward!'

The queen's candour and kindness obliged Adoniram to grow more tender, and this great and outraged man was wounded now to the quick by his own fully justified disdain for Balkis.

'As for Soliman ben Daoud,' the sculptor resumed, 'his opinion does not bother me. He and his breed are parasitical, envious and servile beneath their royal purple disguise. My power is limited by his whims and fantasies. And as for the others who abused and spat upon me . . . a hundred thousand maniacs, weak, virtueless and void of quality, why, I pay less attention to them than to a swarm of buzzing flies. . . . But you, O queen! the only one whom I had singled out among that rabble, the only one who had won my utter veneration, when you reacted as you did, then my heart, this heart which had never before been moved, then it was rent into a thousand fragments . . . let it remain so. Meanwhile, human society has become more odious to me than ever. Why should I care from now on about praise or condemnation, especially from you, when the one follows the other so quickly, when they are mixed on the same lips like absinthe and honey!'

'You are harsh towards the penitent,' murmured Balkis. 'Do I have to implore your mercy? Surely it is enough that. . . .'

'No! You woo success! If I were on the ground you would not hesitate to trample over my head!'

'Now? No! It is my turn to say No and a thousand times No!'

'Then let me destroy my work completely and fall into disgrace again. I shall return here followed by the imprecations of the crowd, but if you have remained faithful, the day of my dishonour will be the most glorious day in my life!'

'Yes!' Balkis exclaimed, unable to control her rapture, 'Yes! Destroy it!'

And at these words, Adoniram himself could not suppress a cry of joy. But then the queen foresaw the dreadful consequences of such a fearful promise.

Adoniram stood majestically in front of her. No longer wearing his usual workman's clothes, he was dressed in the hierarchical costume of the rank he held as master of the labourers. His stature was enhanced by a pleated white tunic, set off by a large girdle trimmed with gold. Coiled round his right arm was a steel serpent with a sparkling ruby on its crest. Half veiled by a conical head-dress, from which two wide bands unfurled to fall upon his chest, his brow appeared to scorn a crown. Dazzled, the queen momentarily forgot the real circumstances of this bold, intrepid individual; she remembered, and regained her self-possession, but could not free herself from the overwhelming respect she felt.

'Sit down,' she said. 'Your defiant spirit justly incensed you against calmer feelings, but let us return to them now. I treasure your fame. Don't destroy anything. You were prepared to make a sacrifice. As far as I am concerned, you have already made it. Should you carry it out in fact, my own honour will be compromised, for you know, master, that from now on my reputation is linked to king Soliman's dignity.'

'I had forgotten about it,' the artist remarked indifferently. 'Yes, I do believe I've heard some rumours . . . the queen of Saba is to marry the descendant of an adventuress from Moab, the son of the shepherd Daoud and Bathsheba, the adulterous widow of the decrepit Uriah. A rich alliance which will no doubt regenerate the divine blood of the Hamathites. . . .'

The young girl's cheeks grew purple. And her anger hardly decreased when she noticed that her nurse Sarahil, who was so distinctly opposed to the alliance, had overheard Adoniram's remark as she allotted various tasks to the attendants lined up at the pool or leaning over it.

'Apparently Adoniram doesn't approve of this union,' Balkis retorted with affected disdain.

'On the contrary,' Adoniram replied, 'as you can see very well for yourself.'

'And what exactly do you mean by that?'

'If I were offended I would already have dethroned Soliman. You would treat him then as you have treated me. You would no longer even think about him, in fact, for you do not love him.'

'What leads you to such a conclusion?' the queen asked him quietly.

'You feel superior to him, you have humiliated him; he will not pardon you, and such aversion does not give birth to love.'

'You are very bold, Adoniram.'

'When we love,' he said, 'we fear.'

At these words, the queen was overwhelmed by a desire to make herself feared.

Balkis had never seriously considered the imminent resentment of the king of the Hebrews with whom she had amused herself at his expense; Sarahil had only wasted her eloquence on the subject. Although this point now appeared to have a stronger basis, she did not admit it to Adoniram :

'It does not appeal to me,' she said, 'to listen to your insinuations against my host, my. . . .'

'Queen,' Adoniram interrupted, 'I have no love for men and I know them for what they are. This Soliman . . . I have studied him for many long years. Beneath his lamb's wool, he is a tiger muzzled by the priests, a tiger who quietly gnaws at his muzzle. So far, he has done no more than assassinate his brother Adonijah, that isn't much, but he has no other relatives.'

'One would really believe,' Sarahil declared, adding oil to fire, 'that master Adoniram is jealous of the king.'

'Lady,' the artist replied, 'if Soliman did not spring from a race inferior to mine, I would, perhaps, deign to glance at him, but I learn from the queen's choice that she was destined for no other.'

Sarahil opened her eyes wide in astonishment, and, placing herself behind the queen, traced a mystic sign in the air which the artist saw but was unable to decipher. Nevertheless, he trembled at the sight of it.

'Queen,' he exclaimed, emphasizing each word, 'since my accusations have left you indifferent, they have cleared away my doubts. From now on I shall refrain from filling your mind with any prejudices against this monarch whom you have already ceased to think about.'

'Master . . . what is the point of harrying me in this fashion? Even if I do not love king Soliman. . . .'

'Before our conversation,' the artist interrupted with quiet emotion, 'you were almost convinced that you did love him.'

Sarahil moved away and the queen glanced around her in confusion.

'O for mercy's sake, lady !' Adoniram erupted, 'let us talk of other things. I am tempting the lightning to strike my head ! One stray word from your lips is life or death for me. O do not speak ! I forced myself to reach this supreme and perilous moment, and it is I who now withdraw. Leave me the doubt . . . my courage is vanquished. I tremble . . . I must prepare myself for this sacrifice. But O the grace, the youth, the beauty which you radiate. . . . Alas ! what am I in your eyes? No. No, I had to lose an unexpected promise of happiness. . . . Hold back your breath, I beg you, for it can cast upon my ears a word which kills. This frail heart of mine has never throbbed — its first anguish breaks it — I feel death approaching. . . .'

And glancing furtively at Adoniram, Balkis was inclined to believe him. This proud, powerful, vigorous individual was pallid now, quaking with deference and robbed of his strength; death lurked indeed around his lips. Triumphant and moved, happy and trembling, Balkis let the world vanish from before her eyes.

'Alas !' the royal maiden stammered in confession, 'I too . . . I have never loved.'

Her voice died away, but Adoniram, afraid of waking from a dream, did not dare disturb this silence. Sarahil drew near again and both of them realized that it was necessary to speak or else they would give themselves away. The hoopoe hovered around the sculptor and offered him a new topic for conversation.

'What a brilliant plumage this bird has,' he said in a distracted voice. 'Have you had it for long?'

But it was Sarahil who replied, and as she spoke she did not remove her watchful gaze from the sculptor's face :

'This bird, Hud-Hud, is the unique offspring of a species which the race of the genii commanded as they commanded the other denizens of the atmosphere. Preserved by who knows what miracle, the hoopoe obeys the Hamathite princes since time immemorial. It is through her mediation that whenever the queen wishes, she can assemble the birds of the air.'

This confidence produced a remarkable change upon Adoniram's features and he looked at Balkis calmly now with rising joy and tenderness.

'She's a capricious bird,' the queen said calmly, 'Soliman overwhelmed her with caresses and dainties, but all in vain, for the hoopoe persistently escaped from his every enticement, and the king was quite unable to make her alight upon his wrist.'

Adoniram reflected for an instant, then he smiled as though he had been struck by an inspiration, and Sarahil grew even more attentive.

He stands up and pronounces the hoopoe's name. Perched upon a bush, Hud-Hud remains there motionless, but looks at him obliquely. Advancing one step, Adoniram traces the mysterious *Tau* in the air, and the bird, unfolding her wings, flies towards him, hovers over his head for a moment, then settles with docility upon his wrist.

'My suspicions were justified,' said Sarahil, 'and the oracle is now fulfilled.'

'O sacred shades of my ancestors !' the artist cried. 'O Tubal-Cain, O father, you have not deceived me, no ! Balkis, spirit of light, my sister, my bride, at last I have found you ! You and I alone in the world command this winged messenger of the genii of fire from whom we are both descended !'

'What !' the queen exclaimed, 'Adoniram is. . . .'

'The last offspring of Cush, grandson of Tubal-Cain, from whom you spring yourself through Saba, brother of Nimrod the hunter, the great-great-grandfather of the Hamathites . . . but the secret of our origin must never be revealed to the children of Shem who were kneaded from the mud of the earth.'

'Dutifully I bow to my master,' Balkis said, holding out her hand to him, 'for, following the precepts of destiny, I am not permitted to welcome any love other than Adoniram's.'

'O!' he cried, falling to his knees, 'it is from none but Balkis that I wish to receive so precious a blessing! My heart hails yours in jubilation. Since the hour you first appeared to me I have been your slave.'

They would not have ceased from speaking to each other now had not Sarahil, endowed with the prudence of her years, interrupted their conversation.

'Postpone these tender avowals,' she said. 'Many an obstacle lies in wait for you and more than one danger threatens you both. Owing to the power of Adonai, the sons of Noah are masters of the earth, holding sway over your mortal existence. Soliman is absolute in his realm and our State is merely his tributary. His armies are invincible, his pride colossal, he has innumerable spies and is protected by Jehovah. Let us find a means to end our perilous sojourn here, and until then let us be prudent. Do not forget, my daughter, that Soliman will be waiting for you this evening at the altar of Zion. To unfetter yourself and break away, that would only provoke him and arouse more than his suspicions. Ask for just one day's delay on the grounds that ominous signs have appeared. Tomorrow, the high priest will provide you with a new pretext. You will have to play carefully upon Soliman's impatience. As for you, Adoniram, take leave now of your servants. The morning advances, the new wall which overlooks the pool of Siloam is already crowded with soldiers, and the sun which seeks us out will bring us to their notice. When the disc of the moon slices the sky above the slopes of Ephraim, cross the Kedron and approach our camp, come right up to the grove of olive-trees which conceals the tents from the inhabitants of the two hills. There we shall discuss the situation thoughtfully and wisely.'

They separated with regret. Balkis rejoined her attendants, while Adoniram's enraptured gaze followed her until she disappeared under the oleander foliage.

9 Phanor, Amrou and Methuselah

Looking up at the ceiling of the temple's interior sanctuary, as though he were seeking a witness to his words, the high priest exclaimed in vexation, 'Once more I say you have no choice! Follow my advice, abandon this project. How can I solemnize a marriage when the bride is absent?'

'Venerable Zadok,' king Soliman sighed, 'I am more affected than you by these unexpected delays, yet I support them patiently.'

'Of course you do, but I, I am not smitten by love!' the levite retorted, passing his gnarled hand over his long, white, forked beard.

'All the more reason, then, for you to be calmer.'

'What!' cried Zadok. 'Guards and levites have been ready for four days. The appropriate burnt-offerings are prepared, but the altar fire might just as well be extinguished, for at the solemn moment everything has to be postponed. Priests and king are at the mercy of a capricious foreign woman who keeps us on our toes with one pretext after another, while she no doubt revels in our credulity.'

Above all, what humiliated the high priest was having himself arrayed in vain each day in his splendid vestments, for the opportunity never arose for him to dazzle the Sabean court with the ceremonial and hieratic pomp of Israel. To Soliman's dismay, he now started walking in exasperation from one end of the interior sanctuary to the other, trailing his magnificent costume along the ground.

For this majestic ceremony Zadok wore his linen robe, his sleeveless ephod and his embroidered girdle. The ephod was a brightly coloured garment of gold, hyacinth and scarlet; the gem-cutter had engraved the names of the twelve tribes upon its two huge onyx-stones. Hanging from vermilion bands and carved gold rings, the pectoral shone upon his chest; square in shape and a handbreadth in size, it was adorned by one row of sardonyxes, topazes and emeralds; by a second row of carbuncle-stones, sapphires and jaspers; by a third row of

186

ligures, amethysts and agates, and, finally, by a fourth row of chryso-
lites, onyx-stones and beryls. Open at the middle, the pale violet linen
robe was embellished by small hyacinths and purple pomegranates
with tiny, fine gold bells between them. The high priest's brow was
encircled by a linen tissue tiara, adorned with pearls, which rose to
a crescent at the top; attached to the front of it by a scarlet band was
a burnished gold plate upon which the following words were deeply
embossed : ADONAI IS HOLY. And it took three hours and six levite
servants to clothe Zadok in his sacred apparel which was fastened
by small chains, golden clasps and innumerable mystic knots. This
costume was indeed sacred : only the levites were permitted to touch
it, and Adonai himself had dictated the design to his servant Moussa
ben Amran (Moses).

For the last four days, then, the priestly finery of the successors of
Melchizedek had been regularly outraged upon the shoulders of the
worthy Zadok, and to such an outrage was added a more personal
affront, for he was supposed to consecrate this marriage which he did
not approve of between Soliman and the queen of Saba. Zadok was
angry and disappointed.

He considered that this union threatened the religion of the
Hebrews and the power of the priesthood. Queen Balkis was learned
and well informed. The Sabean priests, in Zadok's opinion, had been
too indulgent with her; she was instructed in the kind of subjects
which should remain concealed from a prudently trained sovereign :
he was highly suspicious of a queen who was well versed in the
singular art of commanding the birds of the air. These mixed
marriages, which exposed the faith to permanent danger through
the presence of a sceptical bride, never won the priests' approval.
And Zadok, who had curbed Soliman's proud thirst for knowledge
with great difficulty, by persuading him that there was nothing else
to learn, trembled now for fear that the monarch would realize just
how much was still unknown to him.

Zadok's fear was quite justified. Soliman had recently grown more
reflective, having discovered that his priests were at once less subtle
yet more despotic than the queen's. Shaken in his trust, Ben Daoud
had not consulted Zadok about certain secret matters which had
been recently revealed to him. The risk in countries where religion
is controlled by the priests and personified in them is that on the day
the high priest errs or falls — all mortals are fallible and vulnerable
— the faith collapses with them, and even God is eclipsed along with
his arrogant and pernicious upholder.

Cautious, reserved, suspicious, but neither penetrating nor acute,
Zadok had maintained his position without a struggle thanks to his
lack of ideas. Interpreting the law according to the king's whims and

passions, he justified his interpretations with a dogmatic complacency at once fastidious, for the sake of form, yet fundamentally
trivial. Thus the king submitted with docility to the yoke. And to
think that a girl from the Yemen and an accursed bird could topple
over the edifice of such a prudent education !

To accuse them of magic would be tantamount to acknowledging
the power of the occult sciences, a power which he had disdainfully
repudiated. Zadok was confused and troubled. Moreover, he had
other worries : the sway exerted by Adoniram over the workmen disturbed the high priest, who had good reason to be alarmed by any
occult and kabbalistic domination. In fact, Zadok had constantly
discouraged his royal pupil from entrusting Adonai's temple, the most
magnificent temple in the world, to the hands of the sole artist
capable of raising it; he had dissuaded him, too, from drawing the
admiration and the offerings of all the people of the Orient to the
foot of the Jerusalem altar. Zadok was waiting for the completion of
the work, then he would get rid of Adoniram; meanwhile, he did no
more than nourish Soliman's dark mistrust. The situation had grown
worse over the last few days. In all the uproar of an unexpected,
impossible, and even miraculous triumph, Adoniram, you will remember, had disappeared. The whole court was astonished by his
absence, except for the king apparently, since he had made no
mention of the subject to Zadok; Soliman rarely exercised such
self-possession.

Seeing that he was not needed, but fully determined to remain
needed, the venerable Zadok had thus been reduced to concocting,
with vaguely prophetic declamations, the kind of oracular warnings
which would make an impression upon the king's imagination. In
the present circumstances, however, the maxims of the Ecclesiast, far
from being influenced by Zadok's homilies, revolved only upon the
necessity of the master's open eye, upon suspicion, and upon the
misfortune of kings who were betrayed by guile, falsehood and self-
interest. Disconcerted, the high priest retreated into the depths of
the unintelligible.

'Although you speak most admirably,' Soliman said, 'I did not
come to meet you in the temple with any intention of enjoying your
eloquence. Woe unto the king who feeds himself on words ! Three
men will arrive to ask for an audience with me, and their request will
be granted, for I know what purpose leads them here. For the sake
of secrecy I chose to hold this audience in these premises.'

'These men, lord, who are they?'

'They are well informed about certain matters unknown to kings
. . . one can learn a great deal from them.' No sooner had Soliman
spoken than three artisans were ushered into the interior sanctuary.

They fell prostrate at Soliman's feet; their attitude was constrained and their shifty eyes were troubled.

'May your lips speak the truth,' Soliman said to them, 'and do not hope to impose yourselves upon the king. Your most secret thoughts are already known to him. You, Phanor, modest workman in the corporation of masons, you are Adoniram's enemy, because you deplore the supremacy of the miners, and in order to destroy your master's work you mixed combustible stones among the furnace bricks. Amrou, journeyman among the carpenters, you arranged for the joists to attract the flames and thereby weaken the foundations of the sea of bronze. As for you, Methuselah, miner of the tribe of Ruben, you acidified the casting liquid by throwing in sulphurous lava gathered from the banks of the lake of Gomorrah. And all three of you aspire in vain after the title and salary of the masters. Have I not indeed penetrated the mystery of your most secret activities!'

'Great king,' Phanor replied in terror, 'Adoniram's calumnies have woven our doom.'

'Adoniram has no suspicion of this plot, it is known to me alone. Understand that nothing escapes the sagacity of those whom Adonai protects.'

Soliman had only to notice Zadok's astonishment to realize how little credit his high priest attributed to Adonai's protection.

'There is no point, then, in concealing the truth,' the king resumed. 'What you are about to disclose is already known to me, and it is your integrity which is now at stake. Rise to your feet. Let Amrou be the first to speak.'

'Lord,' said Amrou, who was no less terrified than his accomplices, 'nobody's surveillance of the workshops and the sites could have been as attentive as mine. Adoniram has not been there once.'

'As for me,' Phanor continued, 'I decided to hide, at nightfall, close to the tomb of prince Absalon ben Daoud, on the route which leads from Coria to the camp of the Sabeans. At about three o'clock in the morning, a man passed in front of me, dressed in a long robe, his head covered by a turban like those the Yemenites wear. Stepping forward, I recognized Adoniram. He was heading towards the queen's tents, but as he had noticed me, I did not dare to follow him, though I stayed watchfully by the tomb until he passed out of sight.'

'Lord,' said Methuselah in his turn, 'you know everything and wisdom dwells in your spirit. I shall speak the truth, but what I have to reveal is so intimate that my companions may lose their heads merely for listening to my words. Deign, then, to let them withdraw, so that no life but mine be imperilled.'

As soon as the miner found himself alone in the presence of the king and the high priest, he prostrated himself once more, saying :

'Lord, stretch forth your sceptre to assure me that I shall not die!'

'Your own faith saves you,' Soliman replied, stretching forth his hand. 'Fear nothing, Methuselah of the tribe of Ruben. Rise and speak.'

'Dressed in a caftan, my face dyed black, I mingled easily enough, thanks to the night, among the black eunuchs who surrounded the queen. Slipping furtively through the darkness, Adoniram approached her. They spoke to each other for a long time, and the wind carried the tremors of their voices to my ears. I did not steal away until an hour before dawn . . . Adoniram was still conversing with the queen.'

Although Soliman controlled his anger, Methuselah saw the signs of it in his eyes.

'O king!' he cried, 'I had to obey . . . but do not oblige me to add any more.'

'I command you to continue!'

'Lord, your subjects treasure your glory. I shall perish, if I have to, but my master will not be the puppet of these perfidious foreigners. . . . Only the high priest of the Sabeans, the queen's nurse and two of her attendants are aware of these amorous liaisons. Adoniram, if I am not mistaken, is far from what he appears to be, for, like the queen, he is endowed with magic powers. As she commands the inhabitants of the air, so the artist commands the spirits of fire. Nevertheless, these gifted and favoured individuals fear your power over the genii, a power you do indeed possess, although you do not know it. Sarahil talked about a certain ring and explained all its miraculous properties to the astonished queen, then she took the queen's hand in hers and suddenly grew furious. I didn't grasp what followed, for they lowered their voices, and I was afraid that if I drew too near I would give myself away. But I could see clearly enough that the queen looked very repentant. Soon, however, Sarahil, the high priest and the attendants all bowed to Adoniram and moved away, while he, as I have said, remained alone with the queen of Saba. O king! may I find grace in your eyes, for no lies have grazed my lips!'

'What right have you to probe your master's intentions? Whatever our verdict, it shall be just. Have this man locked up in the temple with his fellows. He is not to communicate with them until we decide their fate.'

Who would be able to describe the high priest's amazement as the mutes, discreet and rapid executors of Soliman's orders, dragged away the terrified Methuselah.

'You can see, venerable Zadok,' the monarch said bitterly, 'that your prudence accomplished nothing. Deaf to our prayers, indifferent to our sacrifices, Adonai did not deign to enlighten his servants, and it is none but I, aided by my own intelligence, who unveiled my enemies' conspiracy. As for them, however, they command the occult powers, their gods are faithful, while mine abandons me !'

'Because you disdain him by seeking the hand of a foreign bride. Banish from your soul this impure affection, O king, and your adversaries will be delivered unto you. But how can we seize hold of this Adoniram who makes himself invisible? And as for the queen, she is protected by the laws of hospitality.'

'To take revenge upon a woman is beneath Soliman's dignity. You will see her accomplice, however, arrive here within a few moments. This very morning, he sent me a request for an audience, which I naturally granted.'

'A sign that Adonai is aiding us, O king ! See that he never escapes from these premises !'

'If he comes to us unafraid, you may be sure that his supporters are not far away, but at all events, let us act neither rashly nor blindly. Those three men are his mortal enemies; greed and envy have soured their hearts. They have perhaps slandered the queen . . . she is dear to me, Zadok, and the scandalous tittle-tattle of three wretches will not lead me to abuse her by believing she has sullied herself through a degrading passion. . . . Nevertheless, fearing the underhand dealings of Adoniram, who holds great sway over the people, I had this mysterious individual watched.'

'You presume, then, that he did not actually see the queen?'

'On the contrary, I am convinced that he spoke to her in secret. She is curious, enthusiastic about the arts, she is ambitious, renowned, and a tributary of my crown. Does she intend to employ the artist in her own country and commission him to set to work on some magnificent project, or does she plan to use him as an intermediary so that she can muster an army strong enough to oppose mine? I do not know. As for their supposed liaison, do I not have the queen's word? But I agree that only one of these assumptions is proof enough that this man is dangerous. I shall inform him that. . . .' As he was speaking in this resolute tone in the presence of Zadok, who was dismayed to see his altar disdained and his influence declined almost to zero, the mutes reappeared. Their white head-dress was arranged in a spherical form, their coats were covered with shells, while a dagger hung from one side of their girdles and a sabre from the other. They exchanged signs with Soliman, and Adoniram advanced to the threshold. Six of his men had escorted him to that point, where he halted now and whispered some instructions to them. Then they withdrew.

10 Soliman and Adoniram

His expression full of confidence, Adoniram stepped slowly forward and approached the king of Jerusalem who was reposing on a massive bench. The artist bowed in deference, then waited, according to custom, for Soliman to invite him to speak.

'At last, master,' said the king, 'you deign to consent to our wishes and allow us the opportunity of congratulating you for your . . . unexpected triumph. Furthermore, we wish to express our personal gratitude; the work is more than a credit to me, and to you, too. As for your reward, it could never be as great as you deserve, but at least you may choose it yourself. What do you desire of Soliman?'

'My leave, lord. The work is all but complete, the finishing touches can be added without me. My destiny is to roam the world, it calls me now to other skies. I restore to your hands the authority conferred upon me. My reward is the monument itself, which I leave behind, and the honour of having carried out the noble designs of so great a king.'

'Your request disappoints us, for I hoped to keep you among us and raise you to eminent rank in my court.'

'My character, lord, would not prove worthy of your benevolence. Independent by nature, devoted to solitude, quite indifferent to honours for which I was not born, I would only too often put your indulgence to the test. Kings have unpredictable moods, envy surrounds and besieges them, fortune is fickle . . . as I learned too well myself. What you call my triumph almost cost me my honour, didn't it, and even my life?'

'I did not conclude that your undertaking had failed until you announced the fatal result yourself, while I . . . I have never laid claim to a power superior to yours over the spirits of fire.'

'Nobody commands those spirits, if indeed they exist. Moreover, the venerable Zadok is more qualified to broach these mysteries, they lie outside the scope of a mere artisan. As for what happened on that terrible night, all I know is that the operation didn't proceed at all according to my expectations. However, lord, in an hour of anguish I waited in vain for your consoling words, your support; that is why

I no longer dreamed of expecting your praise on the day of success.'

'Resentment and pride, master.'

'No, lord, humility and sincerity. From the night when I sub-merged the sea of bronze to the day when I uncovered it, my merit neither increased nor decreased. Success makes all the difference, and, as you have seen, success is in the hands of God. Adonai delights in you, he has been moved by your prayers, and it is I, lord, who must congratulate you and utter my thanks!'

Who will rid me of this man's irony? Soliman wondered. 'You no doubt leave me,' he said, 'to carry out other marvels elsewhere?'

'Not long ago, I would have sworn so, for whole worlds revolved within my burning brain; I glimpsed blocks of granite in my dreams, subterranean palaces with forests of columns, and I felt burdened by our present works. But now, my ardour and vitality subside, weari-ness lulls me, leisure smiles at me, and it seems to me that my career is over.'

Soliman glimpsed a certain tenderness shining in Adoniram's eyes. His face was grave, his expression melancholy, his voice more pene-trating than usual. Troubled, Soliman could not help but acknow-ledge how truly beautiful Adoniram was.

'And where do you intend to go on your departure from my realm?' he asked with feigned indifference.

'To Tyre,' the artist replied without hesitation. 'I promised my patron, the good Hiram, that I would return. He is as dear to you as a brother, while he is paternally kind to me. If you consent, I shall take him a plan with a bird's-eye view of the palace, the temple, and the sea of bronze, as well as a side-view of the two immense, wreathed columns of bronze, Jachin and Boaz, which embellish the temple's great door.'

'Your wish is granted. Five hundred horsemen will escort you and twelve camels will bear the treasures and presents which have been put aside for you.'

'You are too benevolent. Adoniram will take away nothing but his cloak. Do not think, lord, that I refuse your gifts. I recognize your generosity when you offer me such considerable rewards, but my sudden departure will exhaust your treasury to no purpose as far as I am concerned. Permit me to speak in perfect candour. I accept these gifts and I leave them in deposit in your hands. When I need them, lord, I shall notify you.'

'In other terms,' said Soliman, 'master Adoniram intends to deliver up his tributary to us.'

'Lord,' the artist replied with a gracious smile, 'you have divined my thoughts.'

'And perhaps he waits for the day when he will negotiate with us, dictating his own conditions?'

Adoniram glanced shrewdly and defiantly at the king.

'Be that as it may,' he added, 'I can ask for nothing which isn't worthy of Soliman's magnanimity.'

'If I am not mistaken,' Soliman said, weighing the effect of his words, 'the queen of Saba has certain projects in mind and thinks of employing you to carry them out.'

'She has made no mention of it, lord, to me.'

This reply led to further suspicions.

'However,' Zadok intervened, 'she is far from being insensitive to your genius. Will you leave without bidding her farewell?'

'Farewell . . .' Adoniram repeated, and Soliman spied a strange glow in his eyes, 'if the king permits, I shall enjoy the honour of taking leave of her.'

'We were hoping,' the king replied, 'to keep you among us for the coming festivities in celebration of our marriage, for as you know. . . .'

'I plan to reach Phoenicia without delay,' said Adoniram emphatically.

'Since you insist, master, you are free. You have our permission to depart.'

'After sunset,' the artist added. 'I have to pay the workmen, and I would be grateful, lord, if you would order your steward Azariah to have the appropriate sum of money brought to the counting-house set up at the foot of the column of Jachin. I shall pay the men as usual, without announcing my departure, in order to avoid the tumult of farewells.'

'Zadok, convey this order to your son Azariah. . . . One further word, Adoniram, what do you know about three journeymen called Phanor, Amrou, and Methuselah?'

'They are ambitious and honest, but quite insignificant, they have no talent. They were eager to be nominated masters and urged me to tell them the password that would entitle them to a larger salary. In the end they listened to reason, and quite recently I had occasion to praise their faithful hearts.'

'Master, it is written : "Fear the wounded serpent that retreats." You should gain a more acute knowledge of men. Those three are your enemies; through their stratagems they brought about the disaster which almost prevented the casting of the sea of bronze.'

'But tell me how you know this, lord.'

'Believing that all was lost, but trusting in your prudence, I searched for the hidden reasons behind the catastrophe. Wandering among the crowds, I overheard a secret discussion between these three men which clearly gave them away.'

'Many perished through their crime, and they may prove dangerous in the future. It is for you to decree their fate. That disaster cost me the life of a child I loved, a skilful artist, Benoni . . . I have not seen him since that night . . . but, in short, justice is the privilege of kings.'

'It will be dealt out to each one of them. Live happily, master Adoniram, Soliman will not forget you.'

Pensive, Adoniram appeared hesitant and at odds with himself, then he suddenly gave way to a moment of emotion :

'Whatever happens, lord, be for ever assured of my respect, of my pious remembrance, of my upright heart. And should you ever hold any suspicions, say to yourself : Like the majority of men, Adoniram did not belong to himself; he had to fulfil his destiny !'

'Farewell, master . . . fulfil your destiny !'

And with these words, the king stretched forth his hand; Adoniram bowed low, but did not kiss the monarch's proffered hand. Soliman trembled.

'Well . . .' Zadok murmured, seeing Adoniram withdraw, 'well, what are your orders, lord ?'

'Absolute silence, my father. From now on, I trust no one but myself. Know that I am king ! Obey, or you will fall into disgrace, be silent, or you will lose your life : that is your lot. . . . Come now, old man, don't tremble. The sovereign who reveals to you his secrets in order to instruct you is a friend. Have those three workmen brought before me. I wish to question them again.'

Amrou, Phanor and Methuselah appeared. The sinister mutes, their sabres now in their hands, placed themselves behind the workmen.

'I have weighed your words,' Soliman said sternly, 'and I have seen my servant Adoniram. Is it a sense of fairness or is it envy which provokes you against him? How dare journeymen judge their master? If you were notable men and chiefs among your brothers, your testimony would be less suspect. As it is, you are wilfully ambitious to be nominated masters, and, unable to obtain that title, your hearts have grown sour with resentment.'

'Lord,' said Methuselah, prostrating himself, 'you wish to put us to the proof. But even if I lose my life, I still maintain that Adoniram is a traitor. In plotting his ruin, I wanted to save Jerusalem from the tyranny of this perfidious individual who intended to subjugate my country to foreign hordes. My reckless candour is the surest proof of my integrity.'

'It does not become me to give credit to despicable men, to the slaves of my servants. Owing to the recent catastrophe, however, there are vacancies in the ranks of the masters. Adoniram has asked for a rest, and, like him, I wish to find among the new chiefs persons worthy of my trust. This evening, when the wages have been distributed, entreat him to initiate you. He will be alone . . . persuade him to listen to your reasons. I shall thereby recognize that you are hard-working, eminent in your art and well-considered by your brothers. Adoniram is intelligent, his decisions are law. Has God abandoned him so far? Has he indicated his reprobation by one of those ominous warnings, by one of those terrible blows with which his invisible hand can strike down the guilty? Then let Jehovah be the judge between you! If Adoniram decides to honour you, I shall regard it as a secret sign that the heavens favour you, and I shall have Adoniram closely watched. But if he refuses you the title of master, then you will appear before me tomorrow with Adoniram. I shall hear the accusation and the defence between you and him. The elders will then pronounce their verdict. Go, meditate upon my words, and may Adonai enlighten you.' Soliman rose from his seat, and, leaning on the shoulder of the impassive high priest, he slowly withdrew.

The three men were at once inspired by the same thought:

'We have to wrest the password from him,' Phanor said.

'Or else he dies,' Amrou added.

'Make him tell us the password of the masters and assassinate him!' Methuselah exclaimed.

And they joined their hands together to reinforce their decision.

About to cross the threshold, Soliman turned round and watched them from afar. A violent breath broke from his lungs. Then he turned to Zadok and cried:

'Nothing but pleasure now! Come, let us find the queen!'

11 Soliman and Balkis

As the sun began to set, the burning desert wind harrowed the countryside which reflected the glow from a mass of copper tinted clouds. Lying in the shadow cast by the hill of Moriah, only the parched bed of the Kedron received a current of cool air. The dying leaves drooped, the crumpled flowers of the oleanders dangled, lustreless;

chameleons, salamanders and lizards wriggled among the rocks; no songs ascended from the groves, no murmurs from the streams.

During this mournful day of scorching heat, Adoniram had remained frozen in distress. With Soliman's permission he had now come to bid the royal mistress of his heart farewell. Balkis was prepared for this temporary separation, for she herself had requested it. She gave her reasons as she welcomed Adoniram in her tent.

'Our leaving together would be a challenge to Soliman. Besides, there is no need to humiliate him in front of his people and add an insult to the grief which the eternal powers have already obliged me to inflict upon him. But remaining here after my departure, dear husband, you would court your death. The king is jealous of you. In my flight I would leave behind no other victim than you at the mercy of his resentment.'

'Then let us share the destiny of our race,' Adoniram replied, 'let us be scattered wanderers upon the earth. I have assured the king that I am going to Tyre. Let us be frank, now that your life is no longer at the mercy of a lie. This very night, I shall make my way towards Phoenicia, but instead of staying there I shall hasten to meet up with you in the Yemen, crossing the frontiers of Syria, of stony Arabia, and following the narrow passes in the Cassanite mountains. Alas! Beloved queen, must I leave you already, abandon you on foreign soil to the mercy of an infatuated despot?'

'Be calm, my lord, my soul is wholly yours. My servants are loyal, and acting prudently I shall dispel the dangers that lie ahead. The night will be stormy and overcast, protecting my flight. As for Soliman, I hate him; he covets my lands, he has surrounded me with spies, he has tried to win over my servants, bribe my officers and negotiate with them for the reduction of my fortresses. If he acquired any rights over my person, I would never see the blessed Yemen again. He extorted a promise from me, it is true, but what is my perjury compared to his treachery and double-dealing? Besides, I am forced to deceive him . . . I have no alternative, for quite recently he made me understand that his love is boundless and his patience at an end!'

'I can incite the guilds to insurrection! They will obey me and . . .'

'Not when they are waiting for their wages. What is the point of taking such a perilous risk? But your fiery resolution does not frighten me . . . it pleases me. I expected it and I was waiting impatiently for those words. Go in peace, my beloved; Balkis will never belong to anyone but you!'

'Farewell, my queen. . . . But must I leave this tent where I have known a happiness I never dreamed of? Must I cease to look upon the one who is my very life? Will I ever see you again? . . . Alas!

those precious moments of bliss may well appear as nothing but a dream to me, indeed, only too soon ! . . .'

'Listen, Adoniram, we shall be reunited, for ever. My own dreams and presentiments, in accord with the oracle of the genii, assure me that the Hamathites will triumph. And I take away with me, remember, a sacred pledge of our wedlock; your arms will welcome a son who is destined to revive our race, liberating the Yemen and the whole of Arabia from the feeble yoke of Soliman's heirs. More than one attraction awaits you, more than one affection should bind you now to your love. We shall see each other again, Adoniram !'

Deeply moved, Adoniram pressed his lips against the queen's hand; it was damp with tears. Mustering his courage, he took one long, last look at her, then, turning away with an effort, he let the tent curtain fall back into place behind him, as he returned to the banks of the Kedron.

Soliman, in a state of acute distress, torn between anger and love, mistrust and remorse, waited at Millo for the smiling but heartbroken queen, while Adoniram, striving to bury his jealousy in the depths of his sorrow, made his way to the temple to pay the workmen before treading the road of exile. Each of these individuals believed that a rival would be overcome and counted on a secret which was known, in fact, to both parties. The queen concealed her purpose, and Soliman, only too well informed, dissembled in his turn, but his ingenious pride permitted him a doubt.

Standing on the flat roof of his palace at Millo, the king surveyed the queen of Saba's retinue which wound along the path of Emmaus, then he turned his attention to the red tinted walls of the temple where Adoniram still reigned; the vivid, notched arrises of the walls shone like a torch in the gathering gloomy mist. Soliman's forehead and his pale cheeks were damp and cold, but he kept his eyes wide open and carefully scanned the whole region. No incident occurred to arouse his suspicion. The queen made her entry, accompanied by her chief officers and by a few of her servants and attendants who mingled with the king's.

Soliman was perplexed and thoughtful during the evening. Balkis was aloof and almost ironic, for she knew that he was helplessly captivated by her. They dined in silence. The king glanced at her furtively or looked aside with simulated indifference; his eyes seemed to flee the queen's eyes, which, lowered one moment and raised the next, stirred up Soliman's illusions, however much he wished to master them. From his preoccupied air, it was clear that he was hatching one scheme or another. He was a descendant of Noah, and the princess noticed that, loyal to the tradition of the father of the vine, he resorted to wine for the resolution which he lacked. When the courtiers withdrew, mutes replaced the king's officers, and as the queen was attended by her own people, she now replaced the Sabeans by the Nubians who did not understand the Hebrew language.

'Lady,' said Soliman ben Daoud gravely, 'certain explanations are required.'

'My lord,' Balkis replied, 'you anticipate my own request.'

'I had thought that faithful to her word the princess of Saba was . . . a woman, yes, but above all, a queen. . . .'

'On the contrary,' Balkis interrupted sharply, 'I am more than a queen, my lord, I am a woman! Who is not liable to error? I believed that you were wise, then I believed that you were in love. . . . It is I,' she added with a sigh, 'who suffer the greater disillusionment.'

'You know only too well that I love,' Soliman replied at once, 'otherwise you would not have trampled over a heart which, in the end, rises up to rebel.'

'I have exactly the same reproaches to make against you,' Balkis retorted. 'You do not love me, lord, you love the queen. And frankly, am I already at an age to desire a marriage of convenience? Yes, I admit that I wished to probe your soul. More delicate, more fragile than the queen, the woman, setting aside the interests of the State, pretended to revel in her power over you, but in fact she never ceased to dream of being loved. Postponing the hour when she would have to fulfil a promise won from her by guile, she put you to the proof. She hoped you would seek to claim a victory over her heart alone, but only too quickly her hopes were proved unjustified. You pursued with summons, with menaces, you resorted to stratagems among my servants, and already you are more their sovereign than I am myself. I longed for a husband, a lover, but I have come to fear a master. You cannot deny that I speak in all sincerity.'

'If Soliman were so dear to you, surely you would have pardoned faults provoked by his impatience to belong to you. But no, you thought of him as nothing but an object worthy of your hate. It is not for him,' he emphasized, 'that. . . .'

'Enough! Lord, do not add insults to the injuries which have wounded me. Mistrust incites mistrust, jealousy intimidates the heart, and I fear that my freedom and tranquillity would have been the price for the honour you wished to confer upon me.'

The king made no reply for fear of losing all by continuing to found his arguments upon the word of a base and perfidious spy.

'Listen, Soliman,' the queen resumed with friendly and enchanting grace, 'be truthful, be yourself, be amiable. My illusions remain dear to me . . . my spirit is overcome, but I long . . . I long to be reassured.'

'O Balkis! you would banish all doubts if you could look within this heart where you reign supreme. Let us forget my suspicions and yours, and consent at last to my happiness. O fateful power of kings! O that I were only a poor desert Arab at the feet of Balkis, daughter of herdsmen!'

'Your desires accord with mine; moreover, you have understood me. Yes,' she said, drawing her frank and passionate face close to the king's beard, 'yes, it is the austerity of the Hebrew marriage which chills and frightens me. Love, love alone would have called me here if . . . if. . . .'

'If. . . .' Soliman encouraged her. 'The tone of your voice pierces and inflames me.'

'No, no — I forget what I was going to say, I was suddenly confused. These wines are mild, but they are treacherous all the same. I confess I feel quite . . . quite bewildered. . . .'

At a sign from Soliman, the mutes and Nubians refilled the goblets; the king emptied his with one gulp and noticed with satisfaction that Balkis did the same.

'I must admit,' the queen resumed playfully, 'that the Jewish marriage rites allow no concessions for the benefit of queens, they are in fact quite troublesome for us.'

'Is that what disturbs you?' Soliman asked, darting her a glance weighed down now by a certain languor.

'Indeed it is. Without mentioning the unpleasant prospect of having to prepare myself by fasting, which would spoil my figure, at the very least, I can think of nothing sadder than having to surrender my hair to the scissors and wearing a tightly fitting coif for the rest of my life. It is true, though,' she added, displaying her beautiful ebony tresses, 'that I would not be obliged to lose all my finery and apparel.'

'Our women,' Soliman said, 'are free to replace their hair by charmingly curled crests of plumage.'

'Moreover,' the queen pursued, not without disdain, 'you have another custom. The man buys the woman as a slave or servant; she even has to come humbly to her bridegroom's door and offer herself to him. In short, religion plays no part in this contract which is nothing but a market deal. The husband, as he welcomes his wife, stretches forth his hand and says in only too excellent Hebrew : "Mekudescheth-li", You are devoted to me alone. And, what is more, you are allowed to reject her, deceive her, and even have her stoned to death at the slightest pretext. Proud as I would feel if I were loved by Soliman, I would be terrified if I were married to him.'

'Loved!' the king cried, rising from the divan where he was reposing, 'Loved! Has any other woman ever exerted such an absolute dominion? I was angry, incensed : you calm me just as you wish.

Ominous preoccupations disturb me : I strive to banish them. You betray me, I can sense it, and I conspire with you to take advantage of Soliman !'

Turning round voluptuously, Balkis raised her goblet above her head. Two of her attendants refilled both drinking-cups, then silently the mutes and Nubians withdrew.

The banqueting hall was deserted now. As the lamps grew dimmer, they projected weird beams upon Soliman; his features were pale, his eyes feverish, and his colourless lips trembled. An uncanny languor took possession of the king, and Balkis watched him with an ambiguous smile. Suddenly he recovered himself and quickly regained the divan.

'Woman !' he cried, 'give up all further hope of toying with a king's affection. Night protects us with her veils, secrecy surrounds us. A violent flame scorches the whole of my being, rage and passion intoxicate me. This hour is mine ! And if you are sincere, you will no longer withhold the happiness I have purchased at so exceptional a price. Reign, be free, but do not spurn a prince who abandons himself to you, who is consumed by desire, and who, at this moment, is ready to contend for you with the powers of hell !'

Confused and palpitating, Balkis lowered her eyes :

'Leave me time to collect myself,' she replied, 'this language is quite new to me. . . .'

'No !' Soliman interrupted in delirium, as he managed to empty the goblet from which he drew such audacity, 'no ! my perseverance is at an end. It is a question now of life or death for me. Woman, you will be mine, I swear it ! If you were deceiving me, I shall be revenged . . . if you love me, an everlasting love will gain my pardon.'

He leaped up and stretched forth his hands to embrace the girl, but his arms encircled a shadow, for the queen had quietly stepped away. The arms of the son of Daoud fell like lead to his side. His head wobbled, he kept silent, and, with a sudden tremble, staggered back to the divan. He struggled to keep his astonished eyes open. He felt all his desire seeping out of his body, he could hardly focus on any object in the room, for everything appeared to be spinning around him. A nameless terror marked his mournful, sallow face, framed by his black beard; his mouth gaped open, but he was unable to articulate any sound, and his head, weighed down by his turban, collapsed upon the cushions of the divan. Pinioned by heavy and invisible fetters, he mentally shook himself free, but his limbs no longer obeyed the power of his mind or will.

Slowly and sedately, the queen approached. Terrified, he managed to see her; she was standing upright, her cheek propped against her folded fingers, while her other hand supported her elbow. She was watching him.

'The narcotic is working,' he heard her say.

Soliman's two black pupils whirled around in the white sockets of his large, sphinx-like eyes, but otherwise he remained immobile.

'Very well, then,' Balkis said, 'I obey, I yield, I am yours! . . .' She knelt down and touched Soliman's glacial hand. He uttered a profound sigh.

'He can still hear,' she murmured. 'Listen, king of Israel, you who impose love with bondage and treason, according to your power, listen! I have escaped from your domination, but if the woman deceives you, the queen does not betray you. I love, but it is not you whom I love; destiny forbade it. Descended from a line superior to yours, I had to choose a husband of my race in order to obey the genii who protect me. Your power expires before theirs. Forget me. Let Adonai choose you a consort, he is great and generous. Did he not give you wisdom and thereby well reward you for your service? I abandon you to him, and I take back from you the support of the genii whom you disdain and whom you are unable to command.'

And seizing hold of the finger on which she saw the brilliant talismanic ring she had given Soliman, Balkis attempted to remove it, for she had promised Sarahil that she would retrieve it at the last moment. But the king contracted his hand with a violent effort, making his breath shudder in his lungs, and he kept his fist tightly clenched and as firm as iron. The queen strove in vain to reopen it. She was going to speak again in order to persuade him, but suddenly Soliman ben Daoud's head fell backwards. His neck muscles slackened, his mouth hung open, his half closed eyes grew dull and bleary; his soul had flown already into the world of dreams, but his hand still grasped the ring.

Everybody was asleep in the palace of Millo, except the queen of Saba's servants who had put the narcotic into the king's goblet. Thunder growled in the distance and lightning streaked the blackness of the sky, while the unleashed winds scattered the rain over the mountain. An Arab horseman, as dark as the tomb, was waiting for the queen; she immediately gave the signal to retreat. Winding their way along the gullies around the hill of Zion, the procession soon descended into the valley of Joshaphat. They forded over the Kedron whose swelling waters would protect their flight, and, spurring their horses left of mount Tabor, which was wreathed by flashes of lightning, they arrived at the mountainous route of Bethany close to the Garden of Olives.

'Our horses are nimble enough, we can follow this route,' the queen said to her guards. 'Our tents are folded by now and our people are heading towards the Jordan. We shall meet up with them during the second hour of the day, beyond the Dead Sea, from where we shall gain the narrow passes of the mountains of Arabia.' And loosening the reins of her horse, Balkis looked up at the tempest and smiled as she thought of her partner in disgrace, her beloved Adoniram who was no doubt wandering now along the road to Tyre.

Just as they started to climb the track to Bethany, a flash of lightning revealed a group of people crossing over it in silence. At the sound of this phantom procession riding through the darkness, they halted in amazement. Balkis and her retinue passed by, but one of her guards rode aside to find out who they were.

'Only three men,' he explained to the queen, 'carrying a corpse wrapped in a shroud.'

During the pause which followed, there were heated arguments among the audience. Some denied the truth of the tradition elaborated by the storyteller; they claimed that the queen of Saba did in fact beget a son from Soliman and nobody else. Owing to his religious convictions, the Abyssinian, above all, was highly offended at the assumption that his sovereigns were nothing but the descendants of a workman.

'You lied!' he shouted to the storyteller. 'The first of our Abyssinian kings was called Menilek, and he was definitely the son of Soliman and Belkiss-Makeda. One of his descendants still reigns over us at Gondar.'

'Brother,' a Persian said to him, 'let us listen quietly until the end, otherwise you'll get thrown out again as you were the other night. From our point of view, this legend is orthodox, and if your little Father John of Abyssinia claims to be an offspring of Soliman, well, we shall concede that it is thanks to some black Ethiopian girl, and not to queen Balkis, whose colour was the same as ours.'

The Abyssinian spluttered with fury, but the proprietor managed to restrain him from further assertions. When calm was finally restored among the audience, the storyteller continued as follows.

12 Makbenash

While Soliman welcomed Balkis at his country residence, a man, crossing the heights of Moriah, looked pensively at the twilight dwindling in the clouds and at the blazing tapers which pierced the shadows around Millo like a multitude of stars. He bid his beloved a silent farewell and took a last look at the rocks of Solyme and the banks of the Kedron. The weather was cloudy, and before the pallid sun fully set, it had time to see the night advancing upon the earth. At the noise of the hammers on the bronze bells, sounding the call to muster, Adoniram struggled free of his thoughts and hastened on his way. Soon he passed through the crowd of assembled workmen to preside over the distribution of salaries. He entered the temple through the west door and emerged at the partly open east door to place himself at the foot of the column of Jachin.

Lighted tapers below the peristyle crackled under drops of tepid rain to which the panting workmen merrily offered their sweating limbs. The crowd was large, and Adoniram had at his disposal, besides the book-keepers, stewards in charge of the different categories. To divide the workmen into the three hierarchical grades a watchword was used, replacing in these circumstances the hand signals which would have taken up too much time. Then the salaries were distributed on the declaration of the password.

The apprentices' watchword was Jachin, the journeymen's Boaz, and the masters' Jehovah. Arranged in their appropriate groups and lined up one behind the other, the workmen presented themselves to the stewards at the counting-house. Before each one received his wages, Adoniram touched his hand, and the workman whispered a word in his ear. The password had been changed for this final day. The apprentices said Tubal-Cain, the journeymen Shibboleth, and the masters Giblim.

Gradually, the crowd thinned out, the precincts grew deserted, but when the last petitioner had withdrawn, it was clear that not all of the men had attended the ceremony, for there was still some money in one of the coffers.

'Tomorrow,' Adoniram said to his stewards, 'summon the men

together again to discover whether they are ill or have been visited by death.'

As soon as Adoniram's officers had left, Adoniram himself, zealous and vigilant to the last day, took hold of a lamp, as usual, to inspect the empty workshops and the various locales of the temple, to make sure that his orders had been executed and that the fires had been extinguished. His footsteps echoed sadly along the flagstones. Looking once more at his monuments, he stopped, for a long time, in front of a group of winged cherubim, the last work of the young Benoni.

'Sweet child,' he sighed.

Once this pilgrimage was over, Adoniram found himself in the temple's huge hall. The dense shadows around his lamp unrolled into red volutes, revealing the high mouldings on the vaults, and also the walls of the hall, the exits of which were three doors facing north, west, and east. The north door was reserved for the people, the west for the king and his warriors, the east for the levites, and outside this latter door stood the bronze columns of Jachin and Boaz.

Before leaving by the west door, which was the nearest to him, Adoniram glanced at the dark recesses of the hall, and, deeply moved as he remained from looking at the innumerable statues, his imagination evoked the shade of Tubal-Cain in the shadows. Concentrating his gaze, he tried to penetrate the darkness; the phantom grew taller but glided away; it reached the very depths of the temple and vanished close to the walls, like the shadow of a man spotlighted by a torch which slowly withdraws. A woeful cry seemed to resound among the vaults. Then Adoniram turned round and prepared to depart.

Suddenly, a human form detached itself from the pilaster and said to him in a ferocious voice :

'If you wish to leave, tell me the password of the masters.'

Adoniram carried no weapons upon him. Respected by everyone, accustomed to command by only a sign, he did not even dream of defending his sacred person.

'Wretch !' he exclaimed, recognizing the journeyman, the Hebrew Methuselah, 'step back at once ! You will be welcomed among the masters on the day that crime and treachery are honoured ! Flee with your accomplices before the justice of Soliman falls upon your heads.'

At these words, Methuselah lifted up his hammer in his muscular arms and brought it down with a crash upon Adoniram's skull. Stunned but still conscious, the artist staggered towards the north door, but the Syrian Phanor was waiting for him there.

'If you wish to leave, tell me the password of the masters.'

'You have not worked for seven years,' Adoniram managed to reply.

'The password!'

'Never!'

Phanor the mason thrust his chisel into Adoniram's entrails, but he was unable to aim a second blow, for aroused by the pain, the architect of the temple flew like an arrow towards the east door in order to escape from his assassins. There, the Phoenician Amrou, journeyman among the carpenters, was waiting for him, and he, too, cried out in his turn:

'If you wish to leave, tell me the password of the masters!'

'This is not the way that I learned it myself,' Adoniram gasped. 'Request it from the one who sends you here.'

As he strove to open the door, Amrou plunged the point of his compasses into Adoniram's heart.

At that moment the storm erupted, heralded by a mighty stroke of thunder.

Stretched out upon the temple floor, Adoniram's body covered three flagstones. The three murderers reassembled at his feet and linked their hands together.

'This man was great,' Phanor murmured.

'He won't take up more space in the tomb than you,' Amrou said.

'May his blood fall upon Soliman ben Daoud!' Phanor exclaimed.

'Let us lament for ourselves,' Methuselah added, 'for we are masters of the king's secret. We must destroy all proof of the murder. The rain is pouring down and the night is black as pitch. Come, let us quickly carry this corpse far away from the city and commit it to the earth.'

Then they wrapped the corpse in a long apron of white leather, and, heaving it up in their arms, descended in silence to the banks of the Kedron, directing their steps towards a solitary spot beyond the route to Bethany. As they drew near to it, troubled as they were and shivering in their hearts, they suddenly found themselves confronted by an escort of horsemen. They halted in apprehension. And then the queen of Saba passed by the terror-stricken assassins who were hauling away the remains of her husband Adoniram.

When one of the escorts rode directly up to them, they were too dumbfounded to move, but he merely glanced at them, turned his horse aside and rejoined the procession which rapidly disappeared in the darkness. Then they went further away and dug a hole in the earth to conceal the corpse of the artist. When their work was done, Methuselah uprooted the trunk of a young acacia tree and replanted it in the newly turned-up soil under which their victim reposed.

During this time, as lightning continued to rend the sky, Balkis was fleeing across the valleys, and Soliman was sleeping. His wound was a cruel one, too, for he had to awake.

When the sun had turned completely round the earth, the lethargic effect of the philtre which he had drunk passed away. Tormented by nightmares, the king struggled against a host of visions, and he returned to the domain of the living with a violent shock.

He rises to his feet in astonishment; his bewildered eyes appear to search for their master's reason . . . and at length he remembers. The empty goblet stands before him and he recalls the queen's words : 'I obey, I yield, I am yours!' . . . but unable to see her any longer he grows disturbed. A beam of sunlight which hovers ironically upon his forehead makes him shudder . . . he divines everything, hurls the goblet to the floor and utters a cry of fury. He makes inquiries in vain. Nobody saw her leave the room. Her retinue, however, has disappeared from the plain, and nothing but the traces of her tents is left behind.

'So!' Soliman cried, casting a look of rage at Zadok, 'so that is the kind of help which your god offers to his servants! Is that what he promised me? He delivers me up like a toy to the spirits of hell, and you, you imbecile of a minister who reign in his name owing to my impotence, you abandoned me, without foreseeing anything, without preventing anything! Who will give me winged legions to overtake this perfidious queen! Genii of the earth and fire, rebellious angels, spirits of the air, will you obey me?'

'Blasphemy!' Zadok rebuked him, raising his voice. 'Jehovah alone is great, and he is a jealous God.'

Just as Soliman was about to retort, the prophet Ahijah the Shilonite entered the room. Ascetic and awesome, he resembled a pure, disincarnate spirit; his features were sombre and stern, his gaze acutely penetrating, and his eyes blazed with divine fire. Turning towards Soliman, he addressed him thus :

' "And the Lord said unto him, Therefore whosoever slayeth Cain, vengeance shall be taken on him sevenfold. And the Lord set a mark upon Cain, lest any finding him should kill him." And Lamech, offspring of Cain, cried out to his wives : "I have slain a man to my wounding, and a young man to my hurt. If Cain shall be avenged sevenfold, truly Lamech seventy and sevenfold." Listen now, O king, to the words which the Lord commands me to declare unto thee : "As for whosoever has shed the blood of Cain and of Lamech, vengeance shall be taken on him seven hundred and sevenfold!" ' Soliman bowed his head; he remembered Adoniram and realized that his orders had been carried out. Overcome by remorse, he cried out :

'Wretches! What have they done? I did not tell them to kill him!'

Alone, abandoned by his God, at the mercy of the genii, reproved by Zadok, scorned by Ahijah, deceived by the queen of the Sabeans, driven ultimately to despair, Soliman glanced at his helpless hands. But at the sight of the talisman, he was aroused by a glimmer of hope, for the ring which he had received from Balkis still glittered on his finger, provoking him. He turned its stone towards the sun, and all the birds of the air flocked around him at once, except Hud-Hud, the magic hoopoe. He summoned her three times, thereby forcing her to comply, and then he commanded the bird to lead him to the queen. The hoopoe obediently took to wing, and Soliman, whose hands were stretched forth towards her, felt himself swept up from the floor and carried off through the air at an incredible speed. Gripped by terror, he turned his hand aside, and found himself safely back on the ground. The hoopoe, however, crossed the valley and alighted upon the summit of a hillock to settle on the frail branch of an acacia-tree which was planted there. And none of Soliman's invocations would ever make her move again.

Seized by vertigo, the king dreamed of mustering innumerable armies to devastate the kingdom of Saba, reduce it to ashes, and finally extinguish the flames with the blood of its inhabitants. He often locked himself up alone, cursed his fate and conjured up legions of spirits. An afrite, a genie of hell, was compelled to serve him and attend upon him in his solitude. In order to forget the queen and divert his fatal passion, Soliman had foreign women brought to him from every corner of the world. He married them in accordance with heathen rites, and they, in turn, initiated him in the idolatrous cult of images. Soon, to please the genii, he peopled the high places and raised, not far from mount Tabor, a temple to Molech. The prophecy which Tubal-Cain had uttered in the kingdom of fire to his son Adoniram was thus confirmed : 'You are destined to revenge us, and this temple you are raising to Adonai will cause the downfall of his faithful servant, Soliman.'

But, as the Talmud informs us, the king of the Hebrews did not meet his doom so quickly. When the news of Adoniram's murder had spread far and wide, the people rose up and demanded justice. The king commanded nine of the masters to find Adoniram's grave in order to prove that he had in fact been assassinated.

Seventeen days passed. The search and investigations in the temple's environs led to nothing, neither did the examination of the surrounding countryside. Then, one of the masters, exhausted by the heat, attempted to seize hold of the branch of an acacia-tree so that he would be able to clamber up the mountain more easily. A brilliant bird of an unknown species, perched upon a branch of this tree, immediately flew away, and the master was astonished to discover that the whole trunk yielded now to his hand and no longer clung to the soil. The soil itself, he noticed, had been recently turned up, and he called to his companions to join him. Digging away with their hands and nails, the nine masters soon perceived the shape of a grave.

'The criminals,' one of them said, 'are perhaps traitors who wanted to wrest the password of the masters from Adoniram. For fear that they succeeded, would it not be prudent to change it?'

'What word, then, should we adopt?' another asked.

'If we recover our master from this pit,' a third replied, 'the first word which any one of us pronounces will serve as the password. It will thereby perpetuate the memory of this crime and reinforce the vow we shall make to inflict vengeance for it, we and our children, upon the heads of the murderers and their remotest posterity.'

Joining their hands together over the grave, the nine masters swore the vow, and dug up the soil with renewed vigour. Once the corpse had been identified, one of the masters touched it tenderly with his fingers, and the skin stuck to his hand. The same happened when the next one touched it. The third took hold of the wrist in the manner used by the masters to greet each other, and as even more skin broke loose this time, he cried out :

'Makbenash!' (The skin leaves the bones!)

All of them agreed that henceforth this would be the password of the masters and the rallying cry of Adoniram's avengers. Moreover, through the justice of God, this word also served for many centuries to rouse the people against the progeny of kings.

Phanor, Amrou and Methuselah had taken flight. Recognized as false brothers, however, they were slain by workmen in the States of Maaca, king of the country of Gath, where they were hiding under the names of Sterkin, Oterfut and Hoben.

For a long time afterwards, Adoniram's descendants were regarded as sacred by the workmen's guilds who would swear by The Sons of the Widow, thereby denoting the offspring of Adoniram and the queen of Saba.

Following the decree of Soliman ben Daoud, the illustrious artist was buried beneath the very altar of the temple which he had raised. Adonai therefore abandoned the ark of the Hebrews and reduced the successors of Daoud to bondage.

Meanwhile, greedy for honours, dominion, and sensual indulgence, Soliman married five hundred wives, and at length coerced the appeased genii to aid him in his schemes to conquer the neighbouring kingdoms, thanks to the power of the renowned ring which had been carved long, long ago by Idrad, father of the Cainite Mehujael, and which had belonged, in turn, to Enoch, who made use of it to command the stones, next to the patriarch Jared, and then to Nimrod who had bequeathed it to Saba, father of the Hamathites. In the hands of Soliman now, the ring subjected the genii, the winds, and all the animals to his orders. Satiated with power and pleasure, the sage did not cease from repeating : 'Eat, love, drink, for all the rest is nothing but pride !'

Paradoxically, however, he was far from happy. This king, debased by matter, aspired after immortality, and aided by guile and secret knowledge, he intended, in fact, to become immortal by means of certain stratagems. In order to purify his body of mortal elements, without destroying it, he had to sleep for 225 years, protected from diseases and infections. Returning to its corporal envelope, his exiled soul would then be restored to that state of flourishing manhood which reaches full bloom at the age of thirty-three years.

Grown old and decrepit, Soliman spied in the dwindling of his strength the signs of his approaching end. Then he commanded the genii whom he had enslaved to build him an inaccessible palace in the mountain of Kaf, and in the middle of this palace he had them raise an enormous throne of gold and ivory, supported by four columns yielded by the stalwart trunk of an oak tree. Upon this throne, Soliman, prince of the genii, would pass the time of his ordeal.

Meanwhile, he spent the last years of his life in conjuring up by magic signs, by mystic utterances, and by the power of the ring, all the substances endowed with the necessary qualities to destroy matter. He conjured up the vapour of the clouds, the humidity of the earth, the rays of the sun, the breath of the winds; he conjured up the butterflies, the moths, and the grubs. He conjured up the birds of prey, the bat, the rat, the fly, the ants, and the tribes of insects which creep, gnaw and nibble. He conjured up the metals and stones, he conjured up the alkalis and acids, and even the emanations of the plants.

Once these preparations were made and when he was absolutely certain that he had abstracted from his body all the destructive agents, those pitiless ministers of Death, he had himself conveyed for the last time to the heart of the mountain of Kaf, where he assembled the genii and commanded them to execute prodigious works, charging them, under menace of the most dreadful punishments, to respect his sleep and watch over him.

Then he seated himself upon his throne and arranged his limbs, which were gradually growing stiff and cold, in a fixed and firm position. His eyes grew dull and dim, his breathing ceased, and he slept the sleep of the dead.

The enslaved genii continued to serve him; they carried out his orders and prostrated themselves before their master, looking forward to the day when he would wake.

Soliman's beard grew so long that it spread itself out at his feet like a rug. His nails soon pierced the leather of his gloves and the gilded fabric of his footwear.

But, considering the limits of human wisdom, how could it attain the infinite? Soliman had forgotten to conjure up one particular insect, the most tiny of them all; he had overlooked the mite. Stealthy and almost invisible, the mite advanced. It fastened itself to one of the columns of the throne, and slowly, slowly, but without ceasing, it gnawed away at that column. Even the finest ear would not have heard this atom-sized insect at its scratching. Every year, it cast aside a few grains of sawdust. The mite worked for 224 years, then the corroded column suddenly gave way under the weight of the throne, which toppled down with an almighty crash. Thus the mite conquered Soliman and was the first to be informed of Soliman's death, for the king of kings, hurled across the flagstones, never awoke again.

Then the humiliated genii acknowledged their oversight and recovered their liberty.

The storyteller stood up and declared :

'Here ends the tale of the great king Soliman ben Daoud. It should inspire the respect of all true believers, for it is summarized by the sacred hand of the Prophet in the thirty-fourth sura of the Koran, the mirror of wisdom and the fountain of truth.'

Conclusion

The narration had taken up the better part of two weeks, but I did not wish to divert the reader's attention by describing what I had been able to observe in Constantinople during the intervals. Neither have I mentioned a few short tales, inserted now and then, according to custom, either to entertain the clientele until the whole audience have assembled, or to relieve and at the same time heighten suspense at certain dramatic moments in the tale.

The café proprietors often spend considerable sums of money to guarantee the co-operation of one or another of the more renowned storytellers. As the sequence never lasts for longer than an hour and a half, they can appear at several cafés on the same night. They also hold sequences in the harems, when the husband, after evaluating the interest of the tale, wishes to have his family share the pleasure which he has enjoyed himself.

To arrange a contract, prudent people appeal to the khassideans (trustees) of the storytellers' guild, for it sometimes happens that double-dealing storytellers, unsatisfied with the takings in a café or with the payment made to them in a private house, disappear in the middle of one of the most exciting moments of the narrative, leaving their audience quite broken-hearted at not being able to hear the tale out to its end. Such a situation cannot occur if the contract has been drawn up and signed in the presence of one of the trustees.

I was very fond of the café frequented by my friends the Persians, owing to the variety of its customers and to the freedom of speech which reigned there. It reminded me of descriptions in that philosophical tale, by the good Bernardin de Saint-Pierre, *Café de Surate.* You do indeed find much more tolerance in a cosmopolitan gathering such as this, which included merchants from nearly all the countries of Asia, than in the cafés frequented exclusively by Turks or Arabs.

The tale we had heard was discussed during each pause among the different groups of customers, for in a café in the Orient conversation is never general; apart from the Abyssinian, who, as a Christian,

212

appeared to have somewhat over-indulged his taste for the juice of Noah, nobody questioned the principle notions of the narrative. They do in fact conform to the universal beliefs and convictions of the Orient, though you find in them a touch of that spirit of popular opposition which distinguishes the Persians from the Arabs of the Yemen. Our storyteller belonged to the sect of Ali which is, so to speak, the catholic tradition of the Orient, while the Turks, who belonged to the sect of Omar, represent a kind of protestantism, which gained the upper hand when they brought the people of the south under their subjection.

Glossary

afrite In Mohammedan mythology afrites are powerful demons; in the popular imagination, however, they are generally mischievous sprites.

aga A chief officer, military or civil, in the Ottoman Empire.

alma An Egyptian dancing girl; from the Arabic *almah*, learned (in music and dancing).

besestian Probably an armoury, an arsenal.

cadi A civil judge in Mohammedan countries.

cangia A light boat used on the Nile.

chibouk The long pipe smoked by the Turks.

dragoman Guide, interpreter in countries where Arabic, Turkish, or Persian is spoken.

effendi A Turkish title of respect, chiefly applied to officials and to professional men.

fellah From the Arabic *fellah*, a peasant.

houri A nymph of the Mohammedan paradise, a voluptuously beautiful woman.

moucharaby An external balcony enclosed with latticework.

moultezims Farmer-generals of revenues.

mudir In Egypt, the governor of a province.

narghile A hookah, an Oriental pipe in which the smoke passes through water before reaching the mouth.

okel A native inn or caravanserai.

peri In Persian mythology a good genie endowed with grace and beauty, 'a fair one'.

shereef In this text, the meaning is a Mohammedan priest.

ulema An authority on law and religion, a doctor, divine.

yataghan In Mohammedan countries a sword without a guard, and often with a double-edged blade.